COUNTRY MARGINS

AND

Rambles of a Journalist.

BY

S. H. HAMMOND,

AUTHOR OF "HILLS, LAKES, AND FOREST STREAMS."

AND

L. W. MANSFIELD,

AUTHOR OF "UP-COUNTRY LETTERS."

NEW YORK:
J. C. DERBY, 119 NASSAU STREET.
BOSTON: PHILLIPS, SAMPSON & CO.
CINCINNATI: H. W. DERBY.
1855.

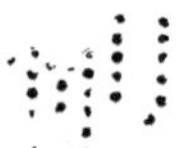

E. O. Jenkins, Printer,
No. 26 Frankfort Street.

DEDICATION.

TO THE HON. THOMAS A. JOHNSON,

A JUSTICE OF THE SUPREME COURT OF THE STATE OF NEW YORK.

My dear Sir :—

You are to some extent responsible for the publication of this book. It was your own suggestion that "Country Margins" should be printed and bound in a volume. Whether that advice was prompted by the kindly prejudices of ancient friendship, or a just appreciation of the merits of the work, you see it has been accepted. I therefore take the liberty of dedicating this book to you. If other excuse is necessary, I trust it will be found in the recollections of bygone years.

I am, very respectfully,

Your obedient servant,

THE AUTHOR OF "HILLS AND LAKES."

PREFATORY.

The Editor of the Albany State Register received one day from an anonymous correspondent, a communication which occupies the first chapter of this book. He published it, with a playful commentary, supposing, at the time, that there the matter would end. A few days afterwards, he received "Margins No. Two," which he published with a commentary in like manner. From such beginning the correspondence grew on, until it acquired the dimensions presented in the book which is now given to the public. The writers were entire strangers to each other until the "Margins" were more than half written, and it was an accident which made them acquainted at last.

At the suggestion and upon the solicitation of many friends, who professed to be pleased with the correspondence, most of which was published in the Register, it goes before the public in its present shape. It makes no claim to any peculiar literary merit. It was simply the result of a digression in the routine of the labors of a daily journalist, intended to lift his paper out of the dull monotony of politics, rather than for publication in a book form. It does not, therefore, challenge criticism, nor affect to compete with the finished productions of popular authors of the day for public favor. The end of its publication will have been accomplished if it shall afford amusement for the leisure hours of those who desire relaxation from labor or severe study.

But little more than one year has gone by since the last "MARGIN" was sent down to the printer, and now the "Up-Country" home, where the writers first met, is lonely and desolate. Of the happy group there gathered on that pleasant summer night, three have departed to another home.

The light, the joy, of the house is gone.

Time itself is but a "margin," dear reader; it is but a step over its borders.

S. H. H.

ALBANY, *June*, 1855.

CONTENTS.

COUNTRY MARGINS.

I.

INVITATION TO DINNER.

II.

THE HALL CLOSET.

III.

COUNTRY LUXURIES.

IV.

EDITOR'S LATITUDE AND LONGITUDE.

V.

A FRIEND FROM THE OLD DOMINION.

VI.

A CHAPTER FOR THE SABBATH.

VII.

ROARING RIVER.

VIII.

HOW POEMS LOOK IN PRINT.

IX.

ISOLATION.

X.

D, WITH A DASH TO IT.

XI.

SEPTEMBER.

XII.

OCTOBER.

XIII.

NELLY.

XIV.

DREAMS.

XV.

THE BRIGHT MORNING—AND JULY.

XVI.

THE DINNER, AND GOOD-BYE—DECEMBER.

COUNTRY RAMBLES.

I.

CANANDAIGUA—PENN YAN—CROOKED LAKE–BATH —HORNELLSVILE.

II.

NIAGARA–PORTAGE—WELLSVILLE—COUDERSPORT.

III.

LAKE CHAMPLAIN—BURLINGTON—KEESEVILLE—AU SABLE FORKS—FRANKLIN FALLS—SARANAC LAKE —ROUND LAKE—TUPPER LAKE—BOG RIVER—ON THE BANKS—THE BLACK FLY.

A.

B.

COUNTRY MARGINS

AND

Rambles of a Journalist.

COUNTRY MARGINS.

I.

INVITATION TO DINNER,

THERE are river margins, and brook margins, the margins of lakes and seas, and of those little beauties in high places (hid away, often, in mountain tops), which we call *ponds.* There are also, of late, book margins. I live, sir, in the country, and am in the habit of filling in my book margins with such notes and exclamations as come uppermost in the course of reading, some of which are possibly highly original, (*quien sabe?*) but quite lost to the great world.

Shall I send them down to you, Mr. Editor? For I think, if handsomely printed, my friends might some day read them, by mistake supposing them to be by some "valued correspondent" other than I. What say you? How do you make it, yea or nay?

Very good. Now I can't go to town to read books, or fill margins for you. In fact, I can't read a book in town. I can let my eyes run up and down its pages, but I do not *take* the book, unless indeed it is hard and abstract. Did you ever read ISAAC TAYLOR'S "Physical Theory of Another Life"? I carried that book all about New York city, some years since, pocketing it at every sally out of doors, and reading it in *omnibi*, and all unheard-of places for meditation and study, being utterly crazed with its enchanting speculations. In the same way, I could sit down on a drygoods box and work out a conic section; but for a *book*—say of travel or sentiment—you need repose; and it is so much the better if you have *all* proper accompaniments and circumstances, harmonies of place, mood, &c., and for this and these there is but one place under the heavens—to wit: *the country*.

Besides, it is necessary to dine before taking up a book, and you can't dine in town. To dine, you must have *peas;* and this, as Ross Brown's Dr. Mendoza says, is *imposs.* Nor can you have salad. *Imposs*, also. You may have shot, and you may have pale round things, which, with infinite buttering, cannot, however, express peas.

We had peas, sir, the other day, for the first time this season. They were, perhaps, the best that ever came on the table since the creation of the world. What peas were before the deluge, cannot now be pronounced. Adam and Eve may have had a few messes equal to ours, but never, probably, after being driven out of that beautiful garden. Your early peas, sir, are abominations.

I have undertaken peas in town, before now, and

the memory of those undertakings, even to this day, is fnll of wrath and indigestion. After repeated failures—Waterloo defeats so to speak—I have been again cajoled by the sight (optical delusion entirely) of peas. Drawing the dish carefully up, I have said, "Ah, here we have them at last—*at last*, thank the sweet heavens. My dear wife, hold your plate; these, my excellent wife, are the thing, eh? (a little nearer, my dear) so tender as they look, so delicate." "Yes," says my wife, "and so little, so young." "Of course, my darling, so little, so young, so—" and here I raise to my mouth a spoonful, and wait for the sensation. It *comes*, the sensation; and as it comes, my wife and I compare notes with a *look;* but oh, my countrymen! Don't ask me to enlarge. Think of a mouthful of pills, or of soft-boiled gravel! and this, in the hope —the joyful anticipation of peas.

Why, sirs and madams, the pea is the most gentle and delicate thing in all the garden. It is not to be forced, but must have time, as all things must, to be good. Don't force it, therefore; don't undertake to improve it; don't water its life out, but give it a fair chance, soil, and sun, and showers; and let it grow, as God designed it, into a properly perfected pea. The frost should approach, but not touch it; and then, as it matures into podhood, I incline to think that lightning (round about) is good for it—a cutting up of the air giving that freshness to the atmosphere which the pea takes into its heart, and makes a part of its life. Whence it gets its meltingness (as of strawberries), its pure apple richness, and its creamy fulness of satisfaction to the palate, is known only to the little round body itself, which has a way of its own, and is taught, doubtless, by heaven itself.

But I was talking of books. I have been reading, of late, in the afternoons of two days, before and after Sunday, "*The Old House by the River*," a book which I like at once, for its fair margin and handsome look. It is a book, also, to the temper of which Sunday is no interruption. It will prepare you for the day, and the day prepare you again for the book. But on that holy day there are few books that I care to read, save the one Book of all. For in that I find better sermons, better sentiment, better philosophy, better news, better poetry, and better and more glorious facts (good for all eternity), than in all the utterances and exclamations of men since the world began.

But "*The Old House*" is written with extreme purity of style, almost matchless in this respect, and with the clearness of sunlight, and I thank God that a man can be found to step out of the whirl of city life, and write a pure book like this.

Dr. Tyng, I have been told, can write *only* in the tumult of the city. But his nature is a fiery one. Whereas the secret of this author's success is, that his true life is *not* in Wall street (eminently successful as he is there), but in the forest, and on the sea, and in that world of beautiful sentiment which surrounds, as with a glory, the heart of woman. Touches of humor appear occasionally, but the author's range is mostly too high for humor. He does not care to come down to it. There is one charming exception in the Bear Hunt, which is the most exquisite piece of comicality I have seen for many a day. Hot as the weather is, I would be willing to ride twenty miles, without stirrups, to see that bear performance. But the author has touched the picture so perfectly, that one can sit at home, quite at ease, and see the whole thing to the life. There are, elsewhere, passages of great power, as in "Ben's Death" in *Delirium Tremens*, "The last leap of the Panther," "Mr. Stewart's Story," etc., but I like best, for my especial humor, "The old Chuch and its Pastor," "Old Friends," and chapters of a kindred nature. But any one who enters "The Old House by the River," will find none but pleasant company; and if any one can read the book without finding that, he is a better man for his intercourse with that company; he ought to retire, at once, to private life,—his being abroad is dangerous to the commonwealth.

And now, Mr. Editor (stopping a moment to bracket my thanks to the author for having written this book, which I should like to have written myself), I will say—as to peas—that we shall have another mess in a few days, and very soon every day, or as often as the weather will permit. After a week, you can scarcely come amiss. I have never seen your face, but if we have peas that day for dinner, I'm sure I shall see a glad one. Will you come? Yours, ——.

Our correspondent has placed us in a dilemma. We like the country, and we like peas—and we like an invitation to dinner. But it is always convenient to understand two or three preliminary matters before accepting such an invitation. In the first place, it is a great advantage to know *where* you are invited to dine. It will not do to indulge in conjecture on that subject; you might go to the wrong house, and get down by, and possibly *under* the wrong table. You might tax the hospitality of John Smith under an invitation from James Brown. Then, again, it is well to know *with whom* one is invited to dine. Not that we are aristocratic, or insist upon associating (especially about dinner time) with "the first families." We can eat a good dinner at almost any body's expense. We're liberal in such matters, *we* are. But we are of the national school, silver gray, and no mistake. Suppose, on sitting down to table, we should find ourself cheek by jowl with a rank woolly, oran out and out abolitionist. He wouldn't let politics alone, of course, *he* wouldn't; he'd take his stand on his platform, he'd denounce the Union as "an unholy league" and the Constitution as "an atrocious bargain," and drawing the esculents on his side of the table, demand of us concessions in favor of his opinions, or leave us to go away empty. That would be subjecting our principles to a test unnecessarily severe.

An anonymous invitation "to eat peas," is all very well in its way, but it isn't according to our taste. There is too much of the ideal about it. It lacks the solid ingredient of sober fact. If our correspondent will certify us of the place *where* we are to "eat the aforesaid peas," and the person with *whom*, and upon whose invitation we are to eat them, he will have to lay the venue a good way off, and have a pretty hard customer for a host, if he finds we decline, provided—the trimmings are all right. We take it for granted we shall have something besides "peas," something solid, something savory and pleasant to the taste, such as spring chickens, nicely broiled, or speckled trout fresh from the brook, or maybe, a brace or two of woodcock, or snipe, or a pair of fat wild ducks, and we shouldn't be at all offended to see them come on the table in succession, one after another like, together with salads and such vegetables as relish with them. And then a bottle or two of old port, or sherry, or Madeira, or even Champagne, wouldn't "rile" us in the least. The whole affair might conclude with delicate pastry and fruits, ices, and such cooling things as add to the comforts of the inner man in the warm summer days. We never take offence at such trifles. But we can't really think of accepting an anonymous invitation to eat peas—we can't, indeed.

II.

THE HALL CLOSET.

YOU have confused me a little, Mr. Editor. The blood has been mounting up and about my temples all the long day, at the thought of your unparalleled impu—— I mean your remarkable effront——, or at least, your peculiar comment—upon my invitation to peas.

But I am cooler now, and touching the great topic of dinner, I will say briefly, that wine with me is a memory—a reminiscence—or, if you please, an abstraction. To many it is a *dis*traction; I make it an *ab*straction, by putting it in the hall closet, and turning the key. My wife, I will not deny, was a little elated at the idea of having a city Editor to dinner; but when I repeated, one by one, your extraordinary expectations, she became very thoughtful and silent.

Why you see, sir, the "spring chickens" we could count upon, by-and-bye; but the "trout," the "woodcock," the "snipe," the "wild ducks," and, coolest of propositions, that all these should be brought on consecutively, keeping half a dozen cooks busy, and quite confounding my father and my dear old aunt with such unheard-of proceedings—all these, and ices, and wines, in our quiet country home! Oh, sir, I blush at the thought of it. Moreover, I withdraw the invitation. Don't come to dinner. I forbid it.

The other day, reading an account of three sunrises*—one on a high Northern river, one on Lake Champlain, and one from the Berkshire Bowl—I said to myself, "Here is a true poet; and, moreover, a philosopher. *Genial,* I warrant you. In short, a man to throw both arms around!" "Doubtless," I continued, "this man, like Milton, drinks water only, and feeds upon peas and pond-lilies, and the like wholesome things. How calmly and gloriously he writes of the morning! How handsomely he poises himself above the world! Like a great white cloud, close up to the sky, with a sunny radiance about him, and earth, and all shadows and undercurrents far away below, quite out of his beat."

Now, who would have thought, Mr. Editor—I put it to you, yes, sir, to you—who would have thought that this man of brilliant sunrises was holding forth, even then, through the strength of yesterday's dinner? Yesterday's snipe and woodcock, or (more shocking) yesterday's wine?

I have wine, sir. It is in a dark closet under the hall-stairs; and there it will remain. I have turned the key and hid it away; and no man will find it. Sauterne and Claret, and Old Port and Heidsick, and with them also, "Old Q." and Otard!

* See Appendix, A.

There they are, and sometimes I talk to them a little through the key-hole. "Lie still, my darlings," I say to them, "no one shall touch you. You are all locked in, and the key lost forever. No Editor shall come nigh you. Keep cool, and above all, keep your tempers. You, my pleasant Sauterne, my charming Sauterne, my ambrosial Sauterne; you, who quite flattered me last summer that a half-bottle every day was building me up into a strong tower, only to break me down in the fall, like the confusion of Babel: you, Old Ports, costly old chaps, but doubtful, I am sorry to say, as to your integrity: you, my only two Heidsicks; two only of the many silver tops we had, what time my wife and I "came home forever,"—lie quiet, all of you, and take your ease. Let us have no souring from neglect; no poppings of summer wrath, my excellent quondams, but be patient, all, and bide your time."

In this manner, sir, I keep them under, and in a healthy way. As to "Old Q.," the oily old fellow, there is no danger of his exploding. He is as strong and as firm as the stars, and as *high*. He has great command of himself, "Old Q.," he never effervesces or runs into sour humors. Stand him belly-down, or on his feet, it is all one to him. Besides, as I have said, the key is lost, and they all know it.

Wherefore, Mr. Editor, until I may suddenly find that key, or until you can dine in a plain way, with say for wine, a glass of *eau de sucre*, or the like, I see no way to meet your wants.

Lastly, as to who and where I am, the motion is not now in order. Perhaps I am a country clergyman recreating in a country paper. (I *shall* preach to you; aye, sir, I shall lay on and spare not.) Perhaps I am a country farmer, trying to get his wife to read the news. Perhaps a retired valetudinarian, amusing himself with a city Editor. Perhaps, and perhaps, and perhaps.

In any case, for the present, my special invitation is (and my wife joins me heartily), DON'T COME TO DINNER. Yours, ——.

There it is again, just our luck to a dot. We knew 'twould be so. We'd have made our affidavit to the fact beforehand. Just because we indulged in an imaginary dinner, (a poetical license,) on an anonymous invitation, we're to lose a matter-of-fact meal. Surely this never could by possibility have happened to any body but ourself. See the hardships of the matter. When a man fancies his legs *under* a gentleman's table, he may as well fancy any variety and amount of good things *upon* it. Where it is *all* fancy, why not swing loose, give rein to the imagination, and let it choose its gait? It costs no more to eat an imaginary good dinner, than an imaginary poor one. And yet we're to be struck off the list of invited guests, and denied even the consolation of "peas." Well, we're used to such misfortunes.

"We never loved a plant or flower," &c.

"My wife, I will not deny, was a little elated at having a city editor to dinner; but when I repeated, one by one, your extraordinary expectations, she became very thoughtful and silent."

We give up the "woodcock" and the "snipe." We surrender the "brook trout" and the "wild ducks," let them all go—they're no great things at best; good enough in their way, but by no means a *sine qua non* for a good dinner. We give up our "extraordinary expectations," and settle down on the "spring chickens." We would not bring a shade of thought or sadness to the face of a good wife for worlds. We'd have her smile. There's heaven in the smile of a true woman. We would not have her silent for a gold mine. There's music in her voice sweeter than the song of harps. We would have her always happy, always cheerful. No cloud should ever darken the sunshine of her pure heart, if we could rule her destiny.

"Now who would have thought, Mr. Editor, I put it to you, yes, sir, to you, who would have thought that this man of brilliant sunrises was holding forth even then, through the strength of yesterday's dinner, yesterday's 'snipe,' 'woodcock' or (more shocking) yesterday's 'wine?'"

All illusory, all a mistake, but we can bear it.

We're used to such things. It isn't the first time we've been made the victim of man's imperfectibility of judgment, or his positive injustice. The "Yesterday" was a dark day with us, 'twas washing-day with our wife at home, a day of cold meats, of half-picked bones and attenuated coffee, a day (and who is not thankful that it should be so?) that comes but once a week, a day of all days that brings no inspiration to the poet's fancy, no buoyancy to its wing. "Yesterday's snipe or woodcock," quotha! Our very dear friend, these things are not even "memories" with us. It may be we're getting old, that the mists which hang around the memory when we pass into the sear and yellow leaf, obscure our vision of the past; but try as we will, we can recall no such incident within the circle of half a dozen years as "snipe and woodcock." Good things we've eaten at home and abroad, things savory and pleasant to the taste, but of "snipe and woodcock" we're innocent, indeed we are. And "yesterday's wine," too, is a fancy, pure ethereality; we derived no strength from wine—we made no terms with the "deceiver." Wine never had a place on our table, nor in "our closet under the stairs." We never took it into our dwelling, never associated with it on any terms. We look upon wine as our enemy, we do indeed. Wine floored us once, and only once, and then 'twas by treachery. Under the influence of "repentance and soda water" we cut its acquaintance forever. Aye! laugh as you will, 'tis gospel truth; point to the imaginary dinner we sat down to at your table, still we affirm its truth.

> "I have wine, sir, it is in a dark closet under the hall stairs, and there it will remain. I have turned the key and hid it away, and no man will find it. Sauterne and Claret, and Old Port and Heidsick, and with them also, "Old Q." and Otard. There they are, and sometimes I talk to them a little through the key-hole."

Don't do that—it's dangerous. Hold no communion with them. Eve talked with the serpent, maybe at first "through a key-hole." She talked too often; she ate the forbidden fruit after talking, and the woes that darken human destiny followed. Have no word to say to them. Rather go boldly among them with a club and slay them, smash them into ten thousand pieces, throw them away to perish as they deserve upon the dunghill. It is this talking to the bottle "through the key-hole" that has ruined thousands, aye, millions of men; that has snatched an army of souls from Heaven, and peopled the dungeons of perdition with fallen spirits. It has broken the hearts of thousands upon thousands of mothers and fathers, and sent thousands upon thousands of wives in sorrow and desolation of spirit to the grave. It has given thousands upon thousands of sons to the prisons, and daughters to shame. It is not enough that you "have locked them in a dark closet under the stairs, and hid away the key." Doors grow rusty upon their hinges, locks fail in their office, wine grows in strength and power of seduction, with age. You are not safe, your children are not safe, your servants are not safe, while the wine bottles are in that closet. Turn them out, break them in pieces. 'Tis your only sure protection. Talk not of your strength, your power of resistance. Look around you, see how many strong men, strong in intellect, strong in moral power, who mocked at the warning of danger, and derided the prophecy of their fall, who, in the face of all these things, became victims at last. Aye, victims! and in spite of the admonitions, the prayers of mother, father, wife, children, all that could strengthen resolve, went down through the drunkard's infamy to the drunkard's grave. Don't talk to those bottles "through the key-hole."

"Wherefore, Mr. Editor, until I may suddenly find that key, or until you can dine, in a plain way, with—say for wine, a glass of *eau de sucre,* or the like, I see no way to meet your wants."

That's what we call sensible talk. Don't waste time, our dear sir, in looking for the key. Let it go. Get your "plain dinner" ready. Never mind the "sweet water." The pure element that bubbles up from beneath the rock, at the foot of the old birch, or the ancient maple, will answer our turn. Certify us of the time and place, and we'll be there. Prepare your "spring chickens." Let them be broiled to a demonstration, over hard wood coals—crisped and browned, but not burned. Baste them with fresh sweet butter, and sprinkle them with parsley. We'll come. Serve them up hot, smoking from the gridiron. Accompany them with peas, young potatoes and beets. We'll come. Don't forget the white wheat bread, baked the afternoon before, as the Patlander would say, and the pure yellow butter, and the sliced cucumbers. Yes, we'll come. We'll be there to a minute. We'll "dine in a plain way." "Better is a dinner of herbs where love is, than a stalled ox and hatred therewith."

"Lastly, as to who and where I am, the motion is not now in order. Perhaps I am a country clergyman, recreating in a country paper. (I *shall* preach to you: aye, sir, I shall lay on and spare not.) Perhaps I am a country farmer, trying to get his wife to read the news. Perhaps a retired valetudinarian, amusing himself with a city Editor."

No matter, our dear sir, your "spring chickens" shall be your warrant of respectability, and your peas the endorsement of your character. If you are a clergyman, you may preach to us. You may "lay on and spare not." We're remarkably patient. We'll listen with commendable meekness, taking our revenge on the spring chickens. We respect the clergy. If you're a farmer, it's just as well. Our father was a farmer, our kindred are all farmers. It's a respectable calling; those who belong to it are coming to be the aristocracy of the land; besides, they raise such fine spring chickens.

We don't, by any manner of means, object to farmers. If you're a retired valetudinarian, it's all the better. Your lack of digestion will augment our share of the chickens. Amuse yourself with us to your heart's content. We're to be amused with, if the chickens are properly broiled and the trimmings all right. Yes, yes! amuse yourself with us. We'll take care of ourself and the chickens.

"In any case, for the present, my special invitation is, (and my wife joins me heartily,) DON'T COME TO DINNER!"

We decline the "*special* invitation," promptly and at once. Our convenience will not suffer us to accept. We regret, on account of our correspondent and his excellent wife, that we cannot, but circumstances must control our action in the matter. We are, of course, grateful for this "*special* invitation," and we hope they will pardon us for declining it.

III.

COUNTRY LUXURIES.

We extend to you, sir, the right hand of invitation. But as only two can shake hands at once, my wife, who is all in white this morning, makes you a courtesy, and sends you her regards. If you could see her, sir, as she stands making you this modest obeisance, you would come, as with wings. You would be charmed through the air, as was Loretto's chapel. "Tell him also," she says, "not to wait for the spring chickens, but to come now;" and so say I, her excellent husband, as she calls me; and I will add, that were we two individuals, or even two very diverse individuals, instead of that consolidated unit which we are (though called from the paucity of language, Mr. *and* Mrs. Margin), I should still say *come.* I should mount the platform, and exclaim as the speech-maker did, in those three immortal words, at the laying of a corner-stone, "*It will do!*" *Come.*

We have, sir, lamb chops, new potatoes, the round squash, peas if possible, and that delicate vegetable, powerful in its way, but still delicate, *the young onion.* How other people's onions may relish this year I know not, but ours have arrived just now at a youthful pungency that is very touching. Boiled to a creamy tenderness, or cut up thin with vinegar, from the pure white globule (about the size, when cut asunder, of an English sovereign), they are alike admirable and perfect in their way. I use the word *perfect*, thoughtfully, for you can add nothing to the young onion; or if you do, as in the more advanced onion, you have *too much*—an excess; a wild and giddy nostril-dilating power; which, as I have just said, is *too much*. Thanks, therefore, that things must grow, and not spring up into rankness in a single night. Why, sir, a young lady and her sister in the great city have just written to us that they are coming up this summer (a journey of some hundreds of miles), expressly to have a good time with that delicate plant. I immediately replied with my very best married man's regards, and conceiving it proper to make a few remarks, added the following: "I thank heaven that there are some people left in these latter days, who are willing and ready to eat onions. It is a good sign. It augurs well for the country. It will give strength and tone to the people—the onion—when all other things may fail."

When will you come? It's a good time now, our hay being well housed, and nothing remaining of an urgent character.

My father remarked the other day, that with one exception he had not succeeded in getting in his grass without rain, in fifteen years. He usually begins on Monday, so as not to have the eye-sore of hay in the meadow on Sunday. Accordingly, on Monday last, my father sent the men into the meadow, although the clouds were ready, at the very moment, to drop with fatness. He merely remarked that it would have to be rained on, and the sooner the better. Before noon the grass was down, and so was the rain. A fine shower began about that time, and continued at intervals all day. My aunt, who had not been watchful of the grass-cutting, walked into my father's room, and taking a pinch of snuff, remarked in her pleasant and thankful way, "What a beautiful shower! how good it will be for the garden!" "Yes," said my father, very briefly, "and for my grass, too."

The little excitement being over, and the grass made into hay and under cover, we are now at leisure again. It remains, therefore, only to point you the way. But I hope, sir, you will not look for a vulgar and exact chart of the route; as, say, "Bungtown train 10:20, stop at Bung, inquire for Bing, and find the same just round the corner." Horrid! How excessively annoying to be booked in that way! Think, sir, of the nervous anxiety as to reaching station at the precise 10:20; then of the great trepidation as to where *Bung* is, the intense scrutiny of your watch and time-table, or, in your final despair, the hurried exclamations to the flying conductor, "Is this Bung? Have we got to *Bung*, yet."

I never do so. When I travel (and the mood may spring upon me at any moment), I kiss my wife *good-bye* between the eyes, and walk directly to the station; she, perhaps, trotting by my side, as I go off with easy strides, hoping, possibly, for more *good-byes* at convenient corners. Well, sir, at the station I *take the cars.* That's all. I never ask the conductor where he is going, or when he expects to get there. I take it he understands his business. We are going,—that is the great point: we are travelling. When it comes night, or whenever I get tired, I motion to the conductor, in an easy way, to let me out; and if there is no coach handy in that part of the country, perhaps I may walk; but then I never programme to do so and so. I programme to do as I please, and as events shall determine.

I would say, therefore, Mr. Editor, in a general way, as to coming to dinner, *take the cars.* Or, to be entirely explicit, take the cars for the country. After riding as far as you think proper, I should say *stop*, by all means; and after taking bearings a little, look about for Small Bob. If you find Small Bob, you are in our neighborhood. Don't overlook that individual, or mark too harshly the width of his hat-brim. Small Bob, seeing a man of your comprehensive appearance, will address you as follows:—"Is this"—

removing his hat-brim—" Is this the great city Editor, come to dine with Mr. and Mrs. Margin?"

Of course, I need not indicate further. Only don't be alarmed at the dogs, as you come up the yard. If Bob is with you, you are safe.

P. S.—Don't come to-day. We are in a revolution—temporary, it is to be hoped. In fact, I suspect it's all to be for your benefit. But the fact is all the same,—we are housebreaking. Half a dozen strong women are about upsetting things, and busy in various burglarious operations. We are to dine on the piazza, and sleep as the strong women may provide. Perceiving that all things would soon be, as you may say, in a state of probation, I saved my portfolio early from the ruins, and have stolen away to a spare corner up stairs, to stop the press with this postscript.

You would smile, sir, to see my young wife order her forces: now with a low tone of suggestion, or a hurried word of caution, and again with a cut-short *oh!* or an unstoppable scream, as some fabric is threatened with destruction: and the next moment turning to me with a woman's composure, all calmness and greatness, saying—" Tell him to come. We will be ready."

My father regards the event from a different point of view, rolling his thumbs, as he sits in his great chair, and looking sharply down the long vistas of piled-up confusion, or chaos, as he calls it.

P. S. No.2.—We have dined as arranged, on the

piazza, under the roof shade and the shade of the pines, and it was, as the little girls say, *be-u-tiful.* I almost wished that we had sent our dispatch for to-day. We had the chops, the new potatoes, the young onions, and (forgotten before, but always immortal; I eat it three times a day) the black raspberry; and you, my aunt, Souchong. We discussed *junkett* also, called in the vulgar, "slip and go down;" and after dinner, I mounted the door-sill and made a speech, quite surprising myself with the youthful vigor of my remarks.

During the speech, I put the question, sir, as to whether the great Editor shall now be invited to come to dinner to-morrow, at say $1\frac{1}{2}$ o'clock, and the result was a unanimous *aye.*

This matter is, therefore, as the French say, *fini.*

Yours, ——.

"We shall have lamb-chops, new potatoes, the round squash, peas, if possible, and that delicate vegetable, powerful in its way, but still delicate, the young onion."

Say no more, our dear sir, we accept the invitation. We won't wait for the spring chickens, or, if it's all the same to you, we'll reserve them for a future occasion. Lamb chops, young potatoes, the round squash and young onions, will do for the present. Mark, we say, for the present. We postpone, only postpone the era of spring chickens.

Talking of onions reminds us of the times of old, when youth sharpened the appetite, and exercise gave a zest to plain fare. How often have we taken a piece of bread spread with butter in one hand, and a spoonful of salt in the other, and gone out into the garden to eat bread and butter, with onions fresh from the ground. We have done this many a time when we were young, and the memory of it comes back like the shadow of a pleasant dream. Onions, young onions in particular, is our weakness. They are healthy, as well as delicious and savory vegetables. We like lamb-chops; we like young potatoes, we adore the round squash, but young onions is our weakness. True, they add no sweetness to the breath, but then let others eat them too, and there will be no trouble on that score.

"Why, sir, a young lady and her sister in the great city have just written to us that they are coming up this summer (a journey of some hundreds of miles) expressly to have a good time with that delicate plant."

Strong-minded women, those who are not to be tyrannized out of their "young onions" by the potentates of fashion. Sensible girls, that go into the country to get free for a time of the bad atmosphere and worse conventional proprieties of a city life. Will they come during the season of young onions, or will they wait for the spring chickens? Let us hear when they come, and we shall not take the least possible offence at being invited about the same time. We'll encourage by our example the young lady and her sister in having a good time with the onions.

"My wife, who is all in white this morning, makes you a courtesy, and sends you her regards."

We like white. It is the true color for a pure-hearted woman. It is the color of the robes that angels wear. It belongs to the spotless beings above, to the cherubims that circle around the great white throne. Let her always wear white of a morning. We accept her regards—we shall cherish them as sacred things—we would not forfeit them for worlds.

"If you could see her as she stands, making you this modest obeisance, you would come as with wings. You would be charmed through the air as was Loretto's Chapel."

We *do* see her in our mind's eye, not as "making" us "a modest obeisance," but as a calm and dignified woman, conscious of her own worth, her value, her purity. Her heart has not been chilled by contact with the cold world, nor her aspirations blighted by disappointment. On her cheek is the rose of life's summer, the flush of health and high hopes. May the rose bloom there for many a year —may the flush continue till life's close, and may that be far off in the future; may children and grand-children be around her then, and may the tear of affection, as it falls upon her cold cheek, be the last sensation that shall remind her of earth's cares.

But we can't come "as with wings"—we are too substantial, too earthly, if you please, for that. We will come in the cars, and speak to the engineer to let on the steam; but fourteen stone weight can't do much with wings. Nor can we go through the air like Loretto's Chapel. We have a natural tendency to sink, a downward proclivity as it were, when we step off from some high place upon nothing. Loretto's Chapel was transferred through a miraculous agency, but the age of miracles is past, and unless we can harness the power that moves tables, and makes chairs, and stools, and stands dance a jig together, into the service, we must perforce be content to go on land, and under the impulse of steam.

"When will you come? It's a good time now, our hay being well housed, and nothing remaining of an urgent character. My father remarked the other day, that with one exception, he had not succeeded in getting in his grass without rain in fifteen years."

You are quite right, our very dear sir. The best time to accept an invitation to a good dinner is always *now*. We are sorry the grass has been mowed. We want to swing a scythe again. We have done so once this summer. We want to rake and pitch; we have done that too. It was away out in old Steuben. We were passing a meadow where six men were mowing, marching forward like a platoon of grenadiers keeping step and stroke together, each swing of the scythe cutting down grass enough to fodder an ox. We climbed over the fence, and throwing our coat upon a swath, took down a scythe that hung on the limb of a thorn bush; we felt the edge, and finding it keen, struck in boldly with the mowers. We understood this business once, and so long as our wind held out, kept up. But editing a newspaper is not calculated to make one enduring in the hot sun of July, and after mowing a bout, we surrendered. Raking was easier work, and we took an hour's turn at that. Then we pitched on a load and pitched it off, into the great bay in the barn. By this time we had taken a sweat that a steam doctor might envy, and we passed on our way. Do you remember when a boy at work in the hay field, how you watched the heavens, when the signs of rain were in the air? Do you remember how merrily the tree-frog piped along the fences; how gently the wind stirred among the trees; how fan-like it lifted the leaves upon the basswoods along the fences, turning the under side to the sun, and making the tree-top shine all over like silver? Do you remember how, when the haze gathered in the air, a great circle surrounded the sun, and how he became less and less bright, until he disappeared in the sky?

And then, do you remember when the small drops of a settled rain came falling gently around you, how you shouldered your rake, and marched to the barn, and then how you clambered on to the hay mow, and listening to the soothing sound of the rain upon the roof, you sunk away into the sweetest possible sleep?

Do you remember how you watched the clouds when a shower was coming up from the south-west? Did you note how the great black clouds came lifting their monster-shaped heads above the horizon, followed by others still more ogre-looking, until the van of the storm stretched in a long dark line across the sky? Did you note the flashing of the lightning, and did you catch the first deep growl of the thunder in the distance? Did you hear the sound of the wind and the pouring rain, while the storm was yet at a distance, and did you look calmly from your bed of loose hay on the barn floor, upon the rushing waters, while the clouds were emptying their floods around you? We remember these things, and we have never lost our respect for a settled rain, or a thunder shower in haying time.

"I kiss my wife good-bye, between the eyes, and walk directly to the station."

Without intending to be personal, you must permit us to say you are wrong, and the more we reflect upon the subject, the more convinced are we that you are wrong. Not in kissing your wife. One may kiss one's wife without blame. We like the practice—we do so ourself, occasionally. It serves to keep the affections warm and the heart soft. Nor do we object to your walking directly to the cars, after kissing your wife good-bye. That may be done with propriety and safety. But what we protest against, is the kissing your wife good-bye "*between the eyes.*" The practice is a bad one. Lips were made to be kissed after their owner has become a wife. The cheek of a maiden may be touched by the lips of a lover, but the lips of the wife should be the recipients of a husband's kiss. This is the true principle and philosophy of the matter, and we protest against any departure from the ancient and orthodox usage.

"I would say, therefore, Mr. Editor, in a general way, as to coming to dinner, take the cars, or, to be entirely explicit, take the cars for the country. After riding as far as you think proper, I should say stop, by all means, and after taking bearings a little, look about for Small Bob."

We begin really to despair of this dinner. We have made numberless concessions. We have surrendered woodcock and snipe, wild-duck and venison, and settled down on spring chickens. We subsequently conceded the chickens and took to lamb-chops, young potatoes, round squashes and young onions, and now we are in danger of losing even them. It's all very well to talk about taking the "cars for the country." The country is a large place. It lays all around Albany, and stretches a great way back. If we go north, we traverse Vermont. The cars go thundering through the gorges of the Green Mountains. We went that way last summer. We stopped at a pleasant village squatted down in a beautiful valley, through which flowed a cold pure stream, to fish for the speckled trout. But hundreds had preceded us, and the trout were all destroyed. We were told of a little lake that few had had the courage to visit, laying just over the ridge of mountains, where the trout were abundant. We started for that lake. Our course lay over Mount Tabor, one of the highest ridges of the Green Mountains. Blazed trees along a blind foot-path pointed out the way. We went clambering up precipices that seemed to have no summits, sweating and sweltering in a July sun. When we stopped to rest, the gigantic hemlocks that grew out from the rugged side of the mountain away down below us, going straight up towards the sky, presented their tall tops almost within our reach, so steep was the acclivity. We toiled on for hours and hours with slow and painful progress, till we entered a region of mist. The bushes were dripping with moisture, and so were we, still we toiled on till at last the summit was gained, and we sat down to rest amid the clouds on the bare top of Mount Tabor. It was cool enough away up there, and we waited for the mist to pass away. It did pass at length, and the prospect that opened upon our vision repaid a hundred-fold the toil of the ascent. There we sat thousands of feet above the level of the sea. Away off to the west lay Lake

Champlain, stretching north and south for a hundred miles. We saw two steamboats ploughing their way through the waters, while away beyond were the mountains of Essex, their bald heads piercing the sky, shining in the sunlight like the glistening helmet of some giant warrior of old. Beneath us were beautiful valleys, winding away towards the level country to the south, with broad farms and green fields spread out, dotted with farm-houses and barns, and here and there a quiet village with church steeples going up from among the clustered houses. We saw the long line of a railroad stretching away towards Rutland, and a train of cars drawn by the iron horse dashing along on its journey towards Rouse's Point. Towards the east was a dense forest standing in all its primeval grandeur, clothed in everlasting green, stretching away far as the eye could reach, with here and there a mountain peak towering towards the sky. We sat there for an hour enjoying the cool breeze, and drinking in the grandeur of the landscape beneath us, and then passed on to the pond where the trout were said to abound. We reached it in half an hour, and were repaid for our labor by two trout and a mud turtle. We returned at night weary enough, but in the morning we remembered the vision from Mount Tabor, and were satisfied.

If we go east, "the country" reaches all the way to Boston, the metropolis of the Bay State. If we go west, it reaches to Lake Erie, and beyond that, thousands of miles, across vast prairies, and over the Rocky Mountains, to the great Pacific. If we go south, it reaches to the Empire City. Here we are, then, afloat without a compass, wandering in a boundless wilderness, with no landmark save "Small Bob." And who, in the name of all the saints, is "Small Bob"? Answer us that. Where are we to find him? What are his distinctive marks? What is his complexion; is it ebony or topaz? Are we to wander all over the land, like Japhet in search of his father, inquiring after "Small Bob," and a dinner of lamb-chops, new potatoes, round squashes and young onions?

We can't do it; and we see the vision of gastronomy fading from our view, as many a bright one has done before. We give it up in despair. Ah me!

IV.

EDITOR'S LATITUDE & LONGITUDE.

I THOUGHT of you this morning, my kind editor, almost with tears in my eyes. Crossing the high bridge over Roaring River, I came upon three boys lying flat on their bellies, their heads just over the edge of the bridge, shouting to a boy below, who, with rolled-up trowsers, was seeking wildly for a mud turtle. The excitement both below and above was extreme. The turtle, in looking down, was in plain sight, floating about in quite shoal water, and evidently having a good time, now with his tail up, going down among the crevices of the rocky bottom, and then with raised paws, coming slowly up and skimming the surface. But to the boy below all was glimmer and confusion; the dazzle of the sun and the ripple on the surface suggesting to him unknown depths, and his own eagerness to accomplish the feat making him almost frantic, set on, as he was, by the cries of the boys above, "There he is—oh, my gracious! Don't you see him? he is coming right towards you—oh crackee! Catch him, Jim, catch him!" All this, I say to my experienced eye, knowing how perfectly safe that turtle was, made up a scene of distress in which I couldn't help exclaiming, "Oh that the editor was here!" For I remembered your experience in turtling, and that large men are always magnanimous and generous to boys. I counted, also, on your length (not breadth) of beam, for I take it, sir, you are a man of symmetry. Your "fourteen stone" weight, I do hope and trust, is not all laid out horizontally. Your downward tendency has not settled you into a rhomboid. You have height as well as depth; longitude as well as latitude. You should be, sir, at least six feet, in your stockings: for the symmetries are as important to men as the graces to woman. Mental, moral, and physical—these are the symmetries; and such is the effort of nature to make them always harmonize, that having one, we invariably look for the others. If a man lack in altitude (the *proportionate* height, I mean), he will be short in something else. Inevitable, sir, inevitable. He will not be gifted in sunrises and large views; though he may be good in trouting, and better still at *chub*-bing. Some of the most patient anglers I know are those who, having seated themselves comfortably on a river bank, find it exceedingly difficult to get up again. *You*, sir, should be six feet high, and well proportioned.

But why is it, I was going to ask—why is it, Mr. Editor, that boys crave mud-turtle? Why hanker after the ugly? For an eel or a bull-head—(I do not deny a certain beauty and philosophical harmony in the turtle—its life in its shell), but an eel or a bull-head is a greater satisfaction to most boys than the handsomest trout you ever saw. There are people, also, who go about collecting strange bugs, beetles, snakes, spiders, and many-legged monstrosities, which they carefully bottle and keep near them, as a kind of refreshment! U—g—h!

And now, sir, I ask you, is there a sort of *Young Harry* in this, leading on to the *Old Harry?* For there are older boys just as intent, just as eager, just as morbidly hungry for moral monstrosities, bottling all manner of vice and ugliness, and deformity, and cherishing them as something very delectable, something really new under the sun, and the only true facts and realities, as though hell itself were not already full of just that kind of material!

As there is a love of the beautiful, so also there is a love of the ugly. I have fought hard and long against this conviction, but I believe it is true as Holy Writ, and the great mischief of our day is the practical unbelief in regard to this matter.

A love of the ugly for its own sake—a love of vice *with* its sequents, and because of them, almost as though it were a pleasure to be damned. There are men in the world who seem to be haunted with the fear that they will see or hear of something pleasant, something beautiful, or good, and so be charmed by some hocus pocus, into a belief in the existence of such things. "Oh my vipers," they cry: "Oh my bugs, my snakes, my excellent big black spiders!"

Nothing is more painful to such men than symmetry, beauty, proportion. They seek always for the ugly, and they find it. No fear as to that. They are sure to arrive at the most hellish capacities, and it is rare that such men die without proving to the world the height and depth of their abilities in that line.

The morning that we have to-day, under these heavens, is exceedingly beautiful. It would seem that on such a morning, everything that hath breath would be saying—*Hallelujah, hallelujah, amen, hallelujah!* But it is safe to say that the Prince of Darkness, and his legions, whether here or elsewhere, have had no voice in these utterances. Their partialities are all "the other way, the other way;" they love the ugly. I have no liking for the freedom with which some people talk of that Great Creature, that "archangel ruined," who is now making such terrible havoc in the world, showing his hand of late with so much boldness and success, and claiming allegiance upon the very score of his supreme hideousness. I am not disposed to make light of him, but I trust there is no harm in offering it as my long-settled conviction, that if this "murderer from the beginning" had ever, by any mistake, made a pleasant morning like this, he would have hung himself before breakfast. Yes, sir, he would have hanged himself high, unless, indeed, he might have gone mad in the first glance at its beauty and glory.

But God made the morning—thanks to His Great and Holy name. God made the morning, and in this is the hope of the world.

I did not expect to be so grave, Mr. Editor, for there is a time and place for such topics, and I fear you may think I am out of both. Permit me one last word about our dinner. I have been thinking, sir, that if you start out alone, you may be charmed away by some inviting vista, and never find us. Your passion for mountains might be too much for you. We should hear of you, perhaps, clambering, coat off, and hat in hand, up some neighboring height, making speeches to the clouds and the country at large; or possibly—and quite possibly, too—stopping somewhere for a sunrise. I am coming after you, therefore, myself.

Yours, ———.

"I take it, sir, you are a man of symmetry. Your 'fourteen stone' weight, I do hope and trust, is not all laid out horizontally. Your 'downward tendency' has not settled you into a rhomboid."

Men's notions of symmetrical beauty differ. Tastes, on that subject, take a wide range. Some admire long men, reaching away up like a liberty pole, a thing to hang flags on, on the Fourth of July. Length has its conveniences, we admit. It's a good thing in cherry time. One can pick the fruit handily from the remote branches. Others prefer horizontal dimension, a spreading out sideways. It gives an appearance of substantiality, of solidity. We never quarrel with people's tastes. *De gustibus non disputandum*, is our motto. We insist that it is a wise one. If the standard of beauty were fixed at six feet and upwards, what would become of the short men and women? For ourself, we are not a "rhomboid." We have more than four sides. We have been accused of having had at least twice that number in politics alone—with what justice "history must determine." All we say on the subject is, we never had but one political side—at a time. We admit that politics has "made us acquainted with strange bed-fellows." We entered upon political life with certain *fixed* principles, and as we affirm, have stood *fast* by them. Parties fluctuate, or rather circulate, revolve, go round and round. We being fixed, it is not singular that we should have come in conjunction with all parties, in their revolutions. True, the world differs with us on this subject, and says that *we* have been circulating —visiting different party orbits in our course. That we deny, and surely *we* ought to know the real truth of the matter.

"You should be, sir, at least six feet in your stockings."

True, we *should* be, but we are not by a long shot. Doubtless it was originally intended otherwise. We were meant for a six-footer, but we got spoiled in some way in the making up. It was a great misfortune, we admit, but by no system of ethics can it be charged against us as a fault. What a man *does*, he should be held accountable for. He should be held answerable for what he *is*, if he made himself such by his follies or his vices. The Deity made men right. He gave them the power of choice in their course of life. He placed good and evil before them, and left them free to choose. The consequences of their choice were not hidden from them. All around the good were scattered peace and happiness, joy and gladness in this world, and the promise of happiness in the world to come. The evil was beset with sorrow. Vice carried its chains, to be fastened upon its votaries. A troubled life, a barren and hopeless hereafter, were the rewards it promised. Between these utter divergents lay the destiny of men; and, strange infatuation, transcendent folly, the evil has an army of followers, in comparison with which the good can reckon only a corporal's guard.

"The symmetries are as important to men as the graces to women. Mental, moral, and physical—these are the symmetries; and such is the effort of nature to make them always harmonize, that having the one, we invariably look for the others."

Doubtless this is all true in theory, but not so clearly sustained by facts. Let us look around us and see what are the demonstrations. CHALMERS was a man of small stature, and lean proportions, but what divine equalled him in mental power, or excelled him in moral qualities? Who has not read with rapture his matchless sermons, replete with thrilling eloquence and grandeur of rhetoric, his "thoughts that burn," his profound and original conceptions? One can almost imagine himself soaring amid the stars, far away in the blue vault of heaven, traversing the milky way, and diving between the rings of Saturn, while reading his astronomical discourses. Newton was a man of medium stature, and yet in intellect almost a god. Instances may be multiplied of great men with bodies by no means proportionate to the giant dimensions of their intellectual stature. The true theory probably is, that there is a secret balance between the intellectual and physical, which depends not so much upon length of bones and size of muscle, as upon a proper connection and development of organization.

"If a man lack in altitude (the proportionate height, I mean), he will be short in something else. Inevitable, sir, inevitable."

Excellent. This accounts for the milk in the cocoanut. We are a living demonstration of the truth of the theory. Lacking in the requisite altitude, we, of necessity, must be short somewhere. We have been so all our life. We have been short in the pocket, short in bank deposits, short in ability to meet promptly incoming bills. In short, we have been troubled all our life with the shorts, and here is the reason of the thing—we lack in length of body. Well, it's a pleasant thing when one enters upon a fight, to understand the *casus belli*, to understand the origin, the why and the wherefore of a thing. We have a friend who is "six feet in his stockings," and well proportioned, and he never had a bill protested in his life. We didn't understand how it could be, till we measured his height, got him to stand up by the ceiling, stuck a knife just even with his crown, and then got on to a stool and measured. It was six feet and an inch to the floor. Our friend always has his "pockets full of rocks," and it is all owing to his altitude.

"Some of the most patient anglers I know, are those who having seated themselves comfortably on a river bank, find it exceedingly difficult to get up again."

This squares with our own observation. We have in our mind's eye a notable example, what the lawyers would call a case in point. We returned last week from an angling expedition to the mountains of Pennsylvania, away up among the sources of rivers. We saw the spring from which the Genesee takes its rise. It comes out of the ground in a stream large enough to propel a mill wheel, and starts at once on its returnless voyage to the majestic St. Lawrence and the ocean. Beyond was a high ridge over which we passed, and then stepped across the remotest branch of the Alleghany that travels west to the Ohio, and then to the great Father of Waters, and so along down by New Orleans to the Mexican Gulf. Beyond again was a ridge higher still over which our road lay, and there we came to the head waters of the Sinnemahoning, that travels through great forests towards the Susquehanna, and finds its final passage to the ocean through the Chesapeake Bay. By the way, will anybody tell us how these great springs, that go to make up these rivers, get up here on these high mountains? We have read about capillary attraction, and the pressure from above that forces them through, and finally out of the ground, to flow away to the ocean obedient to the laws of gravity. We don't want to hear or read any more of that, for we don't believe it. There is not rain enough falling on these mountain ranges to supply evaporation, and these springs that gush in such volume from the ground, that come welling up in a flood day and night, week days and Sundays, always. But we got to the Sinnemahoning, in the woods, in the middle of a vast forest with only little clearings at long intervals along the valley through which it flows. Here we stopped for a week to fish for the speckled trout, and have a pleasant season of communion with nature in her old-fashioned dress. We do not intend to enter upon description of the scenery here, we reserve it for another occasion. We had with us two friends—the one a clergyman, to whom we refer as an example of patience in angling. He is one of a thousand, a Christian man, one fit to be trusted with the care of souls; but he is neither a zealot nor a bigot; of a cheerful, but contemplative spirit, with a mind profoundly stored with varied reading, he can appreciate as well as tell a merry anecdote, and perpetrate as well as enjoy a jest. He was a most patient angler. He would sit for hours under the shadow of some great tree on the bank of the little river, by the side of a deep hole, watching with patient assiduity his hook, as it floated in the water. If the fish were minded to bite, it was well; if not, it was just as well. There was the bait and the hook, the line and pole, and he was ready to draw them out. If they chose to remain under the logs and drift-wood, regardless of his tempting offers of a grasshopper or a worm, it was not his fault. Where you left the dominie, there you would him find, until the sun came round and drove him to another deep, still place, where was a bank and a shade, with the pleasant song of birds about him. He was not a very successful angler, but his cheerful countenance spoke of the pleasant memories, the bright day-dreams, the cheerful thoughts that were clustering around his heart, as he sat there in the cool shade, angling in a troutless eddy.

But he is not a "short" man; he is "six feet in his stockings," and had to stoop as he entered the door of the pleasant little dwelling where we stopped. That dwelling is in a little clearing of some twenty acres surrounded by forest, and high mountains, with tall peaks running up towards the sky, behind which the sun hides himself for hours before he finally goes down to his lodging-place for the night. We fishermen had our wives along, and they were so merry and contented, while we stayed, that we acquiesced in the name given it a year or two ago, and called it the "Saint's Rest."

"And now, sir, I ask you, is there not a *Young Harry* in this, leading on to *the Old Harry?*"

Very possibly, although the generally-received opinion, we think, is that the elderly gentleman spoken of, has most to do with such matters. He is said to be exceedingly busy in his vocation, and takes quite as much interest in the young as in the elders of the human family. Indeed, many think that his policy is to induct mankind into evil ways at an early age, so that as they advance in life, they give him less trouble by their ability to sin without calling upon him for aid in the furnishing of temptations.

"Permit me one last word about our dinner. I have been thinking, sir, that if you start out alone, you may be charmed away by some inviting vista, and never find us. Your passion for mountains might be too much for you. * * * * I am coming for you, therefore, myself."

A most sensible conclusion to an excellent sermon. That's what we call a practical climax, leaving a pleasant sensation on the mind, to aid in the digestion of a discourse. Well, come along. We'll be ready. We're not particular about the day or the hour, only let it be a week day, and not Friday. That's a bad day—a day when they hang people; a day full of evil omens. All the bad luck we ever had was on Friday. We fell into the Crooked Lake on a Friday, and were so nearly drowned that we never knew, save from hearsay, how we got out. We were upset in a stage coach, and had our nose knocked to one side, and our wrist sprained on a Friday. We were in the railroad cars when a collision took place; we were fast asleep at the time, and the shock pitched us headforemost against a lady who sat fast asleep in front of us, and whose husband threatened, in his ignorance of the collision (for he had been asleep too), to do us serious bodily damage, on account of our involuntary rudeness—all this was on a Friday night. Our house was burned on a Friday night, and two as noble stag hounds as ever followed the trail of a deer, perished in the flames. They were shut up in the wood-shed adjoining, and were suffocated before the flames were discovered. We never enter upon any new undertaking on a Friday. We form no new acquaintances on that day. We never accept an invitation for a Friday. We did that thing once "long ago," and we upset a capital dish of roast venison, covered with delicious gravy, in our lap. We had to send home for a pair of pantaloons, to don in the place of our white ones, spoiled by the misadventure. We have a theory on the subject of diurnal influences, and laughing at us won't induce its abandonment. We point to the facts, which to us, at least, are history, as evidence of its truth. Don't come on a Friday; something would surely go wrong, to mar the pleasure of a new acquaintance, and spoil a good dinner. On any other day, we say in the beautiful langauge of the poet—

"Walk along, John."

V.

A FRIEND FROM THE OLD DOMINION.

If you do not hear from me soon again, Mr. Editor, you may consider that I am taking a rest. Perhaps (as I remarked yesterday to my tall friend, L. P., of the F. F. V.), perhaps you carry too many guns for me. Perhaps you blow away my positions, and symmetrical arrangements, too easily. Certain it is, that pleasantly as we have chatted together over our peas and young onions, you have, of late, grown upon me into a kind of overshadowing greatness. Besides, August has come in upon us with great force, and for a space now, I must rest. On the first day of the month, and among the first of those hours which I include in the morning, I was rounding a pleasant dream up stairs, when there was a vigorous knock at the front door. Springing from bed, I put on my dressing-gown, and with unshod feet went down the stairs and opened upon—the *first* event of the day—my Rev. friend and quondam from a neighboring State, whom I had not seen for many years. Our mutual bewilderment in gazing upon each other, was almost at the point of awkwardness. He, so clean and clerical, so firm and close-buttoned; and I, like a ragged cloud, all wild and loose. He, who, ten years ago, had been spare-bodied like myself, and with eyes full of that intense sensibility with which some people go mourning about the world, was now round and compact; and I, who had been thin and spare, now thinner and sparer still. His face, which, like mine, had been sharply triangular, now presented a projection and squareness of chin, which implied, that let the world roll how it may, he was ready for it. Ready for to-day and for to-morrow, and for next week, built up, expanded, consolidated.

My friend seated himself comfortably by an open window, and gravely searched about me for some reminder of his old acquaintance; finding, however, only ruin and waste, with an occasional feeble flash, like sheet lightning, telling of storms gone by. And I couldn't help thinking there was something exultant in his gaze, as he saw all this change, and that hollow other-world look, which might have checked him, one would say, from coolly remarking, as he did, that, positively, if he had met me in the street, he should not have known me.

Perhaps not; probably not. But accustomed as I am to hear people say—"My dear Margin, how well you are looking," I was taken a little aback. Leaving him the freedom of the parlor, I returned to my chamber, exclaiming to the world, *sotto voce*, "Don't, my dear people, oh, don't let us be too

3

practical in a world like this." And I freely confess to you, my dear Editor, the effort of getting ready for breakfast that morning was more of a labor than I have had for many a day. I didn't pretend to shave, and my endeavors at getting my hair straight were, for a long time, as Longfellow says, "All in vain, all in vain." My young wife, however, during this time, was bracing me up, this way and that, and trying to put me in shape. "Pray," said she, "what does *he* know about you? Why, my dear husband, you are younger now than you have been for years. You are! Yes, for years. Please don't hurry; your cravat is all one side; yes, for years! Why, everybody tells you you are better—wait a moment; your coat; yes, better a great deal; and *you know you are!*"

Strengthened, and built about in this way, I came down to breakfast, prepared to demolish my stout friend instantly, if he continued his vein of remark. But, whether owing to the juvenile look which Mrs. Margin had given me, or to a deep feeling of remorse on his part, we had no further collisions. My friend stopped only for an hour, barely touching upon us, as he said, on his way home. But it was the touch of a strong mind in a strong body, carrying me off as with a whirlwind. I found myself, in a little while, bowling away with him to your city, and whirling and speeding through times past, times present, and the great time to come. Swift as flew the wheels in that lightning train, were our exchanges, shuttle-wise, of the great prominences in our last ten years. Nothing was too great for us. The roar of the train, and that outrageous scream and blast of the steam-whistle, were as trifles to us; for we were piped up higher than that, and in a wider range, discussing as we did, not our affairs only, but the pressing interests of the great world, winding up, of course, with the Thirty-nine Articles and the prospects of the Universe. An hour after reaching your city, we parted; he, stronger than ever; I, ready to descend rapidly into reactions. Strolling along, feebly, by the Marble Pillar, I looked wishfully over to No. 46; but weak as I was from my one stout friend, I couldn't think of meeting another. Not all our pleasant exchanges, sir, could tempt me to cross that street.

In this collapsed condition, I came home in the afternoon, to dinner and repose. About that time, also, came a shower opening the very windows of heaven; and after dinner, over which we lingered lovingly, just as the shower ceased, somewhere about four to five o'clock, there was another knock at the door, and behold—*second* event of the day, and tall contrast to him of the morning—my great friend, six feet four and three-quarters, L. P. of the F. F. V.! Yes, sir, my great friend and refreshment, as you may say, from the Old Dominion. All through that shower, he had been on our borders, in a shanty, on the further side of Roaring River, waiting for the floods to subside. And now here he was, in all his extreme length, and with that rich full voice, which, without loudness, could be heard all over the house. I had to turn him around twice in the hall, to enjoy him in different lights, and at all points. My young wife came forward to meet him, almost with a shout, and I some expected to see him bend down, and leave an impression upon Mrs. Margin; which, however, he did not, but talked a continual stream of music and delight, at the state of things now arrived at.

Well, sir, he has been with us three days, and he grows taller every day. Taller in our esteem, in our heart's regard, and in our determination to keep him, if possible, to the full extent of his furlough. Having preached four sermons a week, for the last ten months, now, he says, is the time for rest. *Dulce est desipere in loco*, and what loco like this (so he flatters me) with his friend, Mr. Margin, whose appreciation of rest has reached a perfection scarcely to be found, perhaps, in all the round world. Now for easy chairs and the piazza, the book and the hammock; or rather, the hammock without the book—(books are a nuisance). At this moment, he is lying at full length on the parlor sofa, smoking a cigar. He is calling to me now, and his voice has to travel around through the hall and two doorways, but comes with perfect distinctness.

"I say, Margin—"

"Well, what is it?"

"Did I tell you about the little boys?"

(While I was napping yesterday, my friend walked down to the Rising Sun, a village in the north-east, and there surprised another Virginia friend and rector, and was passed about like a bottle of old wine with the cork undrawn, his friend holding him stoutly by both hands, while he presented him to some half dozen ladies and two clergymen, who were present.)

"Did I tell you about the little boys?"

"No. What about the boys?"

"Why, sir, there were four of them, and they followed me all about the streets!"

"Yes?"

"Yes; and what do you suppose they were after?"

"A penny, perhaps."

"No; because I heard some of their remarks. 'I say, Jim,' said one, 'did you ever see any thing like that?' 'Crackee!' says another, 'just look at him!' And the rascals followed me, sir, to the very door of the rectory."

My friend having unburdened himself of this matter, relapses again into silence, though I dare say he is smoking vigorously, and not unlikely, may continue talking the whole matter over to himself, for some time to come. If I was nearer, I should hear, perhaps, fragments of speech thrown out with considerable force, such as *the rogues! the scamps! the young rascals!* but not unkindly, for all fire and power as he is, he has a heart (as they say out West) "as big as an ox."

And now, Mr. Editor, I will say good-morning, remarking, as once before, that I am not now in the marginal way. We design—my friend and I; I say we design—or rather, we do not design. That is the beauty of it: plans and designs are laid aside. We rest now, and wait for events. All things of easy approach shall be welcome. Nothing more. Cigars that smoke easy, we shall smoke. Dinners that are patriarchally simple, and not distracting in temptations, we shall have from time to time—in fact daily; unless we may arrive at that happy perfection of the ideal when a day *without* dinner may seem to be the maximum of easy enjoyment, in which case we shall *not* dine. Cigars and easy positions will be the general order, with occasional short and celestial remarks. The great point will be not so much to *do* things, as to let them be done. While we pause, the morning and evening will continue as usual: sun and shade, and rains and night-dews, and the great world to whom they are sent; these all will come and go, roll about, migrate, fluctuate, and so forth, but as pictures only to Mr. Margin and his eminent friend L. P., of the F. F. V.

Meantime my young wife, who has finished her jellies—in which seraphic employment, with short gown and up-rolled sleeves, she has been busy for so many happy days—she, I say, will join us at times, waking us from too long naps with some pleasant song, or suggesting occasional novelties, all in keeping with our sublimated life. Of course, if occasion requires, we shall preach to the people roundabout; but we hope there will be no occasion. After our four sermons a week, for the last ten months, we feel more like pardoning everybody out and out. I say we feel more like this, as sailors say, letting things go by the run: but, of course, it's wrong; we are aware of that, and if called upon, we shall hope to be ready. But it would be as wise, perhaps, to let us alone just now, for our style is not of the mealy-mouthed kind. No, sir, and may God preserve me from any levity in this matter: we preach, as my father says, *death, judgment, and eternity.*

Once more, Mr. Editor, good-morning; and till we meet again, good-bye.

Yours, ——.

"If you do not hear from me soon again, you may consider I am taking a rest."

Don't do that, our dear sir—don't do it. Don't take a rest. There's something sad in the idea of taking a rest; something that speaks of decay, of energies exhausted, of life-springs drying up. To us the words come freighted with no pleasant memories. We had an ancient friend long ago, a rough specimen of a man, but every inch a man—

one of nature's nobility—honest and straightforward as truth itself, whose good opinion we lost for a time by "taking a rest." He was a man of eccentricities, of idiosyncrasies, if you please, and it cost us years of effort to get back into our old place in his regards. We said he was a rough specimen of a man, but he was one of giant sympathies and a big heart. He was a man of the back settlements and the woods. He was a mighty hunter, and the game he sighted might count itself as lost. He loved his friends, and was proud of them. He loved his rifle and his dogs. He loved the old woods and mountains, and the wild streams. He was older by a score of years than ourself, but the icicles of age never gathered around his heart, and the coldness of growing years never chilled the genial warmth of his nature. He has passed to his rest now, and sleeps quietly under the shadow of thick foliaged maples on a little knoll selected by himself. Calm be thy slumbers, mine ancient friend, and happy thy long future in the world to come. He loved his rifle and his dogs, and his heart was ready to embrace the man who loved the tangled forest-paths, who loved to hear the music of his hounds upon the mountain, and to bring down the flying deer. A marksman himself, he was ready to love the man who could equal him in skill with the rifle; and to be his superior was a surer passport still to his affections.

On a Christmas day, long ago, when we were

younger by many, many years, than we are now, we went to a gathering, known among the border villages as a shooting match. Turkeys were the prizes contended for. A plank was placed at some five and twenty rods distance, with a hole in it, through which was thrust the head of the turkey, while his body was secured behind it. At this mark the sportsmen fired. If blood was drawn, the marksman was entitled to the turkey. Each competitor paid a small piece of money before taking a shot, which went to the owner of the turkey. Well, we were there with our rifle to take our chances with the rest for a Christmas dinner. A number of marksmen had preceded us, and we ourselves had failed in a shot or two, when it was proposed to "take a rest;" that is, to lay down with the rifle resting upon a block properly arranged, and in that position take sight and fire at the head of the poor bird. Its owner had already pocketed twice its value in shillings, and he consented to the arrangement. The block was placed in position, and the first shot fell by lot to ourself. Among hunters in those days, taking a rest either at living game or a dead mark, was a violation of all the proprieties of woodcraft. It was opposed to all rule, a practice which, if largely indulged in, would cost one his position among sportsmen, and the regards of every true hunter and woodman. As we said, the first shot fell by lot to ourself, and we were about taking our position, when we felt a hand laid upon our shoulder. Turning, we saw our old friend standing beside us, leaning upon his long rifle. We had not noticed him before. "Don't do it," said he; "Sam, don't do it—never take a rest, stand up like a man, and fire off-hand; if you miss, you can't help it, and nobody blames you, but never take a rest." His voice sounded more in sorrow than in anger, but we saw that his confidence in our woodcraft was shaken, and his esteem for us as a hunter fading away.

We *did* stand up and fire off-hand, and the head of the turkey was shattered by our ball. That shot did much towards calling back to us his wandering regards, but it was not until we had hunted with him, and brought down many a noble deer in his company, that the impression of our weakness in "taking a rest" was effaced from his mind. We admonish you, therefore, our very dear sir, in the language of our ancient friend, "Don't do it, never take a rest. Stand up like a man, and fire off-hand. If you miss, nobody blames you, but 'never take a rest.'" There's a moral in the admonition, a moral and deep philosophy in the advice. Always, and at all times through life, whatever temptations may beset you, however misfortune may darken around you, yield not a foot to the tempter, bend not a joint to misfortune, but "stand up like a man and fire off-hand."

"On the first day of the month, and among the first of those hours, which I include in the morning, I was rounding a pleas-

ant dream up stairs, when there was a vigorous knock at the front door."

Served you right, our dear sir, right, to a dot. What right had you, you, blessed with intelligence, eyes to see, and ears to hear, what right had *you* to be "rounding a pleasant dream up stairs," when all nature was awake, joyous, full of gladness, chaunting the songs of the morning? And in the country, too! Talk not of "pleasant dreams up stairs," of a summer morning. There's no such paradox in nature. Dreams, indeed! In the crowded thoroughfares of city life, the thronged streets and clustered houses, where the air is poisoned by the smoke of ten thousand cooking-stoves, and machine-shops, and gas-factories, and forges, and the thousand villanous smells that exhale from the haunts of condensed civilization, "a pleasant dream up stairs" of a morning is within the range of conjecture, but such a thing in the country would be a libel upon nature. No, no! Thank your stars that a worse evil did not befall you. Why, our dear sir, you should have been up when the first bright gleam of the morning glanced upward from behind the eastern summits. You should have heard the first song of the lark, as he leaped from his perch, and went carolling joyjully towards the sky. You should have seen the last stars as they retired from their watch, passing away into the depths of the heavens. You should have watched the mist that went up in the gray twilight, from "Roaring River," and faded like a vision in the air. You should have seen the first ray of the sun, as it lighted upon the tops of the mountains. You should have looked away to the east, and seen the sun, like a great torch, hanging for a moment in the tree-tops, and then noted how gloriously he leaped forward into the clear sky. You should have seen the dew-drops, sparkling like diamonds on the grass blades, and heard the wild, free song of the birds in their gleefulness. You should have snuffed the pure air, loaded with the fragrance of flowers, and the freshness gathered from the foliage of the woods. With these things all around you, you should have looked away to the Providence that spread so rich a feast; to the God that made the morning, and all the beautiful things that belong to it.

"Yes, sir, my great friend and refreshment, as you may say, from the Old Dominion. All through that shower, he had been on our borders in a shanty, on the hither side of Roaring River, waiting for the floods to subside, and now here he was, in all his extreme length, and with that rich, full voice, which, without being loud, could be heard all over the house."

Strange reunions—meetings of old friends under curious circumstances, sometimes take place. Years may have fled away, events may have hurried us along, changing us in position, in appearance, in feelings, in temper, in all things. Suddenly an ancient friend is thrown across our path, and our youth, the long, long past, comes rushing with his presence around us. The present vanishes, and we are again among the pleasant memories of the olden time.

Some years ago we were at Blosburgh, in Pennsylvania. We went there ostensibly to view the coal mines. The entrance to these mines is midway up a mountain of some fifteen hundred feet in height, along the base of which the Tioga River flows, which is here but a good-sized trout stream, in the summer season. We went up to the entrance of the mines. We saw a great dark hole in the side of the mountain, into which our companions entered, and were lost to sight in its cavernous depths. For ourself, we have no taste for dark places and deep holes in the ground. We never enter a cave. There 's something dismal and sepulchral about them. They smell of mortality. We should expect to see skulls grinning at us, and to stumble over dead men's bones. We keep clear of caves. We preferred trout fishing, to groping around in the damps of the mines, away in the carbonized bowels of the hill. We came down to the river, and borrowing a rod and line, started up stream, with a view of fishing down. We travelled a couple of miles along a pleasant path that followed the windings of the river, and then rigged and threw for the trout. They were plenty in those days, and we were having a good time of it all alone in the woods, notwithstanding the affectionate attentions of the mosquito and the black-fly, that phlebotomized us after a fashion peculiar to themselves. We were busy hauling in the trout and fighting the mosquitoes, and as we came round a great boulder, bigger than a haystack, that thrust itself from the bank half way across the stream, there we stood face to face with an old friend that we had lost sight of for a dozen years. "Hallo! Harry," said we, "where on earth did *you* come from?" "And from what cloud did *you* drop?" was his reply, as we shook hands most cordially. We sat down upon that old moss-covered boulder, and talked of the days of Old. We were schoolmates in our boyhood. We were students in the same law office, were examined in the same class for admission to the profession, returned from Albany, with our licenses in our pockets, together, and the week after such return we shook hands and parted, swinging out in different directions into the world. For a year or two we heard of him occasionally; then darkness settled down between us, and we heard of him no more till we met in the middle of the Tioga River, at the spot where that big boulder stands so boldly out into the stream, each with a fishing-rod in his hand. The world had gone well with him. He had gathered largely of its treasures. He was a man known on 'Change.

We parted the next morning, never to meet again. Consumption laid its withering hand upon him. He crossed the great ocean, in the hope that the genial climate of the South of Europe would bring back health and vigor to his frame. He visited Italy; spent a few months at Rome, and then passed on to Venice. But the grasp of death was upon him, and he turned his feeble steps towards home, in the hope of dying in the midst of his kindred. He died on the ocean; and he now sleeps in a New England churchyard, where his fathers sleep. He was the only son of his parents, and he left no children.

VI.

A CHAPTER FOR THE SABBATH.

MY tall friend is gone. Even now, as I write, he is speeding on over the long iron tracks, to the Blue Ridge of the Old Dominion. The round week—seven golden days—he staid with us, finding some rest, we trust; but now all this is of the past. By-gone, so soon! Pictures all, so soon! Oh, the swift certainty of to-morrow; for however we may pause, God has always something for us to do. He, who doth neither slumber nor sleep, how kindly, how safely, he takes us all on through the night, into the beautiful morning!

My friend, sir, was in great demand. All our choice arrangements for repose were of small account. And as life flies by now-a-days, perhaps it is well. We should make no long steps now, for there is little time for rest here. Time enough for that—to those who shall attain to the true life—when they shall have shaken off these working garments and put on the white robes; when the lame shall walk, and the blind see, and the deaf hear; when their halting frames shall be clothed anew with strength and with glory, and their palsied tongues find voice in the acclamations of that great host, "which no man can number." Time enough for that, when the night cometh, that no man can work. When from groping through these swift-rolling years, they shall see, at last, face to face, and walk in the light of God for ever! Time enough for repose, in that great time to come, the time beyond all time, the great circle, the round time, when they shall have gone up to dwell for ever with their master and their king, their Saviour and their Redeemer, Jesus Christ the Righteous!

But now, oh how swiftly speeds the world! No, it is not the place for rest. "My Father worketh hitherto," said Christ, "and I work." No, it is neither the place nor the time for rest. Nor is it to be found here. Health itself, life itself, subsists only in action, change, accomplishment. This tireless spirit, as it came from God, so in some measure like Him, it scarcely can slumber or sleep, even here.

Time has been when, owing chiefly to physical causes, we have loved rather the life of thought and meditation; but the union of both—meditation and action—is the true life, both here and elsewhere. The good deed, the kind word, the helping hand in the right way—and when these are impossible, the bended knee in the silent chamber, the use of that power that "moves the arm that moves the universe;" these are the agencies—these are the powers that be. To whom these are possible, all else is but wind and ashes.

A man may float in deep water, motionless, by looking straight up to Heaven; but he must look out for the heavy seas. In fact, he can float nowhere, save in the still water, and at best, it is but floating: balancing, as it were, between life and death. To make headway, he must strike out right and left, pull and push, and reach on continually: and, moreover (to finish this matter), it is mostly your good swimmers only who can float.

Make no long stay, Mr. Editor, in any "Saint's Rest"* you may find here. The world rolls too fast now for long pauses. As in youth the days were long, and in age they seem to take wings for their travel, so the world of to-day, as it quickens and concentrates thought and action, quickens and shortens the minutes, the hours, the days and the weeks, and the round year itself: so that we can look forward to some approximation to that life in which, even to us, "a thousand years may be as one day, and one day as a thousand years."

Good-bye, my tall Virginian, and may God prosper you for ever, and make all your days as pure as the sunlight, and as bright. Good-bye—but come back again—will you? Come back in the golden October, and wake us again with your clarion tones. John Knox, as he preached to the assembled

* See Appendix B.

royalties of Scotland, could not more have startled our sleepy souls, than did your ringing cadences last Sunday night. Come back, and rouse us from the dull inaction of this hum-drum life. Come back, and leave a few coals of your Southern fire on our Northern altars, and cry aloud to us, "Awake, thou that sleepest, and arise from the dead, and Christ shall give thee life."

Yours, ——.

"He who doth neither slumber nor sleep, how kindly, how safely, he takes us all through the night into the beautiful morning!"

We never think of the good Providence that watches over the world, in the still hours of the night, without connecting with the thought a beautiful little hymn, of which we think Bishop HEBER was the author, although of this we are not certain; a hymn so full of the pure spirit of poetry, as well as devotion, that we venture to give it here:

Hark! 'tis the breeze of twilight calling
  Earth's weary children to repose:
While round the couch of nature, falling
  Gently the night's soft curtain's close.
Soon o'er the world in sleep reclining,
  Numberless stars in yonder dark,
Will look like eyes of seraph's, shining
  From out the veil that hides the ark.

Guard us, oh thou that never sleepest—
  Thou that in silence throned above;

Who through all time, unwearied, keepest
  Thy watch of glory, power and love.
Grant that beneath thine eye securely,
  Our souls from life a while withdrawn,
May in the darkness, stilly, purely,
  Like sealed fountains, rest till dawn.

Strange linking of memories! Speaking of Bishop HEBER reminds us of an anecdote of the excellent Bishop C——. We were in New York soon after Trinity Church was completed, in company with the lamented JOHN YOUNG, late Governor of this State. We visited the church together. We found, upon entering, a venerable man, who stood near the centre of the great aisle, looking with apparent rapture upon the gorgeous and imposing architecture of the interior of that magnificent structure. It was Bishop C——. The Governor was acquainted with him. After a frank and cordial greeting, the good Bishop remarked, "I have been thinking," said he, "how different our place of worship was when I first became the rector of a parish in what is now my diocese, from this splendid edifice. It was a little building, half school-house and half church, and cost less than five hundred dollars. Yet we were a happy and united people, and, I sometimes think, more purely devotional and pious than we were at a later period, when we worshipped in a vastly more costly church. It always seems to me that pride enters somewhat too largely into the devotional exercises of a place like this; and I think of the lines in one of our beautiful hymns:

"Say, shall we worship with costly devotion,
Odors of Eden and offerings divine,
Gems from the mountain, pearls from the ocean,
Myrrh from the forest and gold from the mine?
Vainly we offer each ample oblation,
Vainly with gifts we his favor secure:
Richer by far is the heart's adoration,
Dearer to God are the prayers of the poor."

There was something infinitely impressive in the earnest and solemn, yet simple manner with which the good Bishop repeated those lines. They contained, as he spoke them, a whole sermon—one that went to the heart with far greater force and directness than many we have heard that were vastly more studied and elaborate.

"Richer by far is the heart's adoration,
Dearer to God are the prayers of the poor."

Great and glorious truths, all! Infinite goodness could alone have sent them forth to the world, to give comfort and hope to man. What if we be poor and of mean estate? Our hold on heaven is stronger than theirs who dwell in palaces, and are clothed in purple. When misfortune and sorrow gather around us, when desolation comes down upon us like a flood, and destruction sweeps away the little we may have gathered of the world's goods, when we look forward to a helpless age and see no promise of provision for its dreary hours, when the heart sinks before the darkness of the future, then comes the soul-cheering truth, fresh from the throne of God, a voice speaking from the cloud that encompasses us,

> " Richer by far is the heart's adoration,
> Dearer to God are the prayers of the poor."

" And as life flies by now-a-days, perhaps it is as well that we should make no long stops, for there is little time for rest here."

Aye! "March on!" is the order of the universe, now; no halting by the way—no pausing to reckon with the past, or calculate the future. The world is in motion. A rest under the shadow of tall trees, by the bubbling fountain, leaves you behind. The great army passes on, and you are reckoned, as you are in fact, a laggard in the race of life. Look back for only a quarter of a century, and see the mighty stride that the world has taken. Where, then, were the iron roads over which the locomotive now thunders on his mission of civilization—where the telegraph that mocks at time and annihilates space? Hark! there are new sounds breaking the stillness of night, and startling the mountain echoes from their sleep of ages! It is the scream of the steam-whistle, the snort of the iron-horse, the deep rumble of his long train, freighted with human life, rushing with lightning speed, shaking the ground like an earthquake, as it moves along. A new sight is seen on the ocean. It is the tall ship that goes forward when the air is still, and calmness is on the face of the deep—that moves forward in the eye of the wind, forward still in the face of the storm—that turns not from its course for billow or blast. It is the ocean steamer, that makes but a ferriage of seas, that comes and goes over the great deep regardless of wind or storm. These are but types of the mighty progress of civilization within that quarter of a century. Look back again to the scenes of your boyhood. Where are the landmarks that you loved, the pleasant things around which cluster the memories of youth? Where the tall forest tree that was spared when the old woods were swept away? Where the clustered plum-trees, the wild hazles, the willows along the brook, the maples that shaded the spring that came out from among their roots? Gone! all gone! The old school-house and the play-grounds—the path across the fields that led to them—where are they? Gone again, all gone! The friends, the companions of your youth—where are they? A voice comes out of the deep silence of the grave, from the ocean, from the far-off city — from beyond mountain ranges, bearing the solemn answer—

> "They are scattered and parted by mountain and wave,
> And some are in the cold, silent womb of the grave."

Where are the high hopes, the lofty aspirations, with which we started in our young career?

Gone, all gone! wrecked by the hand of disease laid heavily upon us. Wrecked by the hand of death that tore from us the joy of our being and the treasures of our hearts. Wrecked by disappointment in a thousand forms, that beset us in our path of life.

Yes, yes, onward and onward is the word. Everything is moving. Childhood passes to youth, youth moves onward to manhood, manhood to old age, and the grave devours them all. If we pause, even to linger by the graves of the loved and the lost to us; the tramp, tramp, of the world is heard passing us. If we fall, its onward tramp is over us as it hurries along in the forward movement. Like a mighty river, the tide of human life, the current of human progress, flows on, pauseless and steady, swelling in volume, moving forever and ever towards eternity. But what of that? Better to float on with the tide, than to pause in the turgid eddies, and stagnant bayous, even though our course be over beetling precipices into the boiling whirlpool beneath them. On the spray of the cataract hangs the rainbow of promise. It is the sign of redemption, the seal to the covenant of God, that he will rescue us from the troubled waters, and take us to his "house not built with hands, eternal in the heavens."

"Good-bye."

How many emotions cluster around that word! How full of sadness, and to us, how full of sorrow it sounds! It is with us a consecrated word. We heard it once within the year, as we hope never to hear it again. We spoke it on an occasion such as we hope never to speak it again. It was in the chamber of death, at the still hour of night's noon. The curtains to the windows were all closed, the lights were shaded, and we stood in the dim and solemn twilight, with others, around the bed of the dying. The damps of death were on her pale young brow, and coldness was on her lips, as we kissed her for the last time while living. "Good-bye, my daughter," we whispered, and "Good-bye, father," came faintly from her dying lips. We know not if she ever spoke more, but "Good-bye" was the last we ever heard of her sweet voice. We hear that sorrowful word often and often, as we sit alone busy with the memories of the past. We hear it in the silence of night, in the hours of nervous wakefulness, as we lay upon our bed thinking of the loved and the lost to us. We hear it in our dreams, when her sweet face comes back to us, as it was in its loveliness and beauty. We hear it when we sit beside her grave in the cemetery where she sleeps, alone, with no kindred as yet by her side. She was the hope of our life, the prop upon which to lean when age should come upon us, and life should be running to its dregs. The hope and the prop is gone, and we care not how soon we go down to sleep beside our darling, beneath the shadow of the trees in the city of the dead.

VII.

ROARING RIVER.

How are you now, my friend? Rejoicing, no doubt, on this first wave of coolness and strength. But how were you in the late solstice? Sitting, as we now do, by fires, morning and evening, it seems like looking far away into the depths of last summer, and yet it is but one short week. Midway of that solstice, came our young friends *Snowdrop* and *Honeysuckle*, from a down-river margin, and with the ease and grace of maidenhood, melted at once, into our quiet ways; took attitudes, at once, all in keeping, and were properly silent and musing for so solemn a time. Pleasant pictures—*Snowdrop and Honeysuckle*—and good for warm weather. But not so our friend *Powerful*, who came with them; he being not at all adapted to such high ranges of the mercury. Too fiery and precipitous. Why, sir, he had the madness to go into argument before he had been ten minutes under our roof; and this, when earth and sky were panting and breathless in that hot blast. And my private opinion is, (I must tell you, *sub rosa*, that I like *Power-*

ful, in toto, fire and all, for he is equal to about seventeen of the common young men of these times), but I haven't a doubt that he had been in argument all day. How else, and owing to his plunging nature, and my quick sympathy with it, (for I jump to all humors,) how else could we have tumbled out of that train as we did, while carpet-bags came after, through the windows, and our two large trunks, in the hot haste, slipped fizzing away into the sides of the north, and all the people laughed at our confusion?

Let that pass, for the trunks came back the next day, and three days later the cool winds northwesterly. But then, in view of what might happen with *Powerful* in the house, and of what was happening, the hot, white, quivering sunlight pouring down day after day, I issued the following general order: "Remember the weather, my people, and be wise. Propositions are vain, and arguments all out of place. This day avoid controversy and shun disputation. *Argue with no man*, or woman. If you find a sitz-bath, sit down on it, asking no questions, but don't go spying about. Stop every thing that can be stopped, and let us rest. Stop talking, stop thinking, stop eating, stop drinking, stop walking up and down the room; and in fine, retire as far as possible into a *vacuum*, and there remain until the north wind blows again."

My next grand proposition (for the general order was scouted all over the house) I brought forward as modestly as possible, merely holding it forth, as a stray thought which had occurred to me, to wit: *chairs in Roaring River*—under the bridge, sir. In the shoal water, you know, say about waist deep, and there to sit, making short remarks, and waiting for the wind to blow. The Editor was to be invited, and we were all to form a circle there and talk up ancient events—all in chairs in Roaring River. I say ancient events, for I should know you instantly: you would be to me as an open volume—a folio of rare value—all in chairs in Roaring River. Small Bob would bring us the proper refreshments; sweet milk loaded with ice and one brown cottage loaf, and water from the well, from the old oaken bucket, sitting all around in State editorial—all in chairs in Roaring River.

But what strange mistiming of nonsense was all this, sir, when men were dropping dead in the streets of our cities (as the swift lightning soon reported to us), not in twos, and in threes, but in tens and twenties, and in hundreds! And still comes the report from a far Southern city—*two hundred dead, to-day.*

There's a time for work, and a time for play, says the old adage. But a startling question sometimes presents itself, as to whether the world has not outgrown its play-time, leaving us the work only. Certainly there is not much play-time, now, to the people of that plague-smitten city.

Two hundred dead, to-day! Gone away, that is to

say, to try another mode of living; another mode of acting; another mode of thinking. No, not that. For as a man thinketh, so is he. And as a man dies, so he remains. Whatever moral pestilence he dies with, he takes with him. Whatever poisoned garment he has on, is his forever. He can ship it to no foreign market; and if he cries it at auction, no man will buy. Nor will fire burn, or the moth consume it. Like himself, it is immortal.

But *move on!* say you; and *move on!* shouts the world. *Get out of the way. We can't stop here over a dead-body.*

No, indeed, but oh my friend, *where* are we going? Where, and under whose orders? Who has the command, in this case? Who is Officer of the Night? for the look-out, just now, is like that of night, rather than the light of day. I don't know, sir, about this onward movement, until we establish quite well what we are about. I must be posted on this, before I make the first step. To cast about, with whatever vigor, or with whatever hopefulness that all will be right by-and-bye, will in nowise modify the ultimate fact; and this ultimatum I must not guess at, but know.

For motion, sir, is not life. Momentum is not life. It is a power, or rather it is a result, but it is not life. The iron horse that leaves your city in the early morning and takes his last refreshment this side of Buffalo, somewhere before sundown, has traversed some hundreds of miles; but he has only changed places; and this he has done, only by clinging to the rails. Take away his hold upon earth—his grasp from the iron bar—and though his wheels may flash with a whiz, and his pipes sputter and scream to the verge of madness, he will not have moved forward a hair's breadth. A grasshopper shall sit square before his driving-wheel, and laugh at him all the day long.

No, sir, 45 miles an hour takes no man nearer to Heaven. If we are to march on, let us know the way, and the country whither we go. We have but one day before us, and by night we must rest somewhere, if possible. It would be sad, after a hard day's work, to find no welcome, no glad face to meet us, no news of home, of rest, of peace, no cheering voice to hail us, through the deepening gloom,—"*All right! This way, my friend! All right!*"

Not to hear this, but to take our wearied limbs on into still deeper darkness, and be conscious, suddenly, that we are lost—that we have taken the wrong way—this would be sad, it would be terrible. Yours, ——.

"*Chairs in Roaring River*, under the bridge, sir. In the shoal water, you know, say about waist deep, and there to sit, making short remarks, and waiting for the wind to blow. The Editor was to be invited, and we were all to form a circle there, and talk of ancient events—all in chairs in Roaring River—Small Bob would bring us the proper refreshment, sweet milk loaded with ice, and one brown cottage loaf, and water from the well from the old oaken bucket, sitting all around in state editorial, all in chairs in Roaring River."

We should not have accepted that invitation. We love rivers. We love to look upon them as they flow on forever, and yet are never wasted We love to inquire how it can be, that their ceaseless current, that always has been and always will be moving away and away towards the ocean, should never be exhausted? To ask of science how they gather their constant, unfailing supply, and why the ocean, into which all these gigantic tributaries pour their mighty floods, never overleaps its bounds? To ask philosophy, by what subtle machinery the far-off fountains that come out from away up among the mountains, are fed with fresh water forever? Why they always bubble up in the same place, and run away in the same channel to make up these great rivers? We like to look upon the bubbles that float along on the surface of the water, and see them burst and vanish away. We like to watch the spray that goes up from the cataract and the turbulent rapids, and the mist that rises from the broad, still current. As the river moves along at our feet, never pausing, finding no resting-place in its ceaseless flow, such, we say, is the tide of human life. The bubbles that float upon its surface are the hopes of man. The spray and the mists are his cherished plans and schemes of life. The bubbles burst, the spray and the mists vanish away, but the river moves on to the ocean.

A pleasant place for meditation is "Roaring River," but to sit waist deep in its waters, beneath the shadow of the bridge, does not comport with our philosophy. There is romance, doubtless, in the matter, but it is not *our kind* of romance; and hot or cold, sunshine or a cloudy sky, let the mercury range high or hide itself in the bulb, "we'll none of it." If we must needs "sit around in State editorial—all in chairs in Roaring River," we should claim the highest seat, the longest legged chair—one in which we could sit with our feet on the top round, clear of the water. We would not mind being a good deal doubled up, drawn together in a heap like, for the sake of the company and the refreshments, but we should cut the concern, vamose when the water began to come into our boots.

"Two hundred dead, to-day."

Well, what of that? Remember we speak not for ourself. Ours is not the voice of a disintegrated atom, an individuality. We speak for the world, for aggregated humanity, and we say what of that? Think of the physical suffering that wrung the joints of these "two hundred dead" before the spirit left them. We answer again, what of that? Is physical suffering a new thing under the sun, to startle us by its cry of anguish, and make us to pause by the way-side for its contemplation? Think of the sorrows, the tears that are wrung from the living, the broken hearts, the crushed hopes that followed to the grave these "two hundred dead, to-day." Again we repeat, what of that? Is sorrow a new thing on the earth? Are broken hearts strangers to the world, or crushed hopes a novelty? Talk not to us about physical suffering or mental anguish—what are they to us? we have no time to listen. The bell rings, the steam whistle shrieks, "All aboard!" cries the conductor, and we are off on the train that never returns—the cars that are always running the same way. And herein is the singularity of this railroad of life—there is no return train. The travel is always in one direction. The world is moving, every living thing is whirling with a rush towards the great terminus, and of all the countless millions that have travelled that road, not one has ever returned. Strange fascinations, wonderful attractions must that country have, from which no traveller ever comes back.

But there are "two hundred dead to-day," say you. As an individual, we can comprehend the vast amount of suffering, the aggregated anguish that pervades the stricken city. The plague is no respecter of persons. It strikes every where. The rich, the poor, the high, the low, the respected, and the despised—the mother that breathes out her life in the arms of her children, and the forsaken, that dies by the way-side. The pestilence smites at random every where. Here is a gorgeous hearse, followed by a long train of mourners; the dead is going to his rest beneath the shadow of a tall monument in the cemetery. Handle the coffin tenderly, the ashes it contains are precious—jar it not rudely.

There, is a deal coffin, alone on a rude cart, on its way to the Potter's Field, the resting-place of the desolate. Ask you who goes thus solitary to a nameless grave? The heartless song of the official that sits upon his coffin, answers,

> "Rattle his bones over the stones,
> He's only a pauper that nobody owns."

The spirits that once breathed in these human Antipodes, are immortal. They have gone to be judged at the same bar, under the same law, and to stand side by side in the presence of the Judge, who looks straight into the heart, and from whose vision nothing can be hid. What a lesson is here! Take care, oh! rich man, look to it—that the despised pauper, whose dust is in the Potter's Field, is not chosen of God, while you, whose ashes are beneath marble that is inscribed with a lying epitaph, are rejected.

> "Whatever moral pestilence he dies with, he takes with him. Whatever poisoned garment he has on, is his for ever. He can ship it to no foreign market, and if he cries it at auction, no man will buy."

The moral leprosy of the soul, if uncured by the "healing waters," clings to it throughout eternity; stripped as it may be of physical atoms, the plague spot remains. The miser who barters salvation for treasure, who sells Heaven for gold, carries with him his thirst for gain, which remains raging and quenchless for ever. The debauchee who defied God, and scorned the restraints of His law, finds in his burning lusts the hell he scoffed at. The murderer looks upon his spectre hand, and sees upon it the redness of the blood he has spilled. His awakened conscience, as he wanders an imponderable shadow in the region of banished souls, is the torment of his eternity. The sin that is unrepented of is a fiery and hissing serpent, coiling around the soul for ever, as the serpents coiled around and crushed the Laocoon. But what of that? For this moral pestilence, there is a cure. For the leprosy of the soul, there is a healing balm. The blood-stains may be washed away, and the spirit of man be re-clothed in a spotless garment. A voice from heaven calls to the leper; speaking from the throne of God to the pestilence stricken, it cries: "Ho! every one that thirsteth, come ye to the waters; and he that hath no money, come ye, buy and eat—buy wine and milk, without money and without price." In these waters there is health. This wine and milk will charm away the pestilence, and cleanse from the mark of the plague. They are free. Wealth cannot purchase them, power cannot grasp them, strength cannot control them, kings cannot command them. The earnest soul that asks will receive them; the earnest seeker will find them. They are at the door of the penitent everywhere. Poverty is no bar, weakness no prevention, obscurity no impediment to the enjoyment of them. Strange, then, that men should die of moral pestilence, or pass into eternity with a poisoned garment wrapped around them. That they should turn away from the healing waters; that they should reject the wine and milk so freely offered; that they should be deaf to the call of the helper, to the ten thousand invitations of the Good Physician, urged every day and every hour of a lifetime. Man, only, can be guilty of such madness and folly.

It would be sad, after a hard day's travel, to find no welcome, no glad face to meet us, no news of home, of rest, of peace; no cheering voice to hail us through the deepening gloom, "*All right! this way, my friends—all right!*"

If we have secured seats in the right car, and our tickets are all regular, we *shall* find a welcome, we *shall* meet glad faces—we *will* find a home, and rest, and peace. When the night comes, a cheering voice will hail us, through the deepening gloom, a kind hand will guide us to our eternal habitation. There is no guess work, no uncertainty about this; it is all fixed as the purposes, immutable as the promises of God. But we must see to it, that we take the right train. The conductor we know. His protection is sure. He will not deceive or forsa[illegible] us. What he promises he performs. Have no [illegible]prehension about that. Lean upon Him, trust H[illegible], follow His direction. He will carry us safely and surely to the end of our journey. When we cross the dark valley of the shadow of death, He will be with us. We shall hear his pleasant voice as time, and the things of time, the world, with its troubles and its sorrows, pass away, welcoming us within the gates of the city of God. There we shall have a place of rest, where weariness can never come where age cannot visit us with its infirmities; where death cannot rob us of our heart's treasures. Care and sorrow cannot enter there. Tears are never shed there. Angels will be around us. The spirits of the loved ones that preceded us, will be around us. There are no summer heats to oppress, no winters cold to chill us, no night of darkness, no day of storms. Calm, and quiet, and peace reign forever there. Years and months, the seasons, days and hours, are all unknown there. Forever is written upon all things.

What matter, then, how soon we accomplish our journey? Nay, if we are in the right car, will we not cry to the good conductor, "Faster, faster still, press on the steam, wait not for the night of age, for the going down of the sun; land us safe in the great city at noon, or even in the morning of life?" Why should we tarry by the way? Why sigh as we pass along, and the beautiful things of the world fall behind us, and vanish in the distance? Things more beautiful await us at the end of our journey. Why start we, as gray hairs whiten our heads, the brow becomes wrinkled with age, and stiffness takes hold of our limbs, and the steps become slow and careful? These are but the mile-posts that stand by the wayside, to tell us that our weary journey is drawing to its close.

VIII.

HOW POEMS LOOK IN PRINT.

WE send you, sir, to-day, three maidenly courtesies and a poem. The courtesies you may keep, but the poem we want returned, in large and handsome type, so that we may see how the thing looks in proper attire. It has been in type once, some years ago, but in such a way as to make a very sorry appearance.

We all want copies—Snowdrop, Honeysuckle, Powerful, Mrs. Margin—and I can't tell how many distant cousins and friends; including the strong-minded young ladies, who have not yet arrived. Send therefore, as Col. T. used to say, send a *quantity*, marked "*Country,—care of Small Bob, Roaring River.*"

Our friends being about to return to their home in the mountains, we desire to part fair: and as a last expression suitable for a time of good-byes, we put argument aside, and join hands over this little poem. Here it is:

As the rocks in mountain rapids
Become islanded with ice,
So our stony hearts surround them
With the rough, hard mail of vice.

Then we say it's cold—though summer
Airs float round us, soft and warm;
Then—though skies are blue and cloudless—
That all life is but a storm.

Doubtless: and the special wonder,
Not that life doth craze or pall,—
But, this Death in Life while under,
How or why we live at all.

If no finger on the dial
Of this world points how to live,
It were well to make the trial
What the next may chance to give.

Haply something else than sadness,
Want, and woe, and o'er and o'er
Lust and crime, and Hell's last madness,
Something less, or something more.

Haply some bright world of beauty,
Peaceful, glorious, heavenly fair,
Where dwell only God and His angels:—
What,—oh what wouldst thou do there?

Scorner,—thou, who having eyes
And ears, art yet both deaf and blind;
Ever to whom, doth only rise
The pictures of thy own dark mind.

If the world is bad, improve it;
Poor and suffering, heal and give;
Forget not there is one above it;
Seek thou that, and thou shalt live.

But, thou weary one, who bearest
 All the burden of the day—
Mock'd, derided, yet forbearest,
 Holding stoutly on thy way;

Ailing, thirsting, starving, fettered,
 Dogged at, from thy very birth,—
Ah, until the world is bettered,
 Thou hast but one friend on earth!

But that Friend—oh, wondrous glory!
 Angels and archangels bend,
To tell the worlds the matchless story
 Of the love of this thy Friend.

Ask, and trust all things to Him;
 The day, however long, must close;
Welcome the night, or dark, or dim,
 For thou shalt find repose.

Yours, ——.

"The courtesies you may keep, but the poem we want returned in large, handsome type, so that we may see how the thing looks in proper attire."

In regard to the "courtesies," we can, of course, keep them, and we can return the poem in the manner indicated, but we do not altogether like the manner in which we have been treated in this matter. When we started with our friend "MARGINS," we set out solely with a view of having a little friendly chat with him by the way, which chat we took for granted would be held in honest old-fashioned English prose. We had no idea that we were to be confounded by the use of unknown tongues, or led a dance through the mazes of poetry. Time was when we strung rhymes, and thought that we were Byronic in our versification. We have given up that idea years ago. The occasion of our cutting the society of the muses was this:—We had a good many leisure hours on hand when we commenced the practice of the law. Briefs were not as plenty as blackberries with us, and we undertook to fill up the time between them by literary efforts. We resided in a flourishing village then, which rejoiced in a newspaper published weekly. Through the columns of that paper we poured our effusions for the benefit of the reading world, securely hid, as we supposed, behind a *nom de plume* selected from the most celebrated names of the olden times. But this is an envious world. It cannot bear to see merit working its way upward. Genius will be hawked at, and if possible brought down to the level of plodding humanity. It was so with us. A very particular friend of ours undertook to criticise our poetry. And he cut, and slashed, and belabored, and ridiculed our effusions and ourself in a manner in no way pleasant to the feelings of a very vain young man. The worst of it was, his criticisms were, in the main, just. He succeeded in satisfying the world, so far as *our* poetry and *his* criticisms were read by it, that we would never become immortal in that line. What may be regarded as still more singular, he satisfied *us* of the same fact. We cut the muses, and for twenty odd years have not, save on two or three occasions, undertaken rhyme. Some three or four years ago, we listened to GOUGH, the celebrated and eloquent temperance lecturer. As one of the causes which induced habits of intemperance, he spoke of the convivial suppers sometimes indulged in by young men—feasts where the wine flowed freely, and the song, the story, and the merry jest accompanied the circulation of the bottle. He said he never saw or heard of these convivial feasts without imagining that they were got up by the "gentleman in black" for the purpose of ensnaring victims, and that he always thought he could hear his demon laugh above the bacchanalian revelry, and see the print of his hoof among the broken glass upon the floor. Indeed, he said he always regarded them as dinners given by Satan to his followers, to confirm them in his service, and he could, at such times, almost see him sitting with his horned head, dragon tail, and cloven hoof, at the table, encouraging the revellers in debauchery. From that lecture, we returned to our office, and indited the following. We had never any idea of its publication, and it would not have been given for the edification of the world now, had not our friend "MARGINS" cornered us by his effusion. On him, therefore, rests the responsibility.

FEAST OF THE "GENTLEMAN IN BLACK."

"The man in black" made a feast one day,
A dinner for all his friends,
And he sauntered about to invite them out
To taste of his dainties, and dance at his rout,
And stuff themselves with tender regoutte;
For, says he, "the devil's to pay."

He got him a priest to preside at his board,
And he grinned when he sat him down,
For I ween, says the devil, a whining priest
That sins with a sanctified look, at a feast
Is entitled to precedence over the rest,
So I'll honor the cowl and gown.

And he got him a lawyer to sit at the foot,
A jolly old fellow too,
Who had plundered the widow, and spoiled the poor,
And spurned the orphan away from his door,
And cheated by statute and plead, and swore
As cunning old lawyers do.

Then he got him a usurer plump and fat,
A sleek old cent per cent,
Who cut with a razor so sharp and keen,
That few who fell into his hands, I ween,
Were suffered to pass till he'd shaved them clean,
Tho' demure as any cat.

Then the " black man" got him a merchant too,
  Who sold by the shortened yard;
Who kept his accounts in a way of his own—
When he sold two ounces he sat three down;
And charged two shillings as half a crown,
  And proved by his clerk 'twas true.

Then he got him a doctor, a queer old quack,
  With his saddle-bags by his side,
Who physicked and sweated, without remorse,
Every living thing, from a man to a horse,
And blistered, and bled, and tortured them worse
  Than the disease of which they died.

He filled up his table with others, I ween,
  Of right good families old,—
For the Devil is proud, and a common knave;
Who cheated by retail he would not have,
And the sight of a pickpocket made him grave,
  So he tipped him the shoulder cold.

The guests were seated, the board was spread
  With luxuries rich and rare;
Each guest had a dish that suited himself
Reserved in the care of a dingy elf;
As a dessert (the host had spared no pelf
  In procuring a dainty fare.)

The guests were merry, they quaffed their wine,
  Right merry were they that night,
They cracked their jokes, and laughed and sung,
And huzzaed, and roared till the arches rung,
And jests obscene were on each tongue;
  They, in fact, were a little " tight."

The night, oh! it glided right merrily on,
And no one took note of time;
And the old clock bell, in the old gray tower,
He hammered the peals of the midnight hour,
But the guests were too merry, they had no power
To list to the solemn chime.

The host he rose from his iron chair,
And he called for his burning bowl,
And he brought the table a terrible whack,
That startled the priest, and alarmed the quack,
And took e'en the lawyer a little aback,
When he thought of that thing—the soul.

He bowed to the chair, and he filled the cup
With right good liquor, I ween;
That sparkled and flashed with gases old;
That was meet to be quaffed by sinners bold,
Or the burly lips of the knights of old—
Oh, that host he had glorious wine!

"A health!" quoth the host, "here's a health to all!
Ye have served me well and true:
Ye have furnished my palace and filled my ranks
With souls seduced by your merry pranks;
Ye have labored so well that the meed of thanks
Is due from your prince to you.

"I have traversed the earth from pole to pole,
I have wandered from sea to sea:
And the world is full of my followers now,
Whom you 've taught to sin, ye well know how:
And one and all at my feet to bow—
On earth there is none like me!

"Ye have finished your task. Your work is done,
And need ye should take your rest.
Ye will speed with me to my murky home,
Where the rich flames flash round my burning dome,
And our demon orgies, 'mid smoke and gloom,
Have a richer and rarer zest."

Then he winked to his imps, and he flourished his tail,
And he stamped with his iron hoof,
And the guests were grappled and hurled along,
And the merry jest, and the shout and song
Were followed by shrieking loud and long,
As they tore through the riven roof.

There was wonder on earth when the morning broke,
And the lawyer, and priest, and quack,
And the merchant and guests that feasted there,
Were sought for carefully everywhere,
By many a longing, anxious heir,
But none of them e'er came back.

That feast was held in a ruined church,
That stood in a lonely dell,
That had battled with time and slow decay,
And the ivy had crept, in its loving way,
O'er its mossy towers and walls of gray—
Oh! a ruin it loves right well.

The ivy was scorched, and its leaves were black,
As if fire had revelled there:
And the wandering peasant often spoke
Of a sulphur stench and a murky smoke,
That hung o'er the ruin when morning broke—
And then floated away on the air.

IX.

ISOLATION.

Sleep, oh, beautiful sleep, if thou wert an angel, I would kneel down here and thank thee for this hour of cool repose.

So I said or thought this afternoon after waking from dreams and refreshment on the parlor sofa. I had wandered home latish in the day, to find the house closed and desolate. All gone! all but my father, and he asleep in his room—all gone. Of course they were. I had just been to see them off.

Well, as you say, what of that? Why, my excellent Editor, you may say "what of that?" as much as you please, but this crawling into your own house, by the well-door or a back cellar window, is a dismal piece of business. Rooms empty and dark, and with that cold smell, into which you go sneezing, and stepping carefully about like a cat, and the servants so quiet and low-toned as though it were Sunday again. Oh, would it were Sunday—the day of days, the glory of the week—the keystone of the arch.

Ugh! throw open the windows and give us light, *light!* LIGHT!

Ah, sir, I don't ask for Sunday. I am not in the mood for it. No, nor for any day. What can I do with this solemn circumstantiality, this inevitable proceeding, this right foot foremost forever? Give me rather (if I may choose), some cast-off fragment, some rough piece of chaos, not yet fashioned into any respectable day-time, so it be other than this bright, glittering, mocking Monday afternoon, which finds my house desolate, as I have said, and my very particular friend full of travel, and talk, and laughter, a hundred miles away! To go away as I did, so *vive* and *elate*, and come back drooping and wiltered to be as a cheese-paring in the face of this dazzling sunshine! Thunders and red lightnings; it seems to me I should like, but this white light, this breezy Monday I *don't* like, and there's no use in talking about it.

Such was the perverse mood, sir, which sleep has charmed away.

For we have had pleasant days, though they are gone; genial days, and nights all-glorious. Sunrises and sunsets, painted with the hues and tones of the first day. Day-dreams and night-dreams, glad faces, and hearts more glad, and disquisitions, and argumentations solid as the primeval granite. All gone now, but not lost—thank God for that—not lost, but a part of our being, and forever.

Backward, looking into these few past weeks, my eye drops upon many pleasant pictures, and as the artists say, *studies*, of a tempting character; and so looking, I behold on one of those most solstitial days, two men, strangers to me, who were walking up our yard, doubtless seeking for what might happen to turn up. One was stoutish, and as you may say, established in all his ways; the other jaunty in both look and carriage, black hair, if I remember aright, with a twist in it, and a decided cock to his hat. The idea, as it recurs in my mind (for it is all dream-like now, in the distance), the memory is, that after shaking myself a little to make sure that I was awake, I showed those gentlemen into our parlor, just about sunset, while a smart crack of thunder was waking up all our northern sky, and that soon after we all took tea and compared notes somewhat, as was proper to men of high consideration. My people, as I remember it, were in white, (my wife, certainly,) and all was cordial and serene. Doubtless there was laughing, and blushing, and pell-mell talking, and a handsome confusion of exchange and interchange, but the picture, as aforesaid, was in its general tone cordial and serene. But it was all like a panorama; for my new friends straightway lighted cigars and departed over Roaring River, and soon after, were wheeling away swiftly into the south. This is one of the pleasant summer pictures in our gallery, and if you, Mr. Editor, ever meet such stout man with a Webster-like build of face and figure, and that other individual, with a twist in his black hair, and hat at an angle—I say, sir—give them my regards.

Reminiscences are pleasant, but facts remain. You have pictures, but "it is *not* good for man to be alone." If a man withdraws from the world, and still lives a high, pure life, it is not because he is alone, it is because he is not alone. He is living with God. He is in a Presence, to which the coming in of whatever hosts on earth, or in heaven, add and detract nothing. But this is not isolation.

And a child, scarcely as yet conscious of this Presence, save in a remote way (as when with closed eyes, we feel, but do not see the light), will while away hour after hour with something of His handiwork—a streak of sunlight, or a pebble, or a flower. Put it out in the grass, under a rose-bush, and see the thing wonder and philosophize, and laugh, all alone (?) to itself. Not much talking at this time, but what grave exclamations, what wise points of admiration, what profound and questioning looks over a leaf, or a blade of grass! A year or two later, put this curious thing out there again, and it begins to combine and arrange. The pebble, and the grass, and the flower, are worn out. They have talked everything up for the present, and now it says, let us prepare for war, or, if of the gentler sex, for a tea-party! In either case, it is not alone—far from it; nor unhappy—far from it; it is just one bubble of enjoyment. But if you want to hear its reserve force, in full Bedlam exhibition, just put it in a dark closet alone.

I never saw but one child that I thought would

bear that quietly. It was a papoose from the Florida everglades. Col. Harney had been exploring those recesses, shooting and hanging the Indians never before disturbed in those retreats, and on one of the little grassy islands, that are scattered about in those clear waters, this youngster was found, after a fight, and brought up a prisoner of war, to St. Augustine. He was the gravest piece of humanity that I ever beheld. A week before, it is safe to say, he had never seen a white man, or any of his novelties. Very likely all that he had seen of the world was that one island, with the bright water running up and away from its shores. Always there day and night, running up and away again; always clear and bright and sweet to the taste. This, and the high grass waving far away into the distance, overtopped here and there by a palm, was all the world to him. There, perhaps, he had heard of the Great Spirit, whose are all the islands and the waters, and the red men and white men; and who has said, "vengeance is mine; I will repay." There his mother had crooned wild songs over the little red face, and his father had tumbled him in the grass and taught him the war-whoop. He didn't want any other father or mother. They were good enough for him. They were gone now, and here was everything new and strange. Houses, streets, faces, language, all new, all strange. But nothing surprised him, nothing moved him, nothing would make him laugh, and certainly if his face told a true story, there was nothing to make him fear.

His keen black eyes were constantly busy noting this thing and that, but in such a blank, sad way, sad, not from its intensity, but from its want of all feeling, as though he saw nothing to his liking. Very nice, very fastidious was he, that nothing would suit his particular humor. Whether, in fact, this cool, blank look, was that of ignorance and stupidity, I know not; or whether he saw continually before him a picture of his father dangling from the fig-tree on his little island home in the everglades. Hanging there all day in the bright sunlight, but so still and speechless. Hanging there all night, staring with dead wide-open eyes, at the white moon and the stars!

In any case, that boy seemed to me quite alone in the world.

But isolation, literal and absolute, would probably be death; and not merely death of the body, but annihilation of all being. There are lonely beings now in the world, thousands and tens of thousands, who, without leadings of thought and hope from the cloud of witnesses about them, or from the felt presence of God himself, would sink at once into nothingness,—burn out like a candle, body and soul. And there are others of us,—God help us all,—still more lonely and desolate, seeking always for this same isolation, as though in that was the very joy of life. Chalk-marking and laying out the bounds, saying, "That's *mine*,—take care! don't step over there, you are on *my* premises," and so in a general way crying out "*Scat,*" and "*Whee!*" to everything about. The great fact being all the time (as we get to know some day, or die as the fool dieth) that man unassisted, or *independent,* as we say, is but small comfort to himself. And this, because he feels that he is with a stranger; a being with whom, as yet, he has scarcely more than a nodding acquaintance; one who, for aught he knows, may yet turn out a robber and a cut-throat.

Am I exaggerating? Not a bit of it. Every man of thought knows this. He bears his own burden; he carries his own secret with him. If he looks within, it is not his whole being at which he looks, for he can see but one thing at a time, and he is manifold in make—*E Pluribus Unum*—a sort of United States of being—wheels within wheels—a strange mechanism, the motive power of which is all in double darkness—an infernal machine, which may blow him up, he knows not how soon. No man feels that he is his own master. He cannot wholly guide his own being. Any one who imagines that he has any power of his own over his nature, has fooled himself to believe a lie. It is his nature that guides, and has power over, him. It sways about with him this way and that, and it never rests for one solitary moment of time. It is like a star, whose glimmer is unceasing. You can never look it in the face, for it never will be still, for you to do it. While you look for it here, presto, it is there. While you fancy you are having a fair *tête-à-tête,* behold it is in California or the South Seas. While you are bending over it microscopically, it has gone six times around the world, and is back again fresh as ever. Lively, pert, inquisitive, joyous at times, and mourning at times, and at other times puffed with such impudence and deviltry, as hell itself must feed, to give it such an air of royalty and dominion. There is no peace with this strange composition, till a man seeks his Maker, and asks for power over himself, day by day, and night by night, and hour by hour, until he may escape from this wild existence into something pure and rational.

And this something pure and rational—this life, as distinguished from death—what is it? It is not motion, as we have said, or momentum. Nor is it isolation, or inertia, or repose in the sense of rest. It is (as far as we may guess) action, needing no repose. It is health after disease, sanity after incipient madness! It is thought, fluent and burning as a star, high above day and night, and change. It is self-possession and strength. It is a part of the glory of God. It is crowned. It is triumphant. It is a living Hallelujah. It is wisdom, and knowledge, and power; and its utterance—the loftiest speech given to men or angels,—"*Glory be to God in the highest! Amen and amen!*"

And doubtless this life must be begun here, if begun at all; must be entered upon, if at all, here, in this bustling and changing world, amid eating, and drinking, and working, and dreaming, and strife, and trouble, and pain, and whatever apparent confusion confounded—"for there is no work, nor device, nor knowledge, nor wisdom, in the grave;" and life, in its essential elements, is the same in all places and at all times, and, like God himself, is unchangeable and everlasting.

Good-night, sir. We have had a long, *lonely* talk. I will go up, now, and seek for more of that sweet oblivion which I found this afternoon, on the parlor-sofa. Good-night.

Yours, ——.

Sleep! oh! beautiful sleep, if thou wert an angel, I would kneel down here and worship thee for this hour of cool repose.

We worship no such divinity as sleep, angel, or no angel. We are against sleep as an active principle, an entity. We look upon it as a necessity, enforced, thrust upon the world; a thing to be endured with resignation, rather than worshipped as a God. Sleep, indeed! Will anybody tell us what good, what pleasurable thing, what positive emotion, there can be in dull Oblivion—in lying down with closed eyes, the mind a blank, and the physical man utterly prostrate and powerless? Have you a purse? A thief can steal it. Have you a house? The incendiary may burn it over you. Have you an enemy? He may cut your throat, and this same divinity, sleep, say no word against it. Mark, we don't deny the recuperative power of sleep—we confess its utility. When we are weary, sleep is a good thing, a very pleasant thing. But it is all negative, only an absence of weariness, a cessation of pain—nothing more. And as well might a hungry man worship a leg of mutton or a rump steak, because eating it will allay his hunger.

But to sleep! to dream! Very pleasant things are dreams, we admit, sometimes—not always. We can't choose our dreams. They come unbidden, and are the subjects of no volition of our own; shadows all, they come and go, and leave no trace, no footprint on the sand, no mark on the wall. We rather like dreams—they are racy; they have no affinities with the sober experience, the hard realities of life. Natural laws are nothing to the dreamer. He laughs at, he spurns their control, and glancing above them, revels in impossibilities. The birds talk with him. Dumb animals converse with him. Even the trees bend their tall heads, and while their leaves are playing with the summer winds, open their queer mouths and speak to him. We had a dream once: we have had many; but this was impressive, peculiar, and left its strange transitions firmly fixed in our memory.

It was three years ago. We were out in the woods with a guide, sleeping in a shanty built by ourselves on the banks of the St. Regis Lake, one of those beautiful little sheets of water lying all alone in the forest away up north. Our shanty was built in this wise: In front of the gigantic trunk of a fallen tree, and at some eight feet distance from it, and as many feet from each other, we placed two forked posts. Across these we laid a pole, and from each another pole, to the great log. Others still were laid parallel with these as rafters, and over all was spread bark peeled from the trees around. The sides were built up with boughs, in order to keep off the lateral dampness. The front was open, and directly before the *door*, which, by the way, was the whole broadside of our dwelling, was a *smudge*, or fire built to keep the musquitoes and black flies from devouring us. Our bed was of green boughs. We had travelled far that day, and were hungry and weary when we reached the lake. My guide built the shanty while I caught a string of brook-trout, in a little stream that came laughing and scolding from the hills to lose itself in the waters of the lake. These, with a steak from a deer we had killed, afforded us a hearty supper, and we ate as hungry men in the forest are apt to do. As the darkness closed in upon the world, and while the stars were coming out one after another to hold their watch in the sky, we laid ourselves down on our bed of boughs to sleep. The solemn night voices were all around us; and weary from travel and lethargic from a wildwood feast, we soon passed into slumber.

As we slept upon that bed of boughs that night, strange visions passed before us. We were away in a new world, and yet all that we saw was familiar, nothing seemed strange to us; we were among beings that we seemed to know; not men and women, but rather the spirits of men and women; not as of those who had died, and whose bodies were mouldering in the grave—they had form, but not substance; shadows that moved and spoke; that seemed formed after the similitude of men and women, but through whose forms the sunlight passed. We possessed all the attributes of humanity, save a real, tangible body. Hands, and limbs, and body, we seemed to possess, palpable to the vision, but not to the touch. Hunger, and cold, and heat, and pain, were things that seemed to us unknown. Space and time were as nothing. We passed at once without effort, like thought, from place to place. We think of scenes far distant from us—memory calls up the stream, the lake, the meadow, the great trees, the cottage, and the garden; we say thought wanders away to such scenes. Well, this seemed to be with us a reality. If we thought of a scene, a locality, hundreds or thousands of miles away, at once we were there.

We thought of Rome, of the great St. Peter's, and there we stood, beneath that gigantic temple. We thought of the pyramids, and stood at their base, and talked familiar with the mummies that slept within those granite piles. We thought of Waterloo, and there we stood surveying that mighty conflict. We saw legions of men hurled against legions of men. We heard the roar of the cannon, and the rattle of musketry. We saw the smoke of battle wreathing up from blazing battalions. We saw the flashing of swords, as vast squadrons of horsemen mowed down the flying foe. We heard the groans of the wounded, and the wild shrieks of the dying. We passed unharmed through the conflicting hosts, looking upon the dying and the dead. Wherever we chose to be, at once we were there. How we passed we know not—the fact alone we remember. As our body was intangible, it was unaffected by the elements. Fire would not burn it, water would not drown it. We could walk on the bottom of the ocean with a thousand fathom of water above us. We could plunge into the volcano's seething cauldron. Rocks would not crush us, and precipices, down which we plunged, were harmless as the level plain. Such a being were we, and such were those around us. Shadows, mere intellectualities existing palpably to the vision, having form and comeliness, but unfettered and unconfined by a fleshly body. Of such a body, it seemed to us, we had never heard, save in the wild theories of some metaphysical dreamer. Its existence was a subject of derision, and those who upheld its reality were regarded as idle visionaries, nay, as profane rejecters of philosophical truths.

"A change came o'er the spirit of our dream."

We were away in the midst of the broad prairies of the West. They lay there as they came from the

Creator's hand. The eye of civilization had never before looked upon them, and no civilized man had set his foot upon the green grass that vegetated upon their bosom. All around us were vast plains, treeless and shrubless as a shorn meadow. Away off, on the one hand, hanging like a blue dim shadow upon the horizon, was a belt that we knew to be timber; while, on the other, on the very outside boundary of vision, loomed up the gigantic peaks of the Rocky Mountains, moveless and fixed, like sentinels of God, watching the boundless plains beneath them. The tall grass waved like vast fields of grain in the summer winds; rich flowers of the most gorgeous hues sent their wild fragrance abroad on the air, charming the vision by their glory, and entrancing the senses by their sweetness. In all this vast plain we saw no living thing. All around us was silence; vegetation alone seemed to live there—and that grew and flourished in richest and wildest luxuriance. It was like a vast garden, planted and nourished by the hand of nature, unaided, as it was unchecked, by the ingenuity or the industry of man. Suddenly a blight seemed to pass over that vast plain; the flowers faded; the tall grass shrivelled and died; the leaves on the rank weeds rolled together, and were blown away by hot winds that swept over that ocean of land; vegetation withered into a gray and sapless mass, standing where it grew; the streams, that were wont to move in sluggish and tortuous windings, were dried up, leaving channels like the trails of gigantic serpents; the blight of drought was upon all nature about us.

As we stood wrapped in contemplation of the immensity around us, a dull heavy sound fell upon our ear, like the rumbling of a thousand carriages over the rough pavement of a far-off city. Turning in the direction whence the sound seemed to come, we saw in the distance vast herds of deer and antelopes, flying at wild speed towards the spot where we stood. Behind these came an army of elks; their stately horns, glancing and waving in the sunlight, seemed like a forest of dead, low, barkless trees. Behind these came thundering down again, millions and millions of buffalo, making the earth tremble with the weight of their rushing and countless hosts. For miles and miles, in width as well as in depth, this vast herd covered the plain, bellowing and roaring in seeming terror at some terrible destruction behind them. Then came vast droves of wolves, panting and howling in immense numbers, with jaws distended and tongues lolling out, like hounds wearied by the chase. None seemed seeking for prey; a mortal terror was upon all; all were fleeing, as it seemed for life, towards the belt of timber land visible in the distance. These vast waves of animal life swept by us; the roar of their countless voices died away like the tempest in its onward flight. Then we saw the reason of their mortal terror. Away in the distance, was a dense line of dark murky smoke wreathing and twisting heavenward, wrapping earth and sky in its sombre folds. On came the fearful visitation, preceded by a line of fire athwart the whole of that vast plain, flashing and glancing upward as new fuel was grasped by its devouring tongue, and it was hurled onward by the rushing winds. On it came crackling and roaring, like a mighty billow of flame, devouring and overwhelming all things in its terrible career. Onward and onward it came with the speed of the war-horse, and the roar of the tornado. Before it was destruction; in its rear the blackness of desolation. Far as the eye could reach, on the right hand and on the left, it moved in a line of fire, leaving no escape save an onward flight. We stood spell-bound as it approached; that mighty prairie seemed rolled up as it swept along like a vast scroll, while the impenetrable obscurity behind it was like the darkness that was of old on the face of the deep. It approached—it surrounded—it enveloped us within its folds, when———we awoke, and behold it was a *dream!* and "yet not all a dream." The fire we had kindled in front of our shanty had crept along the dry leaves until it reached the foot of a dead fir-tree, among whose thick and withered branches a wild grape-vine had spread its thousand tendrils. That too was dead; the fire had crept up the dry trunk of that dead fir-tree, and having reached the net-work of vines and sapless branches, it burst out into a brilliant flame. When we started from our sleep it was flashing and crackling, and twirling upwards, lighting up forest and lake like a vast torch in the hand of some gigantic demon of the woods.

X.

D, WITH A DASH TO IT.

OH, compositors! oh, proof-readers! and you, oh, printers' devils! if you have anything to do with it, please give us the facts which we send you, as they are. The facts, not imaginations.

We admit that words are poor and inexpressive signs, but they are all we have to talk with. And we can approximate somewhat to each other's ideas, by a proper use of words. Usage has attached to them certain meanings and values, and by judgment and care, a man may sometimes say almost the very thing which he has in mind. But, my dear sirs, it is a delicate business. It is walking a very tight rope, and requires the most careful balance and fixedness of purpose. Moreover, it requires a perfect agreement and unity of action. If we say oh, ah, bah, and so forth, then we expect from you the same oh, ah, bah, and so forth. If we say *ex-plum-bum*, *ex-plum-bum* it is. Ex-bum-plum won't do, or plum-bum-ex. No, sirs, give us nothing else but the great fact, EX-PLUM-BUM!

If you diverge the slightest from this solemn exactness, you depart, at once, into fictions and all uncertainties. In short, you are in a dangerous way. You don't know—you can't conceive—and no man can know or conceive for you—the long-drawn mischief, to which you give such a heedless beginning. Why, sirs, you disturb the harmony of the world—the moral equilibrium of things. You do not merely stand in the light, you bring down midnight. You "create darkness."

This, I grant, is not always the case; for when you merely print *on* for *or*, as in a late paper of ours, a shrewd reader may discover the error; but when you drop whole words, containing the heart of a paragraph, I can scarcely express my astonishment. How you can sleep at night, after putting forth such fragments to the world, it is difficult to say.

But to some rules there are exceptions, and although this belongs to nearly the highest ethics, and is, in fact, almost that perfect law to which exceptions are impossible, there is one exception to this rule, and it would rejoice my heart to see it always recognized.

A club-mate of mine, who had been living a gay life, as he supposed, discovered his mistake and reformed; and in a letter to a mutual friend, cautioned him not to write any more, "*d, with a dash to it.*"

This, sirs, is that exception, which, if always observed in papers and books, would gladden the hearts of thousands upon thousands—this d, with a dash to it. Drop it, Mr. Compositor; drop it, proof-reader, down with it, cast it out; it is a devil. Don't use d, with a dash to it. It is not gentlemanly, it is not manly, it is not decent. It is no part of a man's language. It is that abominable thing which God hates, and why should not you and I? There is no such blot in the heavens, or on the earth. No bird, or beast, no mountain brook, or cataract, or earthquake, or thunders even, that ever utter that word. It is of the Devil's make and man's adoption; applied to everything hot, cold, wet and dry, head, eyes, and body, and (Heaven forgive us) to the soul itself, while it has no fitness for any one thing or person placed, or living legitimately on this our earth. It belongs to that place prepared for the Devil and his angels. It is proper there. It is there for the place and its people. But you and I, my friend, are not yet sentenced. Thanks be to our Father in Heaven, the blue sky is still "bending over us all." *We* have not yet gone down into darkness and despair.

Oh! of all smallest performances under the sun, what a study for a Hogarth, is that of "man, born like a wild ass's colt," calling hastily for the day of judgment, with this d, with a dash to it! What courage! what heroism! what greatness! what a sublimely high purpose! My own life has been so joyous, not to say exultant, that I cannot presume to know how terribly some may be tempted; but I can well imagine that here and there, and more than here and there, in the pressing crowd who are daily moving on to the grave, there may be uplifted hands and trembling aspirations; I can imagine many a sinking heart and weary brain *tempted,* if you please, to cry, "Spare us, Good Lord; Christ, have mercy upon us!"—but to invoke *evil*—to ask for death and perdition, oh! the madness—the madness!

Tastes no doubt differ, and to some, d, with a dash to it, may have a pleasant twang, but I would rather have a pistol fired in my hair, than ever hear it, or any of its horrid combinations, and I never heard it even repeated, as from another, in rounding a story, or giving a fancied point to an anecdote, that it was not accompanied with a sheep-faced consciousness of having done a very small thing. I never saw a man detected in stealing a leg of mutton, but I should think such a man would have just about such an expression of countenance.

There are people who think they feel better, sometimes, for "blowing off steam," as they call it. But swearing is not blowing off steam; it is bursting the boiler. Doubtless, as a people, we carry too many pounds to the square inch—let us blow off, by all means, but don't let us suppose that the final cause and end of steam is to "blow up."

The truth is, we may, with just as much propriety, just as much kindness, and about the same effect, throw vitriol about among our friends, as to foul the pure air of heaven with oaths and blasphemies.

Is it not so, Mr. Editor, Mr. Compositor, Mr. Proof-reader? Then let us make it so. Let us down with d, with a dash to it.

Its force is weakness—its point is bathos. The world is bad enough, wicked enough, wretched enough, miserable enough; but it is not so bad, or wicked, or wretched, or miserable, as to give any logic or fitness to d, with a dash to it. It is not yet in order.

What say you all to giving it the cold shoulder? Eh! What's the vote? Send me, Mr. Editor, the ayes and noes, on the following proposition: Never to print—never to write—never to utter—never to listen to it—never in any way, shape, or manner, open or sly, to use "d, with a dash to it."

Yours, ——.

"If you diverge the slightest from this solemn exactness, you depart at once into fiction, and all uncertainties. In short, you are in a dangerous way. Why, sirs, you disturb the harmony of the world—the moral equilibrium of things; you do not merely stand in the light, you bring down midnight—you create darkness."

Just so! We have laughed and scolded and said a good many things, that to some might sound like profane swearing, over this same matter. We have been victimized ourself, dozens of times—made to say all sorts of queer things, by the mere change of a letter, or mistake of a word. We came to our present position entirely green, as to all matters pertaining to the management of a newspaper. We had not, in all our life, had an hour's experience in proof-reading. We have tried our best to improve in this respect, but we still fall very short of perfection. The types make us say a good many things we never dreamed of, and the worst of it is, when they speak, whatever they say, becomes a fixed fact, unchangeable as destiny, standing there impregnable, defiant of all human agency to change it.

Not long since, we visited a friend in the country, and in giving an account of our ramblings and the pleasant things we had seen, we undertook to describe his beautiful garden, and in doing so, spoke of a thrifty fig-tree and its fruit. We claim some genius for graphic description, and have always been a little proud of our efforts in that line. Judge then of our mortification, when our attention was called to the fact that we had hung all manner of "PIGS" on the oriental tree in our friend's conservatory, from the little green nucleus from which the blossom had just fallen, to the fully ripe "*pig.*"

On another occasion we had been presented with a basket of oranges. Large, ripe, and luscious the fruit was, direct from the sunny South, where it grew. We acknowledged the gift in suitable terms, as all editors who are presented with nice things should. The next day one of those joke-finders, that are permitted, for some inscrutable purpose, to pester the world, stalked into our office and gravely inquired about the basket of "*ourangoutangs*" we had been favored with. "Bring us the paper of yesterday!" we thundered to our devil, (not he of the hoof and horns,) who was sitting cross-legged on a stool, studying the programme of a band of negro melodists, who were to give a banjo and bone concert in the evening. The paper was brought, and sure as fate, we had acknowledged the receipt of a basket of most beautiful "OURANGOUTANGS," from our esteemed friend Mr. JOHN SMITH, who had just received a cargo of the same sort, at his old stand on the Hill.

A friend of ours, who was formerly connected with the press, as the editor of a country newspaper, relates an amusing anecdote on this subject. He had an old chum, whose name was BULLOCK, and who took to himself a wife one day. Our friend, who attended the wedding, undertook to announce, in a becoming manner, through the columns of his paper, the happy event. In the afternoon of the day on which the announcement was made, Mr. BULLOCK strode into his office, with face blazing, and eyes flashing with indignation, one hand grasping a newspaper, and the other closed up into a compact bunch of bones, like a sledge-hammer—"Look you, Mr. D——," said he, with a voice choking with anger, "by what name am I to be called? Answer me that, you type-setting, quill-driving son of a cylinder press." "Hallo," cried our friend, "what's out, now?" "I want to know what my name is—my NAME, that's what's out," cried the enraged BULLOCK. "Your name? Why BULLOCK, to be sure—Mr. J.D. BULLOCK, M.D.—who ever disputed that?" replied our astonished friend. "Look there," said the excited married man, pointing to the announcement of his own wedding in our friend's paper, and there, sure enough, was the marriage of the beautiful and accomplished Miss AMELIA AGNES So and So, to J. D. BULLCALF, Esquire, M.D., with an acknowledgment of the receipt of a large slice of the bride's loaf, and a liberal puff for the wedding, which, under all the circumstances, looked mightily like a burlesque. The evident mortification of the editor, and his solemn word of honor that it was purely a mistake, appeased the injured party; but our friend always insisted that he narrowly escaped a personal assault on that occasion.

We are getting used to these things, and they do not trouble us as they did once. They are vexatious enough, but they *will* happen. Writers will, through all time, suffer from the inaccuracies of compositors and proof-readers. The best remedy we know of, is contained in the prescription of a medical friend of ours, who is principled against curing the toothache by extracting the troublesome molar. "Doctor," said a suffering patient, with his under jaw in a sling like a broken arm, and one side of his face swollen to the semblance of the moiety of a moderately sized pumpkin, "I've got the toothache!" "*Have* you?" said the doctor, calmly. "Yes, I have," replied the patient, "and it's the jumping toothache, too. This infernal grinder kicks like a whole team of mules." "*Does* it?" said the doctor, calm and cold as an iceberg. "Yes, it *does*," was the answer. "What shall I do for this intolerable agony?" "Grin and bear it, and be thankful that you've got teeth enough in your head to ache," replied the Doctor, as he turned his back on the suffering patient and walked away. So we say to all authors, and our friend, MARGINS, in particular, in view of these occasional typographical blunders, "Grin and bear it," and be thankful for the talent that enables you to furnish a work in which the world sees beauty enough to be marred by a "mistake of the printer."

Is it not so, Mr. Editor, Mr. Compositor, Mr. Proof-reader? Then let us make it so. Let us down with d, with a dash to it.

It is all very well to *talk* about this downing "with d, with a dash to it." Reform is a pleasant thing to talk about in a quiet way, to think of, and speculate upon. In our closet we may imagine what a wrong thing this or that popular habit may be—how unproductive of good—how pregnant of evil—how easily its folly may be demonstrated, and how readily it will be abandoned by the people when they come to understand it. All theory! all imagination! our dear MARGINS. Strong as we may be in logic in these closet interviews with ourselves, there is one thing wanting, the lack of which annihilates our theories, and dissipates our imaginings like the mists that go up in the early morning, from the cascades and waterfalls of your Roaring River. Go out into the streets, and preach reform in this matter. Take the swearer by the button-hole, and pour your exhortations, your logic, your demonstrations into his ear. Tell him it belittles humanity, and is a sin against God. Prove its folly, its utter uselessness. It's hazarding the great interest of the soul, for that which is more utterly worthless than a mess of pottage. He won't argue, he won't gainsay a word of your excellent admonition. He'll stand like a post until you have exhausted the subject and passed on. Then, as his companion emerges from around the corner, and comes within speaking distance, he'll point you out as one of those reformers (coupling the latter epithet, may be, with an expressive adjective, made up with a "d, with a dash to it") who go about preaching up the necessity of progress in the moral condition of the world, and boring people with their abstract notions of human perfectibility, and thereupon he and his friend will have a laugh over what they are pleased to term your folly in meddling with that which does not concern you, instead of rolling up dollars, by attending to that which does. The thing we lack in our closet theories, in this as in most matters of reform, is the want of practical applicability of those theories to the actual condition of the world as it is. We forget how impossible it is to make the people pause, to make human nature pause, in its onward rush, to comprehend us, to *feel* the force of our reasoning, and the justness of our admonitions. We forget that something more is necessary to change, or eradicate a popular habit, than the mere demonstration of its folly. Every body, for more than a thousand years, has been convinced of the folly of profanity, aye, of its wickedness, too. Nobody advocates it. Nobody justifies it; and yet about three out of every five of the people of all Christian nations indulge in this most foolish and wicked habit of using the "d, with a dash to it." It may in some sense be called a Christian habit, and goes hand and hand with the spread of Christianity. And yet against this habit Christianity has been warring always. Always denouncing, always execrating it. It finds no word, or letter of sanction, in all the broad range of the Chrtstian's creed, or the wide reach of Christian duties. How shall we account for this, save by supposing that the great Author of Evil goes along by the side of the evangelists, the missionaries, and scatters his tares wherever he finds good seed taking root, dropping an oath wherever he sees the germ of a prayer, thus sending up to Heaven, with the incense of every pious and holy aspiration, an attendant blasphemy, to mar the joy of angels over a soul redeemed?

"The world is bad enough, wicked enough, wretched enough, miserable enough."

True, every word most true; and yet, as a whole, it is a good, a marvellously good world. Could we, friend MARGINS, I mean you or I, or any human power, invent one that would, in degrees of perfection, come within a sightless distance of this, which the great Creator has made for us? Would we venture to point to one thing in the great universe of God, whether in the heavens above, or on this earth, and say this is out of place, this is a deformity, this is useless? Would we, in looking over the doings of Providence in the administration of his visible government, and selecting some great national or individual calamity, one that spread ruin and sorrow even over a whole people, venture to affirm that *this* should have been ordered otherwise? Seeming evils there are doubtless—events ordered by God that may bear hard upon us. Sorrow may darken around us; the hopes that we cherished may vanish away, and we may sit down in desolation of spirit, to weep over the loss of things that we loved. But when we see, all around us, the clustering evidences of the boundless benevolence, the infinite goodness of the Power that controls human destiny, would we venture, were the choice given us, to turn aside even the sorrow that fell upon ourselves? Would we take the hazards of marring the great plans of the Infinite Mind, or bend them to square with our own feeble and narrow perceptions? When we looked upon the pale, still face of a beloved child, its eyes closed in death, with the wreath encircling its marble brow, placed there by the hand of love to decorate it for the grave, would we call the spirit back, or breathe life again into that moveless corpse? The heart might yearn for its darling, but who would not say, it is God's work, let it be as it is?

XI.

SEPTEMBER.

Dear Editor, we despair. For, of course, it is raining again, (just this once,) after all the late floods, and so we are *not* at No. — Broadway, though we tried hard. We went to the station, where, as you know, it is my way to "take the cars," but just then a long line of black cloud rolled up from the west, a white field rolled out beyond it, and certain heavy cannonades in that quarter indicated the same kind of thunderous Saturday afternoon, which has been repeated now for about six times in succession. And so we came back.

Rain, rain, rain! But we are safely housed again, though what with riding home in a whirlwind, my people have a color that will last them into next week.

So brilliantly as we were made up, it is almost provoking—almost, I say—not to have made a little figure this afternoon in North Broadway. In the confusion incident to whether we should go, I took cards to show our intent, mounted into the one freight car just behind the engine, and came on thundering through smoke and cinders, over Roaring River, while my people came back behind *Red Jacket;* but at Bungtown my courage failed, and I dropped (for there was no other exit) from that lumbering concern, and came straight home again. It's useless, said I, to separate man and wife. They should go together in all things.

However, I send the cards: *Mr. Margin, Roaring River; Mrs. Margin, Roaring River, Wild Rose, City.* Having parted with *Snowdrop* and *Honeysuckle,* we take gladly such other blossoms as float our way, and are rejoicing now in the *Wild Rose.* All of one excellent garden, sir, but the world having so many waste places, some must be transplanted to grace other localities. We must be generous.

Did I tell you about Wednesday? We were to start that day also. I had said—the last thing over night—"Remember, to-morrow we are to visit the great City Editor."

"Will it rain?" said Mrs. Margin.

"No,—beautiful night—stars all out, and moonlight too: beautiful night, beautiful! night of nights—*charmante!* No, my blossoms; no more storms: go to bed now, and sleep on into the excellent day that is coming."

Next morning, opening my clouded eyes, behold the rain and the equinox!

I say, sir, we despair. However, what could we expect in September?

Oh breezy September, shady September, equinoctial September, September and oysters for ever! The bivalves we can have, though we see no Broadway, no city editor. But if a man has any thing particular to say about September, let him speak quick, for we are already in the latter end.

Good-bye, sir. Make our regards to Rosebud and all the house, and all the people about the house, and your neighbors, if you think proper. But don't fail to grasp the great fact, that we started and came back again—that it rained and re-rained—that we tried hard, and failed magnificently.

Burr-rr-rr-urr! (that's a train on Roaring River.) *Squib! wish-sh-sh-ish!* (that's a flourish.) *Baw! aw-aw-awh!* (that's the blast.) Let them go. Foolish people to be going off in the rain; but let them go. *Tell that conductor, if you see him, that he owes me one*, for I paid through and dropped at *Bung*. The foolish man called out to me to go with him, but it wouldn't do. Rains and thunders in the west, and my people somewhere in the north country behind *Red Jacket;* it wouldn't do, and I told him so.

Rain, rain, and again the rain! Are you looking for us, sir? Are you on the house-top seeking for the wave of a white handkerchief? spying into the uttermost north, for some dim sign of Mr. and Mrs. Margin? Hallucinated editor, go down immediately. We are not coming. Go down before you are wet through. Go down, sir, and dine, and enjoy yourself. Have you got any plums, I wonder? My people are just now making up for their early dinner, with plums, grapes, and muskmelons—the last about the flattest kind of fruit, according to my digestion. But the plums, sir; oh, the plums! Of all the generous, the bountiful things of the garden, I love the plum-tree with my whole heart. It gives, you perceive, in such a whole-souled way, such a bending fulness. We have but few, compared with our great neighbor, who has his plum in every corner. But our wealth is sufficient—four Bleeckers, two *magnum bonum*, and one sugar-plum. It has been very pleasant to feed out among those trees, finishing or beginning a breakfast, or a dinner, or a supper; for the ripe plum is harmless always. I think I am a better man for those plum-trees; at any rate, my digestion is better. Our tropical summer and heavy rains have brought on all the fruits this year, in great luxuriance. Everything is fat and heavy with summer. Our second corn is just now perfect — large, but tender — and rich with sugar. You are not obliged to nibble at it, but may mow it down, as a heifer cuts away the first grass of spring. But the plum is our stand-by. And let me tell you, you can't do much better than to stop under the Bleecker. Not so very aristocratic, but *good.* The egg is a golden dainty, an up-town plum, and the little sugars, to look at, are beauties, but the Bleecker you may eat all day. Our opposite neighbor, who delights in fat cattle and pigs like a butter-barrel, and who is rather cosmopolitan in his ways, walks daily amid his great variety of fruits, tasting, as a wine-bibber his wines—that is, he did, but he is gone now. He stepped in at Bung as I stepped out, and has gone away into the West, taking the *White Rose* with him, (another from our garden,) where they are to plant nearly half a county with plums, grapes, pears, apples, citron, squashes, corn, and potatoes, and to have all manner of men, women, and children running about the lots, planting, sowing, chopping, harvesting, carpentering, masoning, pond-making, prospecting, and churning tons of butter—all which is very well,

> If all our summers are to be
> Like this fine summer of '53,

which, however, has gone even now while we were looking at it—slipped away in a twinkling—walked off in the night, and forgot to come back again. Ah, if we could surround the beautiful summer days and make them stay with us forever. But they must go; they were only here a little while on leave of absence. We will meet them all again in the day of judgment—all the beautiful days, all the golden days, all the dark days and nights of storm—every one will be there. But now it is good-bye and farewell. And we, Mr. Editor, you and I—stout as you are, and full of blood as my veins are of late—*we* shall soon be saying good-bye and farewell, and to us, plum-time will be over forever.

But meanwhile—for this particular moment, at

least—we live; and whatever winds Antarctic are now ready, let them come. We are to roll on now, amid cool nights and the checkered days of light and shade. Let us take the downhill of the year cheerily. There is no harm in being braced up a little when the leaves fall. Our front maple has already gone into colors. If this were in mid-summer, how untimely would it seem! This is why I like not a certain deadness in Southern vegetation, at this season. Its effort at being perennial falls short of that brilliant success which we look for, while it has nothing of the dying glories of our Northern autumn. The perennial, in fact, is not altogether suited to our world, or to its prosperous administration. Let us have, rather, our blazing and dashing summers, cooling off through the magnificence of autumn, to the snows and ices of winter. So shall we prosper and gather tone and character, and make headway in the great business of life. So shall we not tarry too long in some happy valley, and grow timid and feeble in the mere joy of existence.

After all, it don't rain much, and we *might* have gone. But it's too dark for introductions. No, let them go, all the people.

"*Oh! oh! oh! oh!*"

Another train going North. Let them go. *They*, now, are going home. Sensible people. Coming out into the country where are plums, grapes, sickle-pears, pumpkins, and so-forth. Coming home for Sunday. That is sensible, rational. You may always expect something of people who come home for Sunday—the day *royale*, "day of all the week the best." Perhaps we will sing that to-morrow night, as we did in the old times, with a dozen voices surging about through the four parts, not to say five or six, for there were always one or two traversing, and going crosswise; but we made a noise, you may be sure.

Go ahead, up-train, *home for Sunday!* Carry on! up-train, *home for Sunday.* Pipe away, up-train, and sing it out, through the valley—up the river—over the hills and far-a-way—*home for Sunday!* And you, all aboard there, engineer and fireman, brakeman and conductor, young folks and old folks, inside and outside—*God bless you all*—coming home for Sunday!

I think now, Mr. Editor, I will go out to the west piazza, and make a short speech to the plum-trees, and by that time, Saturday will be gone. I must thank *somebody* for the plums.

Au revoir, sir, good-day, *bon jour*, and so-forth; for *bon* it is, after all its wet and windy distractions. The rain is over; a spot of gold lies here and there upon the landscape, while in the mid-heaven a few clouds sail slowly about—but mostly, the blue prevails. Good! Look for us, suddenly, the first sunny day. Yours, ——.

"Oh! breezy September, shady September, equinoctial September, September and oysters forever! The bivalves we can

have, though we see no Broadway, no city editor. But if a man has any thing particular to say about September, let him speak quick."

We have much to say about September, and in its favor, too. It is a good month, a great month, a glorious month. It is the month of dahlias, and of ripe fruits, the seed-time of the year. Out upon oysters! They have a taint of grossness about them. There is nothing spiritual about the "bivalves." Leave them for the long evenings and cold days of winter. But September has its inspirations. We become poetic in September. It is the month of yellow leaves, of purple and crimson foliage, the month of the Katydids, and the Cricket. They pipe clearest when September is young. The tza! tza! of the one is loudest among the hazle bushes, and the chirrup of the other shrillest in the wall. September makes them musical, but the frost comes, and with it the last song of the Katydid. Did you ever, dear MARGINS, indite poetry, perpetrate rhyme, of a September evening, after listening to the little night warbler among the clusters of hazle bushes, or the branches of the small trees? Did you ever ask the insect tattler what Katy really did to make such a stir in the world and give occasion for its everlasting song of "Katy did?" No! Well, *we* have, and here is its answer.

THE KATYDID'S ANSWER.

Oh, Katy, dear, you know you did, at midnight's silent hour,
Steal softly through the moonlight, to this my pleasant bower,
And here beneath its vines and leaves, by blushing roses hid,
You met the man you love, Kate—you did, you know you did.

And here you leaned upon his breast, his arm was round your waist,
Your hand was locked in his, Kate, and when he stooped to taste
The nectar that was on your lip, how gently was he chid—
You loved to hear his whispered vows,—you did, you know you did.

The moon was in the sky, Kate, the stars were watching there,
The gentle breath of summer night was sporting in your hair;
I listened to your words, Kate, though soft and low they fell:
I heard them every one, Kate, and if I would, could tell.

But never fear me, gentle one, nor waste a thought or tear,
Lest I should whisper what I heard in any mortal ear.
I only sport among the boughs, and like a spirit hid,
I think on what I saw and heard, and laugh out "Katy did."

I sit among the leaves here, when evening zephyrs sigh,
And those that listen to my voice, I love to mystify.
I never tell them all I know, altho' I'm often bid:
I laugh at curiosity, and chirrup "Katy did."

I would not make you blush, Kate, your innocence I know—
I know your spotless purity is like the virgin snow.
And yet you'd better not, Kate, altho' you think your 're hid,
Steal to my bower by moonlight, as once you know you did.

The cricket, too, do you remember how in early September, he piped among the stones in the fields, and how merrily he sang in the wall? We remember one that chirped in the corner when we sat by our father's fireside. His voice was cheerful, and it was a pleasant thing to listen to his happy song. Father, mother, brothers, sisters were beside us then, and we all talked of the little warbler as a thing that we loved. If he came out upon the hearth, nobody disturbed him. If he wandered over the floor, nobody stepped upon or frightened him. He repaid our kindness by his cheerful music, as each evening he regaled us with a lay. But the corner, and the cricket, and the home of our childhood, are all gone. Decay has removed the one, and the voice of the other is hushed in death—and those who sat by the hearthstone listening with us to that cricket's song, where are they? Father, mother, sisters, brothers, where are they?

Of the twelve that composed that circle, six have gone to their rest, and the others have floated out in divers directions on the currents of life.

Time! Time! O! the wrecks that lie scattered along thy pathway!

But will you tell us, friend MARGINS, why it is that all living things that come out in the September evenings, have glad voices given them? Why is it that when the sun is gone down, and the hum of business is still, when the voice of man is hushed and the winds have retired to their caves, the voice of the insect tribes, low and quiet and solemn, comes abroad upon the air? Why does not silence come down like the curtains of night, and brood in the darkness over us? It is that we may not forget the lessons that nature teaches. The heavens may be darkened by clouds; the face of the moon may be veiled, and the stars may not shine out to remind us; the sound of the winds may be hushed; but the song of the cricket tells us, that life and beauty, and joy, and happiness are rife among the creatures of God. Such will your answer be, and we concede its truth.

"Oh! if we could surround the beautiful summer days, and make them stay with us forever!"

We would not do it if we could, indeed we would not. We love the summer, we love its long beautiful days, its broad fields of grain, its rich foliage; we love its haying time, its hoeing time and its ripe harvests. But its hot, burning days, its noxious vapors, its deadly malaria, its fevers, its cholera and cholera morbus, we do not like. We love the autumn, with its ripened fruits, its corn huskings, its potato digging, its fat deer, and the music of the hounds on the mountains. We love the flaunting robes, all flaming in crimson and yellow, and green and deep brown that it throws over the hill-sides, dressing them in beauty like an eastern Houri for the bridal. We love the winter, with its social evenings, its pure white robe of snow. We love the jingle of its merry sleigh-bells. We love to hear the hissing of the north wind, as it whirls around the corners, and over the house-tops and along the streets, looking into the crevices of the windows, and peering under the doors, as we sit with our friends around us, and the coals burning cheerfully in the grate. We can laugh at the north winds, and cry, ha! ha! at the driving snow.

We love the spring, with its opening buds, its growing foliage, and its early flowers. We love the beautiful green fields, and the sweet breath of its south wind, that comes to fan us, loaded with the fragrance of the meadows. We love the glad song of the early birds, and to see them building their nests in the branches of the trees. We love to hear the shrill call of the quail from his perch upon the fence-stake, and the song of the catbird, or the brown thrush, as he sits upon the topmost branch of the shade-tree in the pasture, swaying in the breeze as he sings. We love to see the young things, the lambs, the pigs, the calves, the colts, and the little children, all in their places, joyful and happy, frisking and playing and running hither and yon, in their gleesomeness, full of the spirit of life, and fun and frolicking, as if there was to be no storm, no equinox, no bleak fall days or pinching cold of winter. We love the spring. We love summer, and autumn, and winter. We love all the seasons and all the months. We love the days of the months. They are not all bright, and glorious, and sunny, and we love them the more because they are not so.

"Some days *must* be dark and dreary."

The seasons are the types of human life, and the days are types also. Mark this, friend MARGINS; in human destiny there are bright days, and dark days; days of sunshine, and days of storm. There is spring, and summer, and autumn, and winter. But mark again. *We* have but one set of seasons. Spring will never return to us, and when the winter of life comes, its chill will leave us only at death, and its ice be thawed away only in the grave. But what of that? There is another country, where there are no dark days, no equinoxes, no storms, no winter winds, where spring is perpetual. Are we bound to it?

"Let us take the down-hill of the year cheerily."

Change the word "year" to "life," and you will have brought out the great leading principle of the true philosophy of living. "Take the down-hill of *life* cheerily," is your only true wisdom. You and I, friend MARGINS, have at least ceased to be young. And however we may deny being old, yet so much we will yield for the argument's sake. And, moreover, we cannot stand still. We are moving. White hairs are gathering upon our heads, and wrinkles are invading the corners of our eyes. These are mile-stones on our journey of life. It will do no good to count them—to try to eradicate them is folly. We must march on. We are on the top of the hill at best, and our way henceforth is downward. Well, be it so, and what then? "Take the down-hill of life cheerily." No murmuring at the descent. Millions upon millions have gone before us. There are flowers along the pathway, down-hill as it is. Hope blooms by the way—inhale its fragrance and gather its blossoms. Cheerily! cheerily! cries our guide. Let us follow in his footsteps, submit to his guidance, and all will be well. The way may be rough—he will lead us where we will not stumble nor plunge headlong down the precipices that tower above fathomless depths. The way may be dark. Cheerily! cheerily! sounds from the darkness, and light bursts upon our path. Yes, yes, cheerily is the word.

"Perhaps we will sing that to-morrow night as we did in the old times, with a dozen voices surging about, through the four parts, not to say five or six, for there were always one or two traversing or going crosswise, but we made a noise you may be sure."

There is something about this that awakens memory. The clouds of the past are lifting, and old scenes are rising in the perspective. We are young again. A quarter of a century has been obliterated from the number of our years, and we are on our way to the old brown, weather-beaten school-house, near the clear cold stream that flows along through Pleasant Valley, away out in old Steuben. Blessings on that beautiful valley, and that clear, cold stream. We have caught strings of the speckled trout from its deep eddies, and upon its ripples, and under the old logs that lay across it. But we are on our way to that weather-beaten school-house. It is a clear, frosty night. The stars are glistening like bright gems in the sky, and the moonbeams sparkle like diamonds, in their cold brilliancy on the snow. The oak-trees, that retain their dead and withered foliage, cast their shadows like clouds, on the unbroken crust on the meadows that skirt the road. There is stillness all around us. The night voices are all frozen into silence, but there is nothing sad or solemn in the cold, calm hush of a winter's night. We are on our way to the "singing school." We remember the tall, lathy "singing master," with his earnest and solemn face, his long hair parted on his forehead, and combed straight and sleek over his coat collar and resting on his shoulders. He is before us now, with his long, bony hand and long fingers, and his mahogany pitch-pipe. His nasal fa! sol! la! as he gives the "pitch" to his class, is sounding in our ear. He was a devotional man, and his faith in the saving efficacy of psalmody was perfect. Among all the tunes taught in his school, Old Hundred was his especial favorite. True, he indulged in Mear, Amsterdam, Lenox, China, Greenfield, Coronation, and others of the same centenarian character, but Old Hundred was his weakness, his idol, his great tune of tunes. It was his first, his last, his midst and without end. It was the first given out in the evening; it was sung in the centre minutes of the school, and was sure to be the last at its close. And that class, merry, happy, laughter-loving young people, were they all, full of mischief, frolic and fun. The more the simple-minded teacher loved and venerated his old favorite tune, the more they murdered it by their discords. Bass, tenor, treble, and counter, were sure to be playing at cross purposes. Labor as he would, the bass would be too low and the tenor too high; the treble would push along like a locomotive, while the counter would drag its slow length away behind, all filling the musical ear with the most horrible compound of discordant sounds.

The good teacher has gone to his long rest. The old weather-beaten school-house has passed away. The free trout stream that went laughing and scolding over the clean pebbles, on its crooked path towards the lake, has been harnessed to a great water-wheel and made to grind corn. That class, too, is all scattered—some are on the ocean—some in the far Western States—some beyond the Rocky Mountains, and some dwell in the city of the dead. We remember their happy faces, as they were that last winter that we spent at the old homestead. They are before us now, and we see them as they were gathered in the singing school, worrying the good "singing master," with their mischievous discords. Shadows all, creatures of fancy, hallucinations, memories only.

We visited the old homestead the last summer. It passed into the hands of strangers years ago.

We inquired for the bright-eyed, romping girl, the beauty of the class, and we found her sitting in matronly composure in the shadow of a cherry-tree in front of her dwelling, fat and of rotund proportions, smoking a pipe that was none of the cleanest. She had cattle, and sheep, and grain, and pigs, and may be, money out on interest; but the vision of the singing school had vanished away. Time! Time! The wrecks that are scattered along thy pathway!

XII.

OCTOBER.

HEAVEN seems to come very near to us this morning. It is picture-day everywhere. Overhead, the blue, and the blue only; and below, in the soft air, scarcely a single wave of motion. A mile distant on the islands, a line of white, some hundreds of feet high, runs through the valley, and along the edge of this snowy embankment stand tall pines in bright green. Within those white curtains may be seen other forms, faintly outlined and ghost-like; and underneath the front rank, and nearer by, on plateaus of rock, smaller forest trees, rich in crimson and royal colors.

The golden tint is in the air. This is why the shadows on the grass have not the sharp outline which of late they had in September, but rather the softness as of shadows by moonlight. Sound itself seems muffled, and comes gently to the ear. Without thought as to the why of it, people speak low and in kind tones. Every one strolls about leisurely, saying, in a quiet way, "Beautiful—great!"

No one hurries to enjoy the day. There is no feeling that it is soon to pass away; we *know* that, but incline to think, notwithstanding, that now we are to have, always, days just like this, soft, rich, dreamy, and brimming with a quiet joy. We laugh at anybody who didn't know beforehand that we were going to have just such fine, glorious weather. Of course! isn't it October, my hearty? and hasn't it rained enough, in all conscience? However, let us pause over it, and take it down slowly, as the boys do the pippins in the orchard.

A gala-day, a picture-day, artistic, beautiful. Only a little while ago we had the sharp sour winds and the rains—day after day, the wind and the rain. Those were the sneezing times, the coughing times, the tooth-ache and the face-ache times. It was hard to look upon the world then, as other than a very wet and cold affair. Now we counterpoise in the calm, the repose, the pomp of October.

To-day, all things put on glory. Pureness, and beauty, and glory. These grow up together always; the one from the other. Pureness and then beauty, and then the crown of glory which God places with his own hand on every perfected life. It is the water made wine, by the miracle of death. For death is not the Divine order of things, but life. Not pain and trouble, not sinning and shame, not repentance and prayer, not struggle and labor,—but peace and joy, acclamation and hallelujahs,—the water made wine. Some excellent, well-meaning people think it the reverse of this—to wit: the wine made water. But, oh, no! God does not offer his children any such cup of dilution, but the fulness, (think of this, oh lame, and halt, and blind, and deaf, ailing and struggling and starving world, ponder well the promise,) *the fulness of life.*

One cannot well say, to-day,—"Be not angry with us forever." We revolt at this, as unkind, unthankful. Surely not to-day, not to-day is He angry with us. Where is it written? Let me see the handwriting, the autograph of the Most High. Where is it written that He is angry with us? Not in the blue up there! Not in the little white clouds which just now are forming from the morning mist,—not in the rich fruits of the earth,—not in this air tempered to the most exquisite finish of strength and enjoyment,—not in this soft white light,—not in the hearts of His people, for wherever this morning you find any weakest servant of His, you will find thanksgiving and praise, and a full measure at that, pressed down and running over, a well of waters springing up into everlasting life. Ah, if we could hear the utterance of their hearts, would it not be, "Thou, Thou art the King of Glory, O Christ! Thou, who art the everlasting Son of the Father. Heaven and earth are full of the Majesty of thy Glory."

But these are all God's pure creations, and restorations, without sin, without responsibility. Looking beyond them,—into our own hearts, when not in accord with the true and the right,—into the actions of men,—into whatever will live and bear record always, we then perceive the need of that petition, and the deeper we study the responsibilities of life, the greater the need and the more terrible the significance of those words, — "Be not angry with us forever."

Of late—within a very few years—life has become cheap. Our life, I mean, and not that of cattle and brute things. I do not know it to be true, but it seems to me that cases of sudden death (apart from external violence) are much more frequent than we have ever known before. Of course, there must be a cause for this. We live more upon stimulants than upon healthy nutriment. The stimulants of swift travel, of luxuries of eating and drinking, of music and parade and dress, of appetites, mental and moral, sharpened to indigestible consequences. These we live upon, mostly, and the first child born of this life is unchecked self-indulgence—pleasure—the having a satisfactory to-day, anyhow, and without regard to to-morrow. All this becomes, in the aggregate, a passion so overwhelming as to entirely overlook the very instrument by which whatever pleasure is received, namely: the life itself. Whether we shall so become accustomed to living faster than our fathers as finally to reach a certain poise and equilibrium, a clearness for giddiness, and strength for mere animal spirits; whether we shall arrive at stability and speed combined, I am not shrewd enough to guess; but no one will deny that, just now, we are continually blowing up, or running off the track, or knifeing, or clubbing, or shooting somebody, because something unpleasant has happened. If we can show some sort of reason for taking a neighbor's life, it is counted sufficient; especially if we can make out that others in like circumstances would have been tempted to do the same. If it is natural, it must be right. In such cases, juries acquit, judges pardon, and editors applaud. At this rate, where, in the way of whirlwinds, are we to bring up?

A few days since a young girl in a distant city shot her betrayer, and the *Register*, commenting upon the facts, as they are reported, says, "*She served him right.*" It is probable that most of your readers appreciated the spirit in which you said it, but, you will excuse me for going out of my beat, to show you how it looks to us here in the country. Let us talk it over, in a quiet way.

And first, let me ask *who* has come down from Heaven to say that a ball through the brain is good and right for the seducer? Not any angel,—not Jesus of Nazareth—not the Holy Ghost. Nor is there any message left on record anywhere to that effect. The sentiment therefore must be of human origin. Accordingly, in the same article in the *Register*, we find a law proclaimed, higher than any of God's laws, and this higher law is supposed to rule in this case. This, of course, you do not put forth as anything new, for there can be nothing new in morals. At any rate, it is not new. It is so common that it may be called, *par excellence*, "the common law" of the world. It is the convenient law of human passion. It is the law of sin. It is exceedingly popular, and carries a high hand in the affairs of the world. But it is something new to hear of it as being good and right. If, in this case in hand, there is anything that makes it seem right, it is probably some element of partial justice, to which we can say "amen" and pass on, without further investigation.

One of God's laws commands that we "forgive others, as we ourselves hope to be forgiven." Now there may be existences, there may be groups of worlds peopled with beings of whom such a requirement never has been made, because unnecessary, inasmuch as they themselves need no forgiveness. Such a people fulfilling all law, we can imagine, may have certain judicial authority, over any intruders that may come among them of a lower order, or over any of their own number, who may be transgressors. At first thought this would seem likely, but looking deeper into the matter, we perceive that they would not be fit judges of matters beyond their own experience. It would be necessary to find some one who had been tempted with all manner of evil, and yet remained upright, and so maintained perfect clearness of perception and judgment as to what is right and what wrong. If such an one could be found, it would be perfectly safe to vest in him all judicial authority.

Our case is different. We are all violators of law —State's prison birds, every man of us—and for us to set up judgment is to set up farce. Farce in fact, but tragedy of the bloodiest kind in its results. All we can properly do, is to change the venue to another world, and meanwhile keep the peace as well as we can, and wait until we can all come into court together. And while we wait, this precept of forgiveness is all we have to live upon. It is literally our meat and drink. It is not only (through mediation) divinely right, but it is the highest policy, the wisest expediency that can possibly be devised. Without it, the world would go to pieces before sunset. It is absolutely all that keeps us alive. For we are all, as we say, in the same boat. People on board ship, in a storm, and with the prospect of wreck before them, are, for the most part, exceedingly kind and forgiving. (I speak of men, not devils.) All differences are overlooked—pistols laid aside, as not at all pertinent to the matter—and every man bears a hand to avert the calamity.

But scattered about as we are in the world, and in diverse ways of occupation, we forget the common danger,—the lee-shore and the rocks,—and become hard and judicial. We set up higher laws, and walk about with an assured emphasis.

As I am not addressing you especially, Mr. Editor, but only throwing out a word against the popular drift, will you permit me to talk on a little further? It is refreshing, sometimes, to get into commonplace.

You may ask,—(I am putting up an imaginary editor)—"Do you not see the great moral force of punishment? of justice satisfied? of the fearful retribution which must follow transgression?"

Yes—I see that—and more. I see—murder. I see that as long as reputable papers and warm-hearted men cry "*bravo*," the use of the knife and pistol will become exceedingly facile and convenient. I see a time ahead, when if this continues, no man will dare to step into the street, until he has well pondered whether in his breakfast, or in his prayers, or in the cut of his coat, he has suited his opposite neighbor, who stands ready with a loaded pistol to blow his brains out, unless he is strictly orthodox in all these matters. Kind Heaven forbid that I should compare these cases—I am speaking of tendencies and results.

Furthermore, you admit that the law (human law) may regard this act of the betrayed girl, as crime. This, abstractly, is of no moment. Men differ in opinion as to crime, but crime is not one thing to-day and another to-morrow; one thing to me, and another to you. Facts are not disturbed or even modified by opinion or by human law. We take side views, cross views, wrong views, and *always partial* views, but in all this, we cast no shadow upon the white glory of truth. The shadows all fall the other way. Human action and thought are of course to be judged by facts, not opinions; truth, not guesses or approximations. In this only rests the safety and stability of all of God's creations.

There is trouble enough in the world, however bright it may look to you and me. Men are daily going mad by looking too long into these depths. It is scarcely possible to look down upon punishment, without being smitten and blasted by its near approach. We come back, singed and blackened with its smoke and fire. We take within us something of the spirit of the place. It is better, as it is how much pleasanter, to stay in Heaven's sunlight, where there is a way to meet every trouble and calamity that can happen to man (short of madness), and that is, not with submission only, but thankfulness that God is caring for us in that special manner. We know then that He is close by. He is taking things in hand for us; managing and ordering our affairs, which, whether we knew it or not, were undoubtedly in a ruinous way. To resent this and fly in the face of Heaven with pistols, &c., —oh, this serves no one right, nor is it right in itself.

If it *is*, let us begin the work of death, right and left. It has been quoted as proof of God's omnipotence, as shown in his power over his own holy attributes, that He does not at once punish all transgression, or (as this would be, in effect) drop the world from His hand, as a worthless creation. Carry out the purpose of serving everybody right to-day, and the sun and moon would lóok down to-night upon a dead world. In the fulness of time, this will come, but let us not hasten the day.

But you will perhaps press the question close home upon me—"Did you not, as to that leaden ball which took the life of the seducer, say in your inmost heart, and with all your heart, that it served him right?"

Well, Mr. Editor, suppose I say *yes*, and suppose all the world says "yes,"—every man, woman and child on the face of the earth—what has that to do with it? Suppose the vote were taken to-day, and the mingling *ayes* of all the living hosts were to rise together, might there not possibly be one feeble voice heard thrilling through the uproar, one heart-broken child of sorrow, struggling through tears and agony to drown this mistaken kindness? And might not this solitary "*No*" from a heart humbled and broken before God, be more likely to go up into Heaven than all the noisy affirmations that would go clamoring about the world? And if some one in Heaven were taking an account of the transaction, might it not read something like this—"Vote taken this morning on the earth, as to a question of right and justice. Messengers report that all the world voted aye, but nothing was heard here save one feeble 'No,' from a penitent child. The question is lost."

"But," say you," let us take the world as we find

it. We are not Gods. You have talked over a long string of moralities, which nobody denies, and for which no one is the wiser. Let us have something practical. What is your reply?"

It is this, that I have not the remotest idea of what is right, in such a case. I see no good result in such a terrible conclusion. Another crime is added, which in nowise mends the matter. Another cause for sorrow, and the long, long nights of trembling and fear; of misgiving and doubt, of horrors piled up breaker-like in tossing confusion. I see the vista of life darkened and storm-troubled, in which shadows and lightnings play in fellowship. I hear voices in that gloom, as of people going about, saying "*Served him right, served him right!*" I see no light there, no landscape of peace, no glory of October. It is winter thereaway and night! Oh, thou Christ, who art the joy of the world, stay with us always, and be our noon-day of light forever!

No, I can't take upon myself to know what is right as a just punishment for another or for myself; nor am I required to puzzle my brain about it. But if there is any highway of escape, any ransom, tell me about that. I came into the world only a few years ago, and can't make out to see very far, as yet, or very clearly. The confusion is great; the light and shade intermingle, and cheat the eye continually with false distances, and false bearings, and false magnitudes. Only one thing seems tolerably plain—that light and darkness are diverse—that you can't make one out of the other—that you may as well expect a lamb from a wild-cat, as good from evil. They won't breed together. They won't live together. They go contrary ways, though they meet often, and always to clash, and part, and come together again, fighting to the last gasp. One or the other must go to the wall, some day. This, I believe, is getting to be the general opinion. We can't live so forever. Patience will be worn out, forbearance exhausted, and there will be a general uprising of all souls that have ever lived from Adam down, and a universal prayer and shout will go up to Heaven from men, angels, and devils, that the combatants be parted, and sent, each to some prepared place, with such a gulf and high walls between, as will keep them forever asunder.

With a view to this, God has long ago set apart a special day—the last of this administration—when, without doubt, and without contingency, everybody will be "served right.'

Yours, ——.

"However, let us pause over it and take it down slowly, as the boys do the pippins in the orchard."

There are memories that come clustering about these "boys," these "pippins," and the "orchard." Do you remember the old Cider Mill, friend MAR-

GINS, and the old horse as he travelled round and round, moving with a slow and dignified tread, "hitched" to the long lever that turned the wooden mill that crushed the apples into pummice? Do you remember the great "cheese" in its bandage of straw beneath the press, and how, when the great screws were turned in the massive gallows-shaped frame, the rich juice of the apple came gushing out and running into the great tub placed to receive it? Do you remember how, with a straw, the urchins, as they came along on their way home from school, filled themselves with sweet cider from the bung of the barrel? Do you remember how in the long winter nights you sat around the fire-place wherein logs were blazing, and how the pitcher of cider and the platter of doughnuts were placed upon the old cherry table that sat out in the middle of the kitchen, and how you helped yourself to the cider and the doughnuts, and how happy each one was as he sat with his pewter mug of cider in one hand and a doughnut in the other before that old-fashioned kitchen fire-place? Those were pleasant times. But they are memories now. And then the apple parings, or "bees," as they were called, when the young men and maidens came together to pare apples, and talk and laugh and play old-fashioned plays, and say soft things to one another and eat pumpkin pies, and be happy after the fashion of the country people when you and I were young. Primitive times those were, friend MARGINS, and our proud daughters and city dames would turn up their noses hugely were they to be present at an old-fashioned apple-bee, such as they used to have out in old Steuben when the country was new, and the fashions were primitive.

We remember, when we were young, there was a favorite tree in our father's orchard which bore choice winter apples. It was called the big tree, because it was the largest in the orchard. The fruit of this tree was always left until the last, and was gathered with great care. There was a worthless fellow living in the neighborhood who one year coveted a portion of the fruit on the "big tree," and was not deterred from its acquisition by the divine commandment, "thou shalt not steal." A quantity of the apples disappeared one night, and the tracks of whoever stole them had a strange resemblance to those made by the heelless boots of our dishonest neighbor. There were two inseparable friends on the old homestead in those early days; the one a "colored gentleman," by the name of Shadrach, who came to our father's possession in payment for a debt, and who ran away regularly two or three times a year, and then as regularly ran back again, just as his master began to indulge the hope that he had got rid of him for good. The other was a great dog, half mastiff and half bull, of a noble presence and a fearless courage. "Drive" and "Shadrach" were inseparable. They worked and played together, slept together in the same loft, and Shadrach never ate a meal while the dog lived, at least at home, without sharing it with his canine friend. He would talk with Drive for hours when they were alone, and although the dog didn't say much himself, yet Shadrach said a good many things, and laid down and argued out a great many queer propositions, against which Drive uttered not a word of dissent.

One chilly night in October, Shadrach and Drive had been out along the cornfields on an unsuccessful coon hunt. On their return the dog dashed off through the orchard, and in a minute or two commenced barking, and Shadrach of course supposed he had treed a coon on one of the fruit-trees. Now, Shadrach had an abiding faith in spiritual manifestations, and stood in mortal fear of "the gentleman in black," and all manner of spooks in general. Upon arriving at the "big tree" by the foot of which Drive sat, and looking up among the branches, he saw there in the darkness a great black object, with something which seemed like a winding sheet in its hand. Shadrach's hair began to uncurl as he looked, and hallooing "seek him" to Drive, broke like a quarter nag for the house. He bolted breathlessly into the kitchen, exclaiming, "Massa, Massa! Drive got de debble in de big apple-tree!" "What is that, you woolly-pated rhinoceros?" replied his master. "Drive got de debble treed on de big apple-tree!" repeated the negro. A torch was lighted, and upon going into the orchard, there sat our thievish neighbor among the branches, with a bag half filled with the coveted fruit. Our father said not a word to him, but after giving Shadrach certain directions, returned quietly to the house. Old Shadrach laid his jacket down by the root of the apple-tree, and ordering Drive to watch it, said to the occupant of the tree, "Look hea, you brack tief, you come down, and Drive eat you head off sartain. Ugly dog dat. Eat a white tief up like a coon, sure. Roost up dare like turkey, yah! yah!" Shadrach went to his loft, and laid himself quietly away. When the day broke, there was the thief in the tree, and there was Drive watching him. When the sun rose they were there. The negro gave Drive his breakfast, and left him his jacket and the man in the tree to watch. Our father and the "boys," of whom we were one, went to husking corn in the orchard. Ten o'clock came, and there was the dog at the roots, and the man perched among the branches of the "big apple-tree." The horn sounded for dinner, and when we returned the two were there still. The thief called beseeching to our father to allow him to come down. "Well," was the reply, "why don't you come down?" "This infernal dog will eat me up if I do," said the thief. "Very likely," was the calm rejoinder, and we went on husking the corn. Once or twice the occupant of the apple-tree, after coaxing and flattering the dog, attempted to descend, but Drive's ivory warned him of his peril, and he went back to his perch. There never was another human being in such ecstasies all the day as was that negro. "Yah! yah!" he would break out in an uncontrollable cachinnation, and then roll and halloo, and yah! yah! among the corn-stalks, until you could hear him a mile. The sun went down behind the hills, and there still was the thief and the dog. We all went in to supper, and in the twilight of the evening, in pity to the famished and frightened culprit, the dog was withdrawn, and he was permitted to slink away home. He never stole apples again, or anything else from our father, while Drive and old Shadrach remained on the farm.

"A few days since, a young girl in a distant city shot her betrayer, and the *Register*, commenting upon the facts, as they are reported, says, 'She served him right.'"

We read one day in a Western paper that a man had secured, by the seducer's arts, the affections of a confiding and inexperienced girl; that he had tempted her to leave her home and those whom she loved, and who loved her; that, confiding in his promises, and leaning upon his faith, she had gone with him to a distant city, where he was to make her his wife. That, delaying under various pretexts the performance of his vows, he succeeded in robbing her of her virtue, and then left her desolate and penniless, unprotected and alone, in a strange city. That when she sought him out, and claimed the performance of his plighted word, he threw her from him in scorn, like a worthless weed, away. That in her despair, and smarting under her matchless wrongs, she smote him to death at her feet. Upon reading this account of the gigantic wickedness, the iron cruelty of her betrayer, we said, and we say again, "She served him right;" and herein it will be seen that we struck a chord that roused up the latent energies of our friend MARGINS, and brought forth his inward might.

We spoke of human nature as God made it. We spoke of man as he is, exercising the attributes of humanity; of human instincts and sympathies, and passions, as they are. We took the heart of man as it came from the hands of Deity, fashioned as He fashioned it, quick with all its natural yearnings and finite pulsations. We spoke of right and wrong, as human judgment views them; of retribution weighed in human scales, and, measuring the infliction of the punishment in this isolated case by the vastness of the wrong committed, we said that the act which swept the seducer from among the living, "served him right."

The murderer who is taken with the blood of innocence fresh upon his hand, is doomed by the law to death, and through the agency of the gallows or the axe he is launched into eternity. Does anybody say that the law does not "serve him right?" Who preaches forgiveness to the law? Who talks to the law about exercising the attributes of Deity? Or requires it to leave the punishment of the murderer to God? Who asks the law to uncoil itself from around its victim, and let him go forth to slay anew? Nobody. Well, why does the law hang the murderer, the traitor to his country, the incendiary who fires your dwelling in which your little ones are sleeping? What is the principle of the thing, the philosophy of this matter? "Serves him right" is the maxim underlaying all penal codes—"Serves him right" is the authority, the great fundamental truth whereon is based all human, aye, and divine systems, too, of rewards and punishments. It is useless to argue the propriety or policy of the death penalty now. Wiser men than we are, friend MARGINS, have been arguing that question for a good many hundred years, and have not settled it yet. "Serves him right," says the judge, as he did when the argument commenced. "Serves him right," says the executioner, as he brandishes his axe. "Serves him right," says the law, as the head of the culprit falls. Mark, the act which the law thus performs is one of retribution, based upon the crime of the culprit. It is justice, weighing out punishment for wrong, adjusting the degree of the one to the enormity of the other. Nobody blames the law for inflicting death, or the officers who are the ministers of the law. In the case of the murderer, the law affixes the penalty, and appoints the method of its enforcement. It is legal justice, but based upon a higher principle of natural justice. True, one object of the penal code which affixes the death penalty, is to protect society from the repetition of outrage, and some have claimed that another object of punishment was the reformation of the culprit, but we never knew the morals of a man to be improved by hanging, or having his head cut off.

Well, we assume that the law when it takes the life of the murderer, "Serves him right," deals out to him a just measure of punishment. Do you agree with us in this, friend MARGINS? Yes! Then we have advanced one step in the argument.

Now remember that the law, and the judge, and the executioner are but instruments wielded by justice to do an act of retribution. It is not always right to kill a man because the law sanctions the act. The word of an absolute monarch is the law of his dominions, yet when he says an honest man shall die, and strikes off his head, it is not right. It cannot be said of the sentence and the sufferer, "It served him right." The law doomed the martyrs to the flames, but it did not "serve them right." Why? Because there was no great moral wrong, commensurate with the magnitude of the punishment, committed, to give vitality to the right and power of the law to take life. The great ingredient of crime was wanting. We give these illustrations for the purpose of showing that it is not the might of the law that makes it right. The murderer is deserving of death independently of human laws. Is the culprit who slays at midnight and hides his victim, the less deserving of punishment because his crime cannot be proven in a court of justice? Is he any the less guilty because he has concealed his crime from the clear knowledge of the world, and is he therefore the less deserving of punishment?

In the dark annals of iniquity there can be no crime of a deeper dye than that of him who coils himself in the confidence, nestles in the warm affections of a trusting girl, and under the solemn promise of marriage, robs her of more than life, and then leaves her to the cold scorn of the world, to wander, hopeless and companionless, through long desolate years, to find a grave of infamy and sorrow at last. Think of the mother's heart crushed, and the father's anguish. Such a man commits more than murder. He kills the body by a lingering agony, and destroys the soul. Had he slain his victim at once, you and I, friend MARGINS, would have said, while we looked upon her moveless corpse, and his hand red with her blood, "this man shall die." We would have handed him over to the law, to the judge and the executioner, as the ministers of a just retribution, and bid them spare not. When the sentence that doomed him to death had been executed, we should have said, "served him right." Aye, in looking upon his great crime, and the gallows upon which he was hanging, with the last pulsation of life choked out of him, looking upon only these two great facts, and without a thought of the process which suspended him there, we would say—"This is a just measure of retribution." "It serves him right." But here was a crime greater than a simple murder—a crime which inflicts a lingering death, and destroys a soul, and when we remember the gigantic wickedness of the destroyer, and see him struck down even by a felon blow, will we not still say, "served him right?" Remember, we are speaking now only of *his* deserts—of a just measure of retribution so far as *he* is concerned, neither more nor less. If he points to the wound that is killing him, and claims our sympathy as a wronged man, as suffering a penalty beyond the measure of his deserts, we might be moved to pity for his fate, but when we looked upon the desolate and crushed victim of his heartless villany, every instinct of our nature would still say—"served him right." Were he standing on the verge of the precipice that towers above the boiling eddies of Niagara, with the cry of his victim mingling with the roar of the waters, as she struggled to pull him down, when we saw him reeling to his fall, we might, in mercy, reach forth a hand to save him, but if before we could do so he should disappear over the beetling cliffs, while we might be shocked at his terrible doom, we should still say—"served him right." And what matters it whether this retribution is measured out by the law, or by the hand of the individual wronged, we mean so far as the *wrong-doer* is concerned?

Now we beseech you, friend MARGINS, to understand us. We could say to his victim and his slayer, "You are all wrong; you have broken the law; you have violated the social compact; you have transgressed against the commandment of God." In short, friend MARGINS, we could repeat to her your excellent sermon and endorse it all, and yet say as between her and her seducer alone, "she served him right." Think you, that her seducer, when he stands before the throne of eternal justice, will be heard, when he complains of the wrong *he* has suffered? Wrong there is doubtless, sin to be answered for, but it will not be wrong against the villain seducer, the destroyer of innocence, not against him. The sin is against God and his law, and when this controversy between the seducer and his victim shall be settled in Heaven's chancery, the verdict as between the two will be, "served him right."

XIII.

NELLY.

Dear Editor, have you not a young Bob, or Dick or Tom, to come up and play with our Nelly? If, you have, send him up, and we will return him to you in the spring, fat and strong with corned beef and country air. We want a companion for Nelly, lest she should become philosophical and grand. She has been with us but a few weeks, but is already rather didactic, and asking questions quite impossible to answer. I think some of writing a profound treatise on life, beginning with Nelly as a foundation, and coming up into mature years with the child as a continual reference and standard of values.

I imagine it would be seen (as Macaulay says in the opening of his great history, *it will be seen—it will be seen*), that notwithstanding what St. Paul says of putting away childish things—children are mostly in the right, and that for many of us to walk back instead of onward, would be the wiser course. It certainly is a beautiful arrangement that the world is being constantly supplied with new beginners, creatures direct from God, and that so perpetual newness and freshness is continually kept up.

We talk of ADAM and EVE as having been, before the fall, in a very happy condition; but one thing they missed—they were never children. They never rode horse on a stick, or went to bed with a doll. If they had begun life, little by little, line upon line, seeing, and hearing, and thinking, and acting slowly, and in a small way, but experimentally always, as do their children, and if, like them, they had tumbled down stairs, seen stars on the ice, burned their fingers, and in thousands of ways stumbled and bruised themselves upon certain physical laws, hard thumping evidences of order and sequence, would they, oh my excellent editor, would they have eaten the apple? And may not the order of Providence, in their history, have been to show not merely that all creatures must rely wholly upon him absolutely and unconditionally as their life and strength, but that this life and strength must be that of slow and gradual accumulation; that, in short, we must toddle before we can walk?

And however sad may have been the giving up of that Eden, it was the place where the apple grew. It had its temptation, and what more have we? Day by day thousands are born into life, who, if they stay for any time, must be led out, with whatever kindness and whatever words of hope and love, by the same hand, from the garden of childhood into the cold and dark contrasts of struggling life. The gates are forever opening and closing upon the little ones, and just in proportion as they have deeply felt the joy and beauty of their first days, and the strife and temptation of the days beyond, will they go forth with saddened faces and with careful steps. Thanks be to God, there is ONE who has been before them, and who knows the way right well.

A flower is a pretty thing with its color and softness, and its modest joyfulness of expression; so may be a picture, better than whatever piece of inanimate nature, but when you have the flower and picture embodied in flesh and blood, walking and running about, talking, laughing, singing little songs and hymns and *glorias* all in a mix, questioning, wondering, and rejoicing always, or on its knees talking with the Unseen, telling Him some little trouble and asking for guidance and help—then you have a little piece of Heaven upon earth; a young sprout of intelligence fresh from God himself, placed here to grow up into strength and beauty, and at last, under His care, to return to Him in His own home; accepted, restored, saved it may be as by fire, but crowned now with eternal glory.

Have you never, Mr. Editor, in the dead of night, with some little Nelly lying close by, fast asleep with a doll on either side, and her hair floating over her face, have you never felt the insane desire to have some burglar enter the room, so that you might shatter him into ten thousand fragments? Have you never felt the power which Nelly would give to the right arm which would hurl him down the hall-stairs and smash the wash-bowl on his preposterous brain? And would it be all because Nelly is so helpless? So we say, but that is not all. It is because she is pure, and no breath of harm must come to her. We act, in such cases, in God's behalf. The angels, perhaps, are with us, those who behold the face of the Father. They—it may be—give the strength, or the heart's blood. We take care of these little ones, as the Israelites did of the ark of the covenant. Let nothing profane come here—no rude hand, or word, or thought, for it is holy ground. This is why a man may think or speak evil in a temple of worship, or whatever holiest moment or place, but not before a little child, not before one of God's pure witnesses.

NELLY and I are getting slowly acquainted. Yesterday, being rainy, she was busy for a long time putting my hair in papers, after which she advised a walk on the piazza, to give a *set* to the curls, as that, she said, was the way they did out West. At night some of the papers were examined, but not looking well, she recommended me to keep them on all night, which accordingly I did, and got up this morning with a headache. But the whole thing, my dear editor, was a most melancholy failure. Such was yesterday. To-day she is writing—something important, no doubt—with a sharp stick which she is continually dipping in my inkstand. Her great distress—when she has any distress—is in the b-a-ba, k-e-r ker, line—as in making e-a-r-t-h into *urth*, the philosophy of which is too deep for her. How much falsehood is hinted in this and the like orthographical lies, or how much faith in the necessity of believing such monstrous absurdities, would be a new question to discuss. But these light troubles are soon over. Five minutes after such a tribulation, she will be swinging violently in the great rocker, with both dolls in her arms, to whom she pours forth songs with a die-away sentimentality and occasional cracked-voice *applomb*, that is sometimes very exciting.

Oh, my kind Editor, the world is safe as long as children are born into it. If that arrangement should ever cease, if men and women should spring up, or be dropped down ready-made, we might as well give up at once. There would be such a panic and stampede as the world has never seen. Something approaching to this is unfortunately taking place in these latter days; children are not permitted to be children, but with fearful precocity are made up rapidly into men and women. This is the way you have in town. But the cities—let us be thankful—do not contain everybody. There is a connection with God and Heaven still kept up, through the country and country life. Herein is the safety of the world, and of government, and the perpetuity of good institutions—that you cannot wall in the country, you cannot pave the lakes, and the prairies, and the rivers; you cannot shut out the blue sky and the stars, you cannot fence in the mountains, you cannot bowl out the salt sea, and make streets and build palaces there. God reserves to Himself all these, and permits to those who like them, the self-confidence of streets and common councils, saying, however, that except He keep the city, the watchman watcheth but in vain.

The time must come, Mr. Editor, when we shall perceive that much of our crazy life here, is merely exclamatory—that it is demonstrative of not much more than noise and general dissatisfaction—a continual running up of wrong stairs—an incessant shouting as to views and prospects—one crying *lo here!* another, *lo there!* the great sight consisting, perhaps, in some splendid fog-bank, glittering in borrowed light, and itself continually shifting and passing away. When we shall be willing to come down to simple statements—such as that little Nelly has more life and wisdom than the telegraph can report in a thousand years—we shall get along better. When we shall perceive and carry it out, as we say (but that is not quite enough; we must carry it out, and bring it in, travel with it, work with it, eat and drink with it, and go to bed and get up with it), that the intellect is nearly as much a mere instrument as the body, and of no use save as an instrument; that, with all its glorification, it never creates, but only finds out (invents) what

God had before created, and to which He alone gives form and life; we shall become more quiet (shall we not?) and return again to children and principles.

But that day is not our day, and before it arrives, the world will doubtless continue to try what virtue there is in stones and mortar, and iron and lightning, and all other aggrandizing physical and mental forces, to an extent quite beyond our wildest conjecture. To-day (in this movement) we have the dinner, and the dollar, and the lightning train: generous and magnanimous, but extravagant—and material to the back-bone. When the good day comes, it will be (as far as human agencies are permitted), through the proper training of children, as nearest to God and the true life.

Yours, ——.

"Have you not a young BOB, or DICK, or TOM, to come up and play with our NELLY?"

No. We have no young BOB, or DICK, or TOM, to do any such thing; we have no little boys of that name. We have no *little* children at all; we wish we had a half a dozen of them, if they would always remain so. We love little children. One of our neighbors has a pure artless little girl that we borrow occasionally, when we feel sad, or out of sorts with the world, and her pleasant voice and childish prattle, as she sits beside us, always drive away melancholy, and make us cheerful again. We love little boys and girls. We love their frank, straightforward simplicity, their honesty. They seem like fresh things, pure from the hand of God, unspoiled by contact with the corruptions and the wickedness of the world. What a pleasant place this Earth would be, if grown men and women, with their learning, their gathered experience, their matured intellect, their wisdom, could retain the honest frankness, the freshness, the purity of heart and the sincerity of childhood! It would be a place then that one might be loath to leave. We do not undertake to impeach the wisdom of Deity. We *know* we are all wrong, but the thought will sometimes steal into our mind, that it would have been better had man been created with less natural proclivities towards evil. That the world would have been happier, and human destiny loftier, had man been so constituted that it would not have been his tendency, *prima facie*, as the lawyers say, to sin; had a nature been given him that would have led him through the instincts with which he was endowed, to choose good rather than evil.

"Oh! my kind editor, the world is safe as long as children are born into it."

We deny this, as an abstract proposition. We deny it as a practical truth. We hold it as an absurdity in theory, as well as fact. The past history of the world demonstrates its fallacy. Why, when has the world been "safe," we should like to know? We have its history for seven thousand years, or thereabouts, and it has never been in a substantially safe condition for an hour. Society has never been safe. Civilization has never been safe. The people have never been safe. Human rights have never been safe. Religion has never been safe. Nothing that pertains to the full intellectual or moral stature of manhood has been safe. The great earth has been overwhelmed by a flood. Geologists tell us, and astronomers endorse what they say, that it has, at some period of its existence, been run into by a comet; and how do we know that even now, away off millions upon millions of miles distant, some wandering meteor in outer space is not on its way to knock this our planet into a universal smash? But you mean the intellectual, the moral world. No matter, even in that view the world has never been safe since ADAM and EVE were created and placed in the Garden of Eden. By the way, that was a beautiful allegory of the first man and woman, and the Garden of Eden. It was humanity devoid of sin—living intelligences that had done no evil. They were supremely happy, because they were good. The Garden of Eden, with all its beautiful productions, its flowers, its fruits, its fountains and running streams, its shady groves, its green lawns and its singing-birds, was the human heart overflowing with contentment and joy, before wickedness invaded it, to poison its future, to sow remorse, and sorrow, and strife, where virtue and peace only had before thriven.

But the world was in danger, even while ADAM and EVE were in the garden of Eden. There was danger that EVE would eat the forbidden fruit, and then tempt ADAM to his fall. That danger was realized, and they were thrust forth into the outer world. Was there less danger there? Was there no danger that CAIN should become a murderer, or that ABEL should be slain? Pass along down to the time of NOAH. Was there no danger that the world should become so corrupt that God would destroy it in His wrath? Was there no danger, when there could be found among all the millions of living men and women of the world, but one family worth saving from the destruction which the Deity had denounced against the human race? Was there no danger at a later period, that a time would come when the only just man in all the world, the only one that was without a fault, without one stain of sin, one that was pure as Heaven is pure, should be betrayed, and crucified between thieves on the cross? Further along still, was there no danger when moral and intellectual darkness hung like a pall over Europe, when the religion of the cross had degenerated into a senseless mummery, when its high and holy precepts were perverted to the uses of oppression, when profligacy characterized the priesthood, and a brutalizing bigotry possessed the laity, was there no danger that the world should have gone back to the darkness of idolatry, and the degradation of heathenism? Was there no danger that civilization should have been extinguished, that human liberty should have become an obsolete term, and human rights have been obliterated from the vocabulary of the world? Was there no danger that the light of science should have been put out, and the fountains of knowledge that have since gushed so gloriously, irrigating and fertilizing these latter days, have remained sealed forever? Coming down nearer to the present, was there no danger when infidelity spread over Europe like a consuming fire? When France, then the strongest and the greatest, the most elegant and refined nation in the world, bloated with infidelity, and teeming with unspeakable corruption, in the great legislative convocation of her statesmen decreed that "there was no God, and that death was an eternal sleep?" Is there no danger now, to-day, that the world, in the pride of its fancied progress towards perfectibility, shall forget, in the glory of the present, the mighty sequence of the future? Is religion safe? Are human rights safe? Are governmental institutions safe? Are the public morals of the world safe? If the world is safe, why is it that every philosopher, great and small, whether of science, morality, government, or of religion, are tinkering it, driving a rivet here, and soldering up a crack there, polishing this rusty spot, and placing a strengthening brace in that weak place—all patching, and mending, and hammering at it forever? No! No! The world is not safe, never has been safe, and never will be safe for an hour. And yet, from the time that ADAM and EVE went forth from the garden of Eden, children have been born into the world. Every day, every hour, every second of time there are new intelligences, fresh from the hand of Deity, added to the aggregated intellectuality of the world. New souls are thrown forward on the wing, to perch for a little while in this world, and rest at last *somewhere* in eternity. Childhood, we admit, is an institution that exercises a conservative influence over the world, but the power of rendering the world "*safe*" is a task too gigantic for its accomplishment.

"We talk of ADAM and EVE as having been, before the fall, in a very happy condition; but one thing they missed--they were never children."

True. We never thought of that. ADAM never played marbles. He never played "hokey." He never drove a tandem of boys with a string. He never skated on a pond or played "ball," or rode down hill on a hand-sleigh. And EVE, she never made a playhouse; she never took tea with another little girl from the little tea-table set out with the toy tea things; she never rolled a hoop or jumped a rope, or pieced a baby quilt, or dressed a doll. They never played "blind man's buff," or "pussy wants a corner," or "hurly burly," or any of the games with which childhood disports itself. How blank their age must have been, wherein no memories of early youth came welling up in their hearts, no visions of childhood floating back from the long past, no mother's voice chanting a lullaby to the ear of fancy in the still hours of the night, no father's words of kindness speaking from the grave in the church-yard where he sleeps! ADAM and EVE, and they alone of all the countless millions of men and women that have ever lived, had no childhood.

XIV.

DREAMS.

"WELL," said I to my wife, "there is nothing new under the sun, even in dreams."

A few mornings since, as we sat at breakfast, I had recounted to that lady and our Nelly a curious dream, which had occupied me through part of the night, the novelty of which was, that at a large family dinner I was charmingly surprised by hearing the whole party *chant* a grace before taking seats at the table. The thing was unique, as well as *grace*-ful, and so transparently proper, that I wondered it had never occurred to me before.

Well, sir, as the gentle people say, what do you think? I find, to-night, in a letter from Mr. Charles Taylor, published in the *Tribune*, that chanting of grace before meat is actually practised at this very day among the Chinese; and it's not unlikely, my dear Editor, though I grieve to say it, destroying, unmercifully as it does, the originality of the most exquisite night-thought which I ever had—I say it is quite probable that those shaven-headed, pig-tailed chop-stickers, have been doing it for thousands of years. So much for trying to dream something new.

However, it was new to me, as a new star to an astronomer. I am quite confident the thought had never entered my brain before, unless, indeed, it had crept in slyly and taken a place in some remote corner, without waking my consciousness. Is this possible, Mr. Editor? Is it not an absurdity? Can we be taken possession of by thoughts and mental processes, without being a party to the transaction? as, after leaving our hall door open all day, we may be surprised by an interloper at midnight, who hasn't so much as turned a key or raised a window to effect an entrance. Are we to be confronted by ghosts, who claim an acquaintance, a place in our house, and a seat at our table, whom we never saw in the flesh, and all upon the villanous plea that they had a nice time, one day, in our cellar or garret? Heaven only knows what vividness, what terrible meaning may one day gleam upon us from thoughts light as air, which we play with, or toss from the mind as trifles and things of no account, or from that daily crowd to which we open all our doors and windows, and would take off the roof from our house, if necessary, to let them in. Must we not be amused and diverted? Are we not to have a good time, I ask you? Is not this the object of life—the be-all and the end-all—that we should have a good time; and have it right away, to-day, because we are a fast people, and wide awake?

Any one who follows up the line of these suggestions without a cold shudder, must have a cool brain and high expectations. No doubt, there are thousands in the world who would gladly be excused, if it were possible, from this mysterious life, as being too weighty, too solemn, too terrible in its possible conclusions.

The process of thought—the way it acts—the place where it lives—the *quo modo* of its first pulsation, as a living thing—something which a moment ago was not, had no place in the universe (to me), and now is—has begun life—has character and meaning, and a length of days which is eternal—will always be with me, whether I choose, or do not choose—which I cannot burn, or bury (beyond resurrection), which I can give to another, but must keep always the stereotype from which it was first printed—which, in fact, is now, not a thing external to me, as my coat or my body even; but a part of myself, the destruction of which never can take place, trifling as it may be, without involving the destruction of my whole being, so that if *that* die, then I die with it—all this, not so much from its mystery as from its plainness, its demonstrative horror, and its reach into the infinite and the absolute, I dare not discuss. Nor would I sully, with my tame conjecture, the starry grandeur of this topic—its beauty of possible result—its fellowship of glory with the Father of Spirits.

But it is easy to *imagine* that the perception of this truth in all its bearings would Christianize the world in a moment, so that for the first time since men have gone abroad in the world, there would be a universal pause among all nations, and kindred, and tongues—the noisy business of life would cease, and there would be heard in the crowded city, and upon the seas, and in the valleys, and upon the mountains, only the voice of prayer and praise and supplication to the Most High. Something like this is doubtless imagined by those who hold that the intellectual and the moral necessarily carry with them the Christian influence; whose faith is, that to see, is to believe; to know, is to adopt and to act. But this broad way of suggestion, looking apparently into the darkest mystery of our being, is closed (not far down) by an iron door, whose bolts and bars yield only to the touch of God himself. The palpable sight of Hell and Heaven, the darkness and the light, the confusion and the order, the woe unutterable, and the peace which passeth all understanding, would offer no barrier or inducement to the soul which chooses to be guided by its own will, and to be its own God. This must be; i. e. it must be that the intuitions of this life as to the next, however feeble, are, in the main, correct. One cannot imagine what Heaven is in its extent, but he can imagine, and does imagine, and that truly, whether it would suit him. Therefore it is that all philosophy, all morality, all science, all churches and ministries, all struggle and labor and prayer, are dead as ashes for all purposes of an hereafter, unless given to Christ, who alone, as he created the world out of nothing, can give to these feeble beginnings for him who seeks them, honor and glory and immortality. To every child of Adam, who goes daily and always to Him, and asks, believing, Christ says, *Let there be light!* and in a moment, in the twinkling of an eye, a new creation is made for him, holy angels are sent down to him, and all agencies of trouble, and sorrow, and struggle, and doubt, and fear, and temptation, and all powers and principalities resident on high,—are enlisted henceforth in his behalf; his name is at once written down in the book of life, and a white robe is made ready for him, and a seat set apart for him in the starry courts,—so that now there is no more death to that soul,—it has entered already into life everlasting.

But we were talking, Mr. Editor, of dreams. I trust, sir, that you are still in practice. The magnificent specimen you gave us last summer, proves you a splendid dreamer. After editing, all day, the recreation of dreams, the wide area, the ease of accomplishment, the might Olympian of that nodding land, must be especially refreshing. Or do you merely repeat and worry over things already done, thoughts already stale, and pictures beautiful in the making, but now to the mind only so much paint and canvas? Do you find yourself pulling at the same oar at night, which you pulled in the morning? Lifting trout again, or dropping a two-pounder, just as you have him almost in hand? Do you fall into Crooked Lake, now-a-days? Do you have sunrises at midnight? Do you see great wonders and marvels, bright and glorious, all in the darkness of your chamber? Do you travel before you have so much as thought of your trowsers, and see all the strange lands and stranger people? To whom, also, you make speeches and wind up always with "America and the Albany *Register* forever?" Do you edit in Chinese and Persian, and chat pleasantly with the Czar, as to how he likes the war?

To take a meat supper, quite late, with pickles and old cheese, and in due time have what you may call—the consequences, is one way of dreaming, but dreadfully common. To have faces about the bed-side grinning and expanding and multiplying into hundreds is more artistic, but has the same kind of vulgar unpleasantness. It is not enjoyable.

Perhaps the most common, but full of character and import, is that kind of bewilderment which may be called the dream difficult. To be always striving at impossible things and saying to yourself "it's all fudge, it's no kind of use," but still to go on grasping and pulling again at this intangible something, which, all fudge as it is, quite refuses to be pulled or grasped. To go about a room in the dark involving and revolving, searching for a door-handle. To feel for matches which, when you find them, refuse to go off, and at last, when they do, to wait through long palpitating hours until the full blaze of light pierces the room before you dare put naked eyes afloat in the air. To have a consciousness that the shutters in strict propriety ought to be closed, as your room is on the ground floor and opens into all out-doors. Then, of a sudden, to be patiently busy (though it is a midsummer night) sweeping the snow off the piazza, and saying to yourself "I have now swept away exactly six inches, and if it snows all night I shall know directly in the morning that there is a foot of snow,"—then, on your return, to undertake the shutters, which doing quickly, a sleigh with four horses heavily apparelled with bells goes by on the jump, but as you knew before that you were dreaming, you smile, and immediately detect it all as a deception, "it is merely the sound of your breath in your left nostril; if you listen one way it's like a trumpet, but another way, it's like a bell." As you stand by the window and discuss this, your father, or some friend who occupies the next room, comes to the door, and asks, in a soft voice, "what is it you are talking about so much." To this, you reply, in the same soft way, "that you are very sorry, but positively you did not think you had opened your lips to say any thing, in short, you had said nothing at all, and your friend must have imagined it; the night was dark and the wind was noisy, it was easy to be deceived, and any-way it was of no consequence, as it was all a dream."

The sleeping thought, my dear Editor, (I have done with the dream—the above is an exact copy of one as far as remembered,) I say the sleeping thought tells even better what we are, (*hidden away in the possibilities* of this human nature, which, waking or sleeping, is one always,) than the waking thought. It tells fearfully, but unerringly, and, as I believe, truly. If a man desires not to wrestle with perpetual night-mare in the life to come, let him look well to his dreams, while he has them. For dream-time will soon be over with us, and we shall stand, then, in the broad, unfettered, unsleeping life, with no cloak to cover, no indigestions to father the sins of the heart, and what we carry with us, will be our companion and keep-sake forever. I look upon the dream as my better angel, who shows me, now and then, gleams of the very Hell itself, that I may decide now, whether I will make that my home hereafter, whether it will be pleasant to be a part of that dark confusion. But now, it is morning—thank God, it is still to-day—it is the light of the sun that crowns these heavens—it is still the world of dreams.

Yours, ——.

"'Well,' said I to my wife, 'there is nothing new under the sun, even in dreams.'"

We shall not undertake to follow you, friend MARGINS, in your metaphysical dissertation on dreams. Your theory as far as we, being of unsophisticated and plain understanding, can comprehend it, may be all right; we shall neither dispute nor endorse it, but the fact asserted above, we deny. We insist that there *is* something "new in dreams." We remember one dream of our own, that, by its perfect distinctness as well as its comicality, made a deep impression upon our mind, and it remains fixed in our memory. There was such a seeming reality about it, such vividness and clearness in all things, that were it not utterly opposed to all our experience in life, and the knowledge of its impossibility, we should almost doubt whether in truth it were not sober fact instead of a vision of the night. In order that we may be understood, we must be permitted to describe a certain locality as it was long ago, and as the recollection of our boyhood paints it, for it is "the spot that we were born in." It is all changed now, and has been for many years. And who with white hairs upon his head can say that the scenes of his childhood are not changed? That the ancient landmarks have not been removed? That the things that memory calls up from the long past, the trees, the stumps, the plum-trees, the cattle and sheep in the pasture behind the house, the meadow behind the barn, and the old house and barn themselves, and the fences, are all there still? Go back, our dear MARGINS, to the place of your nativity, with all your young memories clinging around your heart, and note how sadness will creep over you, and how the tear will start, as you miss the things that you remember and loved so well.

Our father's farm lay out at the head of the Crooked Lake, in the pleasant valley that stretches away westward from that beautiful sheet of water. The land rose with a gentle slope from the pebbly beach, and a broad meadow lay between the shore and the old farm-house, which stood some fifty rods from the Lake. Midway between the house and the Lake, a spring of the coldest and purest water came gushing up, around which stood a cluster of some half dozen maples that had been left when the old forest was cleared away. The long arms of these ancient trees lovingly entwined, and the thick foliage that covered them in the summer-time, made a dense cool shade all around the spring, and its waters being soft, it was the place where the washing for the family during the warm season was always done.

There was an elderly woman, who with her half-idiot son, lived in a log house on a corner of the farm, a kind of dependent upon, and was chiefly supported by the family. We remember "Aunt PEGGY," as she was always called, and "Silly DICK," well. They were never for an hour separated. Wherever the mother went, there was sure to be her idiot son. We have no recollection of ever seeing them apart. If "Aunt PEGGY" was at work in the house, DICK would be sitting on the door-sill if it was summer-time, or if it was winter, in the corner waiting, and watching patiently till the work was done and his mother should go home. Among the few words that he was able to learn, that of "mother" was most frequently on his lips. He was a gentle, harmless creature, always obedient and affectionate, leaning upon his mother for protection with the perfect confidence of childhood, though in stature and strength almost a man. The affections and care of Aunt PEGGY were all centered upon Silly DICK, and her mother's instincts clung the closer to him because of his imbecility. Poor DICK and his mother have been dead many, many years. He died on a Tuesday, and on the following Monday she was laid in a grave by his side. The only tie that remained, the last link that bound her to life was broken, and she died from very grief for the loss of her idiot son.

Aunt PEGGY used to do the washing for the family down by "the Spring," in the summer-time, under the shade of the maples. Silly DICK would bring water for her from the spring, and see to the fire under the kettles, and lay around on the grass watching his mother, when he could not be useful in aiding her labors. They seem to be present to us now as we remember them in our childhood, she humming a simple tune, or singing some nursery song or ballad, and he under the shadow of the trees, talking in his silly way to the birds among the branches, or to himself, as he lay stretched at length upon the grass, or looking at his own face reflected from the bottom of the spring, and wondering, perhaps, who it was that was always watching him from away down in the water. Those old maples, that old farm-house, that meadow with all the old things we remember so well, are all gone. A flourishing village, with hundreds of houses, and stores, and small gardens, and streets, cover what was then the meadow, and that spring itself is conducted under ground to the lake. This great change has been going on for a quarter of a century, and it is only by groping among the memories of our boyhood, that we can recall the spot in its primitive beauty, and as it was long, long ago.

Well, not many years back, as we were sleeping upon our bed here in this great city, we dreamed a dream. "We were a boy again," and in the meadow at the head of Crooked Lake as it was of old. There was the farm-house, and our father and mother, sisters and brothers. There was the path down through the meadow; there were the old maples, with their summer foliage, all bright and green, and there was the spring itself, its crystal waters bubbling up and flowing in a little rivulet over the sand and pebbles to the Lake. There lay the Lake, sleeping in calmness and beauty. There were the forest-covered hills on the right hand and on the left, there the high promontories around which the smooth waters seemed to creep and hide themselves. And last of all, there was Aunt PEGGY by the spring washing, and Silly DICK was on the grass watching and talking to the birds that were hopping about, and singing and twittering in the branches above him. The vision was all perfect; not a feature, not a tint was wanting. We saw and felt as of old, as if thirty years of our life had been obliterated, and nothing of its cares or trials, its struggles or hard experience, remained. Everything on this side of our boyhood was clean wiped out. The scene had not to us even the charm of novelty. The sun was shining bright and warm in the sky, and it seemed pleasant to be under the shadow of those old maples, as a refuge from his rays.

Darkness gathered away down on the Lake; a dense black cloud seemed to come up out of the water, and from behind the high promontories, not rising slowly and majestically like thundercaps from behind mountains, but heaving and swelling and rolling at first like the billows of ocean, and then rising in dense columns towards the sky, wreathing and swirling, and twisting upward like the smoke that goes up from a burning building in the night, but infinitely blacker and deeper, and extending all across the eastern sky. Red lightnings flashed upward and downward, and crosswise, and every way, trailing like fiery serpents across the face of the cloud. Wild geese and ducks, and eagles, and osprays, came sweeping in flocks, and screaming in mortal terror to the westward over us. A mist gathered in the air, and though it was noonday, yet a shadowy and spectral twilight gathered around us. An immense ball of fire shot like a blazing comet across the sky from the approaching darkness. The thunder growled with horrible intenseness, shaking the very earth to its centre. To us all this war of the elements seemed neither strange nor terrible. We had no idea of danger, no apprehension of harm. Not so, however, with the poor washerwoman; but one idea seemed to have a place in her mind, and that was that the day of judgment had come, at a time when she least expected it. She tried to pray, but every prayer ended with "The house that Jack built." She essayed to sing a hymn, but every effort ended in Yankee Doodle. Try as she might, exert all her powers, aided by the mortal terror that was upon her, every verse would end in Yankee Doodle. Every strain, however devotional in the beginning, was sure to close with Yankee Doodle, till in utter hopelessness her hands dropped by her side, and in a voice choked by the agony of despair, she cried, "Lord help us, my poor boy, what kind of a song will that be to sing in Heaven?" To us who felt no sense of danger, there was something so infinitely ludicrous in the poor woman's astonishment and dismay, that we could not restrain our risibility, and "What in the name of all that's funny are you laughing at now?" said our wife, starting up in amazement at the vehemence of our cachinnations, scattering the dream, and the tempest, and the meadow, the old maples, and the spring, and poor Aunt PEGGY, and Silly DICK, like visions of the night, as they all were.

XV.

THE BRIGHT MORNING—AND JULY.

THE day has gone by. Like the amen to prayer, comes the night. The night, too, has gone, now, and like the smile of God comes the morning.

The sun is riding high in the heavens, but finds me loitering and dreamy. The intense vitality of this July day,—the richness of this beautiful morning, only make me shrink within myself—paralyzing instead of strengthening; prostrating, not uplifting. I am thinking, too, of a brighter day than this—a purer glory. Oh thou kind Heaven, forgive me if I dream too much, and act too little for that pure day,—that golden morning of which every sunrise here is a prophecy—every noon-day, a witness and proof! For it is not far away from earth, where the sun shines on forever. It is almost as though one might stand on some mountain top and reach up a hand into the living waves where sunrise and sunset meet and clasp each other, destroying night.

How still it is, to-day! Soft as mezzotints, and as motionless on the grass lie the shadows of the maples, spotted with the light. One might think that Nature, all clad with the glory of God, had suddenly ceased to breathe, and were waiting the announcement of something new to be. But it is not that. The announcement has been made already. Death has been busy again, (he who parts the day and the night, so that they meet no more, have no more fellowship, one with the other,) he has been busy again, and has taken one more of our young friends. The swift lightning brought us the news, last night, and to-day the world is changed. It is not the same world it was yesterday. She, who is gone, is not a part of it, to-day. She is living yet; the pulses of her being, in whatever wonderful way God has provided for her, are beating yet, and will live on forever—but not to our sight. And what have *we* had to do with this matter—this new life to her—this change, beyond which, and in which, is no change; we, who in times past, have been near her, for so many bright days, so many evenings made glad with the music and joy of youth? Oh, it will not do to turn away from this question, for it comes home to us, now, and it will come home to us again, in the day of judgment. If through all her bright or clouded days here upon earth, we have been pleading with God to prepare her for something purer, brighter, holier—if we have sought mightily, and as for our own souls, that Jesus Christ, the righteous, would come down and make her His child, and number her with those who shall sit with him in glory—doubtless it is all written down in heaven, and will keep well—the ink will not fade—the print of that record will be bright, even in the great day of account.

If we have *not* done this, it is too late now. We may go to our closets and bend low before the Infinite Majesty—we may know that God is there—as leaning in the dark on the arm of a friend, whom we see not; we may feel the touch, and know that Jesus is there, ready to save to the uttermost, *the living*,—ready to hear and answer petitions for the *living*, for whatever other child of our heart may not yet be on the road to Heaven,—but we can ask nothing more for Susie,—she is gone.

At such a time we pause in our routine, and take new bearings and stand-points. Life becomes touched with a higher value, and we ask as to this question of values, what kind of currency passes in Heaven, what exchange rules there—what transactions are going on there,—what is the fashion of life there, and what the speech and apparel of that High Court. In this way, God calls to us, the angels call to us, the friends gone before call to us, the whole world, and the brute and inanimate things of God, cry aloud to us. The sunshine playing in spots under the trees, becomes purer, brighter, more like a thing of life itself; as though it would plead with us, and win us away from the world and its noisy doings. "Look at me," it says—as we stop musing under the maples--"and see how pure and bright I am, doing only the will of God, for He sends me and gives me wings to travel with, and all the strength I need. Oh, come away from the world, my friend, and busy yourself with something handsome, something worthy of yourself and your Creator."

At such times, also, a passage, say a sentence from a book, some forgotten author, or forgotten prayer, will enter and quite take possession of the mind, driving out all other thought with its incessant repetition, like the face of a child whom we love,pressing, importunate, not to be refused.

Within the last ten years my father and myself have visited occasionally an old homestead near New Haven, of which now nothing is left save a small new stone house, standing however on the old ground, and with the same hills and meadows about it, which were there when it was my father's home—the home of his childhood. Our object is, sometimes, to stop at the old place, or to make a few inquiries among the neighbors, and sometimes merely to take one more look, as we pass by; for there are none that know us there now—not one. If they remember us at all, it is probably only as the strange old gentleman and his son, who sometimes stop and ask questions about people who lived there sixty or seventy years ago—and who cares about such people? Why, they are all dead, mostly. So my father says. There is scarcely a man or woman in all New Haven who remembers him.

"All gone," says my father, "all gone—every one of them that I used to know."

What attraction there is to him in this solitary ride I can hardly say, but perhaps he likes it *best*, that he is not interrupted in his meditations thereabouts, by friends on the look-out. It suits him, perhaps, that they do *not* come crowding about the carriage, and urging him to stop and stay with them. What are they to him, or he to them? They are not of the same generation.

On our last pilgrimage, only one summer ago, we stopped, as usual, at the Park House by the College Green, and after the usual questioning, were recognized by the landlord, who always makes amends for not knowing us, by extraordinary civilities, after making us out. We have, usually, the front first floor rooms, and if in season, the landlord always remembers my father's partiality for the dragon oysters, and supplies us three times a day. Early on the morning after our last arrival, we started for our drive. My father was urgent for a one-horse wagon, and I as urgent for an open double carriage and driver, and so we started in a roomy barouche, with the top thrown back, and a trusty driver, who had driven a coach, as he told us, for more than twenty-five years.

To my mind, it was a beautiful arrangement, and my father, I saw plainly, was soon of the same opinion. There was room to point his cane in all directions, and entire comfort as to cushions and back. A charming arrangement!

In this satisfactory manner, we slowly bowled through the streets, my father marking for me, as we passed, all the places of note, and here and there questioning the driver, who sat high up in the air, as to occasional novelties, which were of late date, and consequently of small significance. "All changed—all changed," said my father, after touching up the driver with his cane, as to some new structure, which was built perhaps six months before. "Here," he continued, turning to me, "on this corner was the old church, where we came to meeting. I see nothing of it now," said he, looking very hard at a plain house which stood there, as if he thought something might be left, "I see nothing of it,—but here, sir, we came and heard the great Dr. Edwards more than sixty, yes, seventy years ago. And here," he continued, as we rolled out into the country and passed the creek, "here is the ground where my father planted his cannon and drove back the British. I was on the hill with my mother, where we had retired in the night. We staid in a barn up there, till the troubles were over,—all the women and children gathered together there, for days and nights, living as we could on what we had caught up in haste, as we left our homes. There your aunt was born, shook into the world by the roar of cannon on the plains. It was a hard time, sir, a hard time."

"Up this road," he continued, "a mile or more, lived a man whom I remember as Uncle Joe Ball, who came down to the old house twice a week, always, to shave my father. The Tories in the neighborhood threatened Uncle Joe severely, to which he replied that as long as Captain M. needed a barber *he* (Uncle Joe) should attend to him, and if they, the rascally Tories, would give him half as good a breakfast as he always got at the old Captain's, he would shave them, too."

We made no stop, this time, at the homestead. Perhaps we had frightened them too much, years ago. On that occasion, I being an invalid and lagging behind, my father walked swiftly in at the front door, and by a side-door passed on through a sitting-room, startling several women who were there, and still moved on without let or pause, to a back kitchen, where he threw his cloak on the floor, and exclaimed to all who might be concerned in the declaration, "The very spot where I was born!" This was his first and last remark. Looking for a moment at the frightened people with exceeding severity, as though they had scarcely a right to appear on the face of the earth, and with his great cloak, which I replaced on his shoulders, swinging in the wind, my father immediately marched out again, by a rear door, and has never entered the house since. I returned a moment to apologize, and learned that they bear our name, but knew nothing about us. The event of that morning they doubt less remember, as we do hurricanes, as something fearful, but (providentially) rare.

At this time, as I said, we made no halt, save for a look, but a mile or thereabouts further south, my father stopped the carriage, and directed my attention to a small two-story building, probably now used as a corn-house. "I remember it well," said he, "for there was where we first came to school. I was a mere child, for it is at least seventy years ago, but I remember it well, because the house was once struck by lightning, and none of us hurt, not one. But I remember it better from another circumstance. It was kept by a school-mistress. I shall never forget that place, or that school-mistress," said my father, looking at me with a smile, "for every morning and evening she prayed for us, closing, always, with this petition,—*that we might all meet again in the bright morning of the Resurrection.*"

As we drove on into the city, my father leaned back, for the first time, in the carriage, and exclaimed, (quoting from one of his own poems—the originality of which we afterwards discussed,)

"*Loud strikes the clock of Time!* This, sir, is probably the last drive that we shall ever have together to the old homestead."

I hope, Mr. Editor, that I have not wearied you with these personal matters. It is that petition of the school-mistress, which has been haunting me to-day. That is the child's face which has been before me all the morning. It was said seventy years ago, or thereabouts, and doubtless it has been said many thousands of years ago, but it is good yet, is it not? It will never become old or tiresome. As time piles up the years and hurries them off into the past, this old-fashioned petition will become brighter and brighter by repetition, and for all the years that remain to this rolling world. And long after we, my dear Editor, have stepped aside from this swift procession—when we have written our last Margins, and all this beautiful arrangement for sunrise and sunset shall have floated away from us, as a dream and a mist, there will still be thousands, and thousands, and ten times thousands, evermore looking up, and uttering, by day and by night, through all the round world, that sweet petition—*that we may all—all meet in the bright morning of the Resurrection.*

Yours, ——.

"THE INTENSE VITALITY OF THIS JULY DAY."

Speaking of July, reminds one of "Independence," and that again of celebrations, of the booming of great guns, the fizzing of fire-crackers, of rockets skiving through the heavens at night, and all the paraphernalia belonging to the commemoration of the birth-day of a great nation. We have done one thing in our day to tell of. What few living Editors, we venture to say, or lawyers either, for that matter have ever done. We once delivered an oration in a state's prison, on a Fourth of July, and our audience consisted only of the convicts and their keepers. Most people in this State, legislators and tax-payers especially, have heard of the Clinton prison, an establishment away up in Clinton County, right in the woods, literally at the end of the road. It consists of a great pile of stone buildings surrounded by palisades, inclosing some dozen or more acres, inside of which is a bed of iron ore, which is wrought by the convicts. This ore is raised and separated at an expense of some five dollars, or thereabouts, per ton, and sold at something like four dollars, leaving a clear profit of about one dollar to the State—out of pocket. However this may be, the State has for the last ten or more years been looking for the "good time coming," when the Clinton prison would sustain itself without the aid of taxation, and the treasury, and that same good time is in prospect still.

Four years ago we were out among the Chataugay woods, tramping over the hills and along the streams, floating over the lakes and climbing the mountains, and playing the savage among the Adirondacks for a fortnight. We had a nice time among the game. We shot all the deer we desired to, and caught as many trout as we pleased. We killed a wild cat and a fisher, and squirrels and rabbits not a few. We floated over those beautiful lakes that lay there all alone in the woods, rowing around their rocky shores, talking with the old forest spirits and weird things that had not yet been frightened away by the tramp and the roar and onward rush of civilization.

Beautiful, aye, most beautiful are those northern lakes, lying among the mountains and surrounded by the ancient forest, just as they were placed there by the command of God. Especially beautiful are the Saranacs, and Round Lake, and Tupper's Lake, studded with picturesque islands, some treeless and shrubless, mere brown moss-covered rocks, great boulders rising up out of the deep water. Others are covered with solemn old primeval trees, against which the woodman's axe has never been swung. Romantic bays steal around and are hidden behind high promontories. Fragmentary rocks in some places are piled up like a ruined wall along the banks, while at others a sandy beach stretches back to the alders and scrubby trees that line the shore. A beautiful river is the Racquet, coming down from among the mountains with a deep and quiet current, save where occasional rapids occur, when it dashes madly along, foaming and eddying, and whirling round, among, and over the rocks, and roaring onward for a little way, and then settling down again into calmness and a dignified flow.

We returned, or as our guide termed it, "came out," from our forest wanderings at the Clinton prison, on the afternoon of the third of July. We accepted the invitation of the Agent to spend a day or two with him. In the evening the good old chaplain called upon us, and stated that the convicts were to have a prison holiday and an extra dinner on the morrow, and requested us to give them an oration. We prepared one during the night, and delivered it on the Fourth, in the presence of some three hundred or more convicts and their keepers, in the chapel of the prison. It was a new thing to talk about liberty, and progress, and social order, the glories of a free government and the advance of civilization to men whose view was circumscribed by the palisades of the prison, who were slaves to the State in the hands of their keepers, and with whom freedom of word or action was a memory only. When we rose from the chaplain's desk to address them and looked upon the faces before us, every one of which wore a settled melancholy, a sorrowful, almost hopeless expression, an indescribable feeling of sadness overpowered us, and we had to sit down to wipe away the tears that obscured the pages of the manuscript before us. We had addressed a good many audiences in our day, but never one like that. We saw, before we had spoken a word, the big tears coursing down the cheeks of those with whose hearts memory was busy—memory that brought their little ones around them, with their childish prattle and innocent faces, from whom their crimes had banished them, and no doubt conscience was doing its work. No man ever had an audience that listened with a more earnest attention to his words, than did those three hundred convicts to ours, and the memory of that Fourth of July oration, in a State's prison, will remain with us always.

" So my father says. There is scarcely a man or woman in all New Haven who remembers him." " All gone," says my father, " all gone, every one of them that I used to know."

Herein is one of the mysteries of being. We see those who started with us in life dropping away, falling like the Autumn leaves around us, the circle growing smaller and smaller, the weak and the strong falling alike, and if we are spared only a few years longer, we too can say of the companions of our youth, "they are gone, all gone." We remember a Scotchman, a neighbor of our father's, who was a middle-aged man, when we were a boy. He left his native village in Scotland before attaining his. majority, and came to this country in pursuit of fortune. His industry and frugality secured that, and after the lapse of near half a century, he was seized with a longing to go back to the scenes of his childhood, to look once more upon the things he loved so well, and which memory had treasured so fondly in his heart. He was absent some three or four months, and we met him here in the city on his return. He was an old man, numbering nearly or quite three-score years and ten, but vigorous and hearty as an ordinary one of fifty. We inquired of the friends he expected to find, and deep sadness gathered on his features as he answered, "I found only their graves. None knew me. I was a stranger alike to the memory and traditions of my kindred."

There is small philosophy in pausing to inquire why *we* are spared. The mystery of this everlasting change, this dropping into, and dropping out of life, is a matter upon which we may speculate, but one that we cannot solve. This we know, that busy and successful as death is, and has always been, in recruiting his ranks, the great army of the living goes on increasing always. Being born, is a prerequisite to death, and although it be a fixed fact that it is appointed unto all men once to die, yet it is an equally certain thing, that more men have been born into the world than have died. When one, or a hundred, or a thousand, disappear from among the living, one, or a hundred, or a thousand, together with a few extra numbers, step into their places, and it is doubtless a fact that there are more people in the world to-day than there were yesterday, or at any previous period, and there will be more to-morrow than there are to-day. The number of living men and women is increasing, and has been, we have no doubt, since the ark rested on Ararat, and that number will go on increasing until——when? The world is not full of people yet, by a long shot.

"We have usually the front first floor rooms, and if in season, the landlord always remembers my father's partiality for the Dragon oysters, and supplies us three times a day."

Do you think, our friend MARGINS, that the Landlord of the "Park House by the College Green," could be induced to extend his civilities in this respect to a new customer? Would the editor of the *Register* be likely to be treated to those same Dragon oysters? If so, we shall be likely to patronize the "Park House by the College Green," for we confess that of all the delicate morsels a fresh Dragon oyster right from his oozy bed, is our weakness; we hold him to be the prince of the bivalves; not the largest, certainly, nor the fattest, but he is the sweetest, the one that is just right to a dot. We have small respect for the college or institutions of learning of New Haven—not that we would speak in dispraise of them. They may all be, and doubtless are, well enough in their way. They have doubtless sent out many men who have made a noise in the world, and there may be many more like them to follow; but there are a hundred other places where great men are manufactured, where colleges and institutions of learning abound; but New Haven alone can boast of the genuine, unadulterated Dragon oyster, and this great fact is its crowning glory. It is the Dragon oyster that links New Haven to history, and makes it immortal. Ask of a Virginian where New Haven is, and he will tell you it is where they have the Dragon oyster fresh every day—ask him its principal attraction, and he'll answer the Dragon oyster—ask him its principal production, its chief article of manufacture, he'll tell you the Dragon oyster; and his mouth will moisten, and his eyes dilate while he sums up his geographical knowledge of the locality in the great fact, THE DRAGON OYSTER.

XVI.

THE DINNER, AND GOOD-BYE—DECEMBER.

Now that we have dined, Mr. Editor, let us shake hands, and part.

Some years ago on the Kaatskills, I wrote a little poem about the country near *Stratford-on-Avon.* In that, I discoursed, very much to my satisfaction, of

> "The journeying hills that wind away
> Slowly, as to a passing-bell;
> Like friends who say good-bye, yet stay,
> And still repeat—good-bye—Farewell.

That was very proper for Ould England, but don't let *us*, Mr. Editor, copy after such nonsense. For it is time, sir, to have done with Margins. Unless we stop soon, your readers will think that we have set up for an institution, "most tolerable, and not to be endured." The year, too, draws to a close, and it's hardly worth while to carry over the old year's talk into the new. I am, as you know, a little slow, at best, although you have waked me some, (I rise, now, perhaps an hour earlier, than when we began our discussions:) But I need all the helps of appositeness and picked time of *entrée.* Now that we are to part, it will not be taken in any begging sense, if I confess myself *behind the times,*—*not* up with the rising generation. Not that I care exceedingly about this. Probably not. If there is any one body in the round world, or say any two or three, (counting in my wife and Nelly,) who carry their days along with more high content than do we in this quiet up-country, I should like to make their acquaintance. So that it is not, you perceive, that *we* care as to being not quite so enterprising as the world that dashes by us,—but that others do. Mrs. Dash, I suspect, has a feeling in this matter—so have other neighbors, and so, perhaps, have you and your readers. People well out at sea, and under full sail, don't care to be straining their hearing, to please some idler on the shore, who is shouting to them through a trumpet.

And now, sir, if only that dinner deals kindly with you, I shall be more than content. It was *the* dinner to which you were invited, six months ago, and now that it is accomplished, I see no occasion for further talk. Six months ago, we were to dine. The six months have gone, and we *have* dined. That is to say, *Quod erat demonstrandum, et demonstratus est.* What's the use of margins, when we have found the text, the very heart of the matter?

The talk, then, was of peas, young onions, and spring chickens; but we can't bring June up into mid-winter. You must be content, sir, with having had a Christmas dinner. I flatter myself, however, that we did a fair thing in the way of onions,—the boiled and the pickled;—and the chickens had *been* spring chickens, which, I take it, satisfies the conscience, the moral sense, as to that matter. If a chicken has been young in its day, what more can you expect? Oh, my Editor, in this age of progress, when there's a chance of attaining to the full cackle, the perfected crow, it's quite ridiculous to expect that spring chickens are *always* to continue and remain spring chickens!

How did you rest, Hammond? Did you go through without landing? Did *Roaring River* trouble you? "All in the solemn midnight," (not centuries ago—but this same last night, Dec. 27th–28th, now gone past, and at this moment hanging somewhere, all cold and dark and starry, on its way over the lakes and the prairies,) did there come up any ghosts of dinner—nice things that ought to be quiet,—tit-bits, that wouldn't be kind to you?

One thing is certain—the *fire-water* we did not have, nor the *Claret*, nor the *Sauterne*, nor the *Old Port*, nor the *Heisdick.* We did *not* find the key to the hall-closet.

Of course, sir, it would be highly improper for me to speak of the pre-arrangements for this dinner. It would scarcely be fair to Mrs. Margin. For instance, it would never do for me to say, that the last six weeks, more or less, have been and gone chiefly as antecedents to this event—that we began to smell onions and scolloped oysters (I think) in November—that the draft in the parlor chimney though powerful, was the wrong way—that I placed there an old-fashioned Franklin grate, which from its look of high satisfaction I was anxious should have a good time, and which itself evidently had its whole heart in the matter, burning and smoking in the most generous manner, straight into the room—that I talked with it, and argued, and theorized, and threatened, for days and nights—fired it up this way, and that way, tried it with the north wind, with the south wind, with a powerful west wind, and found all winds alike to it, the honest old Franklin taking all, and giving nothing back to the chimney—that finding, at last, a combination of flues, such as no decent stove could submit to, and after working hard all day, carefully noting the smallest hints, the slightest coquetry of agreement, filling and opening, and again filling and opening certain dark and sooty chambers, that same old stove suddenly put on a bright and complaisant face, smiled through all its brass headings, and drew to a charm!

This, sir, would never do to mention out of the family. I will only remark, therefore, that having established that chimney communication, we held it with a firm hand, so that a perpetual flame went up those ancient flues, to the hour of your arrival.

So, also, as to apparel, especially *boots*, of which

I found an elegant pair, which have been on my feet three times, I believe, in the last five years. Some weeks ago (to be forehanded), I pulled my astonished feet into those boots, and perhaps the happiest moment of my life, was when I pulled them out again. However, I keep them safe. I lay them up choice. They will be good for exercise in stormy days, when we can't get out doors. I have made a calculation, that if I begin to pull them on right away after breakfast, I shall just be able to get dinner, when it will be time to begin immediately at getting them off again. This will fill up the whole day with vigorous exercise, and be excellent for the arms and chest. Any tendency of blood to the head, can be kept down by cold applications.

They were put aside, therefore, as useful in that view, but not for a holiday. For the struggle with those boots, sir, opened my eyes, as to the folly of all such vain and windy endeavor; and when the fitness, the simplicity of *shoes* presented itself, I was at once a better and a stronger man. Having conquered the glistening temptation of boots, other troubles were light as air; so that since that day, and the establishment of the upward current in the parlor chimney, the whole house has been a-blaze with the liveliest satisfaction, up to the breezy moment when you and yours stepped in at our front door.

But, oh my dear Editor, my commentator, and

alter ego of the Margins, you perceive that all this is entirely a private matter. Exclusively, sir, exclusively. It is due to myself—it is due to my wife—and I think, too, that even Nelly might have a feeling in this matter—a nice and delicate sense of the proper, that you should *not so much as dream* that anything of the kind has taken place. I say, therefore, *nothing about it.*

Good-bye, Hammond—good-bye, and *addio.* Now that we have dined, and supped, and slept, and breakfasted, while the wheels are still rolling that carry you home, and the white breath of that fire-horse goes up into the gold of sunrise, we send after you this last greeting and farewell.

With the day, especially the early morning, are light, and strength, and hope. With the night, are darkness and dreams, prophecies and mysteries. I like, always, to shake parting hands in the morning.

Addio, sir, and take our best up-country regards to all your household. Especially my wife's and Nelly's, I trust you will keep in your choicest remembrance. And as you travel down to that last hour to which we all journey on together, may you and yours prosper continually; may you greet many another Christmas; and with the same firm step with which you just now crossed the high bridge over *Roaring River*, may you walk on into the mornings of many, and happy, New Years to come.

Yours, ——.

"Now that we have dined, Mr. Editor, let us shake hands and part."

Don't say that, friend MARGINS, don't say it. Parting is a hard word, indeed it is. Have you so many friends, that you can throw off even one without a feeling of loneliness about the heart? We know that modern friendships, those formed when white hairs are gathering on the head, are not like those of our early years—at all events, they are less easily formed, and herein is a curious matter pertaining to human character. It is more difficult to form friendships as we grow old. We become cautious; we weigh character carefully; we start at any inconsistency, any weakness, that we entirely overlook in an old friend, and close up our hearts against that confidence which in our youth we so freely entertained. No matter how many of our old companions may fall from around us, no matter how we may see ourselves, year by year, isolated, contact with the world, a practical knowledge of its insincerity, its hollowness, and its vanities too, make us shrink from filling the void which death has created, by new intimacies. Besides, we become cold and frigid in our natures. Icicles form around our heart, and the hot tears, over the graves of our early friends, will not melt them away. We should cherish the friendships of our youth the more, because it is so difficult to form new ones, and we should prize a new one, formed at our years, as a diamond set around with rubies; as gold that had passed the refiner's ordeal.

Say that we shall cease our discussions, if you please; that this is the last of the MARGINS. Retire to enjoy the *otium cum dignitate* of your literary labors, but don't say, "let us shake hands and part," don't say it.

* * * "And the chickens had *been* spring chickens, which, I take it, satisfies the conscience, the moral sense, as to that matter. If a chicken has been young in its day, what more can you expect? Oh! my Editor, in this age of progress, when there is a chance of attaining the full cackle, the perfected crow,—it 's quite ridiculous to expect that spring chickens are *always* to continue and remain *spring* chickens."

Precisely so—the theory looks plausible, and so far as the argument goes, we cannot gainsay it. But it won't stand the test of fact: and how many of the ten thousand theories originated by human wisdom will stand that test? The world once believed that this little earth was the great centre of created things. That it was a vast plain stretching out every way, consisting of oceans and dry land, lakes, mountains and seas, rivers and islands. That when a man started to go west, west he might go forever, until he came to the outer edge, the jumping off place, if any edge there was. That the sun travelled round the earth by day, and the moon by night, and that all the stars were only shining things set up in the sky for ornament. This theory was a great thing for human pride, and the men of those times had a great opinion of themselves and their mighty world. No wonder that "there were giants in those days." But the demonstrations of science knocked this proud theory into fragments. Great ships swung out upon the ocean, and sailed away westward, and sailed on, traversing unknown seas. Onward they went, westward and westward still, until one day they made their appearance in the East, returning to the harbor they had left. People still insisted that the earth was flat; but there stood the fact, of a voyage always in one direction, straightforward, that terminated where it began. Here was a practical demonstration, a solitary fact that scattered the logic and the learning of ages, and a great theory that had stood as truth for centuries, to the winds. It proved that this earth was not flat, but round. Science again applied its cold demonstrations of fact to our planetary system, and proved that this mighty earth was a wonderfully small matter in the great visible universe of God, that it travelled round the sun as a sort of tender only, and that the little stars that twinkled away up in the sky, were glorious worlds, to whose vast magnitude this earth is in comparison as a grasshopper to the mastodon.

And now, friend MARGINS, let us test your theory in regard to spring chickens—and remember we are discussing a theory, not a dinner, and especially not the "Christmas dinner," for that was all that an epicure could ask, to say nothing of the generous hospitality, the pleasant conversation with which it was seasoned. Ask a "diner out" who has a taste for that choicest of delicacies, the spring chicken, if he is contented with the argument that he should feed upon an antiquated rooster, because it had at some remote period been a spring chicken? Every tooth in his head would cry out against such a forced conclusion. Reason with him as you might—pile Pelion upon Ossa and Ossa upon Olympus, in the way of theoretical demonstration, still his aching jaws, that had in vain essayed to masticate the muscles and ligaments of the venerable game-cock, and his sense of taste that had detected no delicacy of flavor, would, by the simple application of palpable facts, demolish your learning and your logic. No, sir, a spring chicken is *sui generis*. It never exceeds a partridge in size. When it "attains the full cackle, the perfected crow," as a spring chicken it ceases to have an existence; call it a fowl, a hen, a rooster, anything you please, but it is not a spring chicken. It may be, and I affirm it is, a good and edible thing, but a spring chicken it is not. It has not the delicate flavor, the juicy tenderness—in short, the perfection of all that is pleasant to the palate, that belongs to the spring chicken.

"One thing is certain, the fire-water we did not have, nor the *Claret*, nor the *Sauterne*, nor the *old Port*, nor the Heidsick; we did not find the key to the hall-closet."

And therein we insist upon it we were right. Will you tell us, friend MARGINS, why it is, that rational men, who can reason accurately from cause to effect, should indulge in this same fire-water? Why they will insist that they cannot be jolly, without invoking to their aid the wine-God, or the still more dangerous potentate, King Alcohol? If you will look over our pleasant correspondence you will find, somewhere in the back numbers, this expression in regard to ourselves:

> "Wine floored us once, and only once, and then 'twas by treachery. Under the influence of repentance and soda-water, we cut its acquaintance forever."

We have smiled over the memory of that occasion more than once, notwithstanding certain twinges of conscience, which tempered our propensity to laughter, for be it known to you, friend MARGINS, that there is "a mirthful sadness as well as tears of joy."

We had just finished our term of study required as an antecedent to being admitted to practice at the bar (we mean, of course, as a lawyer); and as the court was in session in New York, went there for the purpose of passing the ordeal of an examination preparatory to obtaining a license to put "Attorney at Law" at the end of our name. It was of a January day when we, with some forty or fifty others, were examined, and cold enough to satisfy the conscience of a Laplander. Much as we had dreaded the examination, and diligently as we had applied ourself to be prepared for it, it finally turned out to be a very commonplace affair, the principal object of which seemed to be, to occupy the time until a supper to the examiners, at what in those days was a celebrated restaurant's in the neighborhood of the City Hall, could be prepared. When that event was announced the examination, of course, terminated, and we were all pronounced uncommonly learned young men, in every branch of legal science; and as the supper was excellent, we may be said to have graduated with great honor. We are green enough, mercy knows, now, but were much more verdant then. The greater part of our long clerkship of seven years had been spent in the rural districts where Champagne was a mere rumor, an ideality, a thing to hear spoken of by travelled gentlemen; besides, our finances, if such cheer had been plenty, would have been a barrier between us and indulgence.

Beside us at the table sat one that might have been called, in modern parlance, a fast young man; so fast, indeed, that he ran himself out of constitution, out of health, and into the grave at last, before he was thirty years of age. He was the son of wealthy parents, highly educated, and of brilliant mind. But a career of dissipation squandered one of the noblest intellects that God ever gave to his creatures, and made his mother's head white, and her brow wrinkled long before their time, and the memory of his last hours, when the drunkard's delirium was upon him, broke her heart, and she sank childless into the grave. He sat beside us at the supper-table. Upon him wine had small effect. Inured to its use, his brain seemed almost proof against indulgence, however copious his libations. The Champagne was choice, and we remember well that it was pleasant to the taste. Our neighbor drank and urged us to drink, descanting all the time upon its harmless nature, and we were foolish enough to drink one glass to his two, during the sitting. We had a jolly time of it; just such a time as lays up repentance and humiliation, and self-abasement, when the *sober* second thought calls up the follies of the past. We were entirely regular, so long as we remained at table, and in the equable atmosphere of the room, but when we got out into the piercing cold outside, all at once the lights seemed to be dancing a quadrille with the houses, and the streets with their lamps seemed to go up in a long vista towards the sky. Everything seemed in motion. The buildings got out into the middle of the streets. The Old City Hall was turning a somersault, and the horses and carts, and carriages seemed to be all standing straight up on end, or going perpendicularly up towards the stars, that were dodging about in a manner that was a sight to behold. The side-walks were steep, very steep, and it was an up-hill business to travel upon them. We remember catching around a lamp-post that was hurrying up Broadway, on a two-forty gait, just as the glass came down in a crash around us, a friend of ours having thrown his hickory cane at it to stop the runaway. At that instant, a kind gentleman, who belonged to the night watch, introduced himself to our acquaintance. What the subject of his remarks was we do not remember, but when *he* said watch-house, *we* said "a carriage, Western Hotel, call in the morning, all right, go ahead." The rest is a blank. We awoke in the morning about ten o'clock, in our own room at our hotel, with ten thousand bees humming and swarming in our head, temples throbbing with pain, and a deep sense of shame in our heart. That night's experience satisfied *us.* If we cannot be jolly without a recourse to artificial stimulants, we have made up our mind to "go mourning all our days." It is a bad thing, a dangerous thing, to trifle with this "fire-water." Better play with the forked lightning, better grapple with the locomotive when he comes crashing and thundering along, screaming and roaring with the voice of the arch-fiend, and hurling forward with the speed of the wind, his ponderous train.

"ADDIO."

Well, friend Margins, if part we must, so be it. To us, at least, our season of communion, brief though it be, has been pleasant. We shall look back upon it as one of the green spots of a life that has been to some extent a barren one. There are many desolate places along which its course has been, and few flowers have bloomed by the wayside. But "addio" be it, and God bless you and all those that you love. May health and strength return to you, may no sorrow cast its dark shadow around you. May your life be a long and a happy one, and may your last hour be the happiest of all, by reason of "the faith that leans upon God."

COUNTRY RAMBLES.

COUNTRY RAMBLES.

I.

CANANDAIGUA — PENN YAN — CROOKED LAKE— BATH—HORNELLSVILLE.

I AM at Canandaigua, certainly one of the most beautiful country towns in the State. The scenery about it is not grand or sublime; there are no rugged mountains rearing their tall heads to the clouds, frowning in eternal barrenness upon majestic rivers sweeping around their base, or lakes sleeping in quiet valleys below them; there are no waterfalls rushing down from the hills in foaming cascades, or winding in deep ravines among old primeval woods; but there is that which is better. There are rich farms spread out all around, far as the eye can reach, fields of grain waving in the summer breeze, meadows covered with rich grass ready for the mower, and pastures in which flocks and herds are feeding; fine farm-houses hid away among the tall trees and shrubbery, and barns filled with the products of agriculture, are in view. On the south is a beautiful lake winding away around low promontories, with cultivated fields or patches of green woods stretching away from the beach. Such is the scenery around Canandaigua. There are pleasant drives in every direction. The road that winds along the shore of the lake will afford a delightful ride of a summer morning or evening, and the other avenues leading away into the country are scarcely less pleasant. Everywhere are the evidences of wealth, of progress, and of civilization. Fine horses, fine cattle and sheep, and rich harvests, are constantly in view. These things are around Canandaigua, outside of the village, within range of a walk or a drive. But the village itself affords a greater display of quiet beauty and taste than I have seen elsewhere. The houses are massive and elegant, surrounded by large and tastefully laid out grounds and gardens, decorated with the rarest flowers, and the richest shrubbery. There are "solid men," as Daniel Webster would say, in Canandaigua—"solid" in intelligence and social qualities, in moral and political influence, and solid in dollars. Men who live for something beyond the mere accumulation of wealth; who will leave behind them a monument in the taste with which they have adorned the spots they occupy. These beautiful residences, the grounds decorated with rare shrubbery, and abounding in the richest fruits; these gardens, sending abroad upon the air the fragrance of flowers that charm the vision by their beauty, and entrance the senses by their sweetness, are better than railroad stocks or vast investments in the funds, to leave as a monument when one dies. The tree one plants, survives him; the grape-vine remains when the hand that plants it is cold; the rose-bush blossoms when he who placed it in the garden is alone in the quiet house of death; and while the tree bears its fruit, the grape-vine its rich clusters, or the rose its sweet blossoms, his name will remain connected with them, as if chiselled in marble. I remember that in one of the old towns of New England, I was conversing with a lady who is not unknown to fame, when she pointed to some elms that stood on the lawn in front of her dwelling, and said, "these trees were planted by my grandfather," and then pointing to some venerable pear-trees that hung with then unripe fruit, said, "those were planted by the original proprietor of these grounds, of whom my grandfather purchased them." The name she gave I have forgotten, but it was associated with the old pear-trees, and had been for more than a hundred years. And so it will be with the trees and shrubbery of these beautiful grounds. They will preserve the memory of those who placed them where they stand, and for generations be a monument to their virtues and their name.

From an observatory on the top of one of the most splendid dwellings in the village, I had a view of the country around. The glass was slightly stained, of the windows through which I looked, and it gave a mellowness to the picture that was exceedingly beautiful. I have never been in Italy; I know about an Italian sunset only from descriptions by tourists and from paintings by masters of the art, but if an Italian sunset exceeds in beauty the prospect that was before me, as I looked from that observatory, it is then beautiful indeed. The lake, the farms and avenues lined with trees in the distance, the village residences, the gardens and grounds near by, and the delightful walks and trees, and rich fruits and flowers immediately beneath and around me, formed a landscape which, seen in the mellow light afforded by the stained glass of the windows through which I looked, no painter could transfer to canvas, or Italy excel.

I dined with the owner of this residence and his excellent lady, in the true style of Scotch hospitality. They were among the pioneers of what years ago was known as the Genesee Country. They have seen the ancient forests standing on the site of Canandaigua, and stretching away to the great lakes, and they have watched the progress of that war which civilization makes upon the old primeval things, sweeping away the woods and spreading out broad farms, planting churches and school-houses, and building up cities and towns. They heard the first blast of the stage coachman's horn, on the great stage route through the centre of the State, and they heard its dying echoes as it was succeeded by the scream of the steam-whistle and the snort of the iron horse. They shared the trials and hardships incident to the settlement of a new country, and in their declining years they are reaping a rich harvest, as the reward of their perseverance and energy. May they be long spared to enjoy the fruits of their labors; and when their appointed time shall come, may they pass away quietly and calmly as the last lingering stars pass from the twilight of morning into the brightness of the perfect day.

As we were walking in the garden after dinner, among the beautiful and rare flowers and shrubbery, I said to the excellent lady of the mansion, "It seems to me that you are blessed, certainly not beyond your deserts, but beyond the ordinary lot of the people of this world. You have wealth, and you have the taste to use and enjoy it. You have this beautiful mansion, and these delightful grounds, these flowers, these fruit and shade trees, these pleasant walks, and all that can make life pleasant. You have health, and spirits to enjoy it all. While I, who have all the love for all these things, have neither house nor grounds, can cultivate no shrubbery or flowers. My life is a long struggle for bread."

"My friend," she replied, and a shade of sadness came over her countenance as she spoke, "we do not differ so much from you. We have no children to bestow our affections upon. You have. Would you exchange them for all that you have seen here? They are your garden."

And I thought of the cherished flower that death had so recently plucked from the garden of my home, and how I missed its perfume, and that I would give all the treasures of earth, were they mine, to look upon the sweet blossom again.

There is, at Canandaigua, one of the finest hotels in the country. It is spacious and new. The rooms are large and airy, and furnished with great taste and neatness. In no hotel have I found more care or attention paid to the comfort and convenience, and even the luxury of the guests. To those who love quiet, who would be away from the bustle and noise of a city, who have no taste for the excitement of the watering-places or fashionable resorts, Canandaigua offers peculiar inducements to tempt a stay. The hotel, I repeat, is among the very best in the State. The country around is charming, the drives delightful. Everything that can add to the luxury of quiet and repose during the heat of summer, is to be found here.

I am at Penn Yan, the county seat of Yates County, a neat and prosperous village in one of the smallest, but richest counties of the State. The farms around it are productive, admirably managed, and the farmers are rich. In no part of the State has there been a more rapid progress in improvement and wealth made. It is a pleasant thing to see the great fields of grain, of wheat just ready for the harvest, of barley ripening for the sickle, of oats yet in their coat of green, and corn even with the fences, just in the gorgeous livery of a thrifty growth. Time was when Penn Yan by no means enjoyed the best name in the world for morals. It was once emphatically a hard place, a place of horse trading, horse racing, card playing, of drinking, and the other proclivities which go to make up an evil reputation. But all these things belong to the past, and Penn Yan is now as distinguished for its public virtue, its high tone of public morals, as it was, in days long gone by, for its evil practices. Churches and school-houses, and the persevering effort and example of good men, have wrought an utter revolution in its moral character. Its vices have been forsaken, its evil practices abandoned. The bad men who stained its reputation with their evil courses, have passed away, or forsaken their bad ways. Penn Yan is a sober village, full of enterprise, energy and industry, where the right tone of morals prevails.

In sight of Penn Yan is the Crooked Lake. This beautiful sheet of water has, to me, a thousand charms, and as I look upon it a rush of pleasant memories come clustering around my heart. I was reared upon its banks; I have floated a thousand times upon its surface, and bathed and fished in its waters; I have caught hundreds of salmon trout out in the deep water, and thousands of yellow perch and sunfish along the shore, or on the points of the bars, where the equatic weeds grow thick and luxuriant, like a cane-brake or a wild meadow away down in the water. I remember when my father's log house stood at the head of the lake, some forty rods back from the shore, with a gentle slope of meadow to the water's edge. Great maples that had been spared when the old forest trees were swept away, stood a few rods apart in that meadow, spreading abroad their leafy arms, and rising in the summer time like pyramids of green towards the sky. Midway from the door to the lake was a cluster of some half dozen of these beautiful trees, from among the roots of which a cold pure spring came gushing up, and ran in a little brooklet over a bed of pebbles to the lake. It was a new country then. No highway or road extended beyond my father's clearing. He lived eight miles from a mill, and the same distance from a store or a physician. But all this is changed now. Where then was that meadow, and fields full of stumps, or old primeval woods, is now a thriving village of some fifteen hundred busy people. All the ancient landmarks have been removed. Civilization, in its onward progress, has swept everything that then was to oblivion. The old maples are gone, the clustering plum trees, the tall sycamores, the hickory, the butternut and the wild cherry trees are all gone. That beautiful spring is in the cellar of a village store. The house that "I was born in" is gone, and its place occupied by a pleasant village residence.

This was a beautiful sheet of water long years ago, when there were few clearings along its shores, and it is a beautiful sheet of water still. The forest that grew in dense luxuriance to the water's edge, by its gigantic growth indicated the strength of the soil. Where that forest stood, are now rich farms, giving back wealth to the descendants of the hardy pioneers that swept it away. The scenery around this lake is most beautiful—not like that of Lake George, where rocks and mountains are piled up in stately barrenness, opposing their bald heads to the storm, or hiding their summits in the mists of heaven. The scenery of Lake George is grand, sublime; but is the grandeur of sterility, the sublimity of desolation. Civilization can never beautify or adorn its rugged acclivities; agriculture cannot thrust its sickle into ripened grain, nor the ploughshare penetrate the granite soil that surrounds it. It may be a resort for the traveller in the summer months, to enjoy the freshness of the mountain air, and the coolness of the mountain breeze, but civilization cannot winter there.

The scenery about this lake is of a different character. It speaks of wealth, of comfort, of intelligence, of civilization and progress. The farms that stretch away in gentle acclivity from the shore are rich in agricultural products, great fields of wheat, just passing into yellow ripeness, waving like an ocean in a gentle breeze. Meadows, which are now being shorn by the mowers—acres upon acres of oats and corn, now in their richest robe of luxurious green—pastures where flocks and herds are grazing. Painted houses and great barns, patches of woodland left to supply fuel, and timber for fences and building. These make up the landscape that skirts the Crooked Lake. There is no lack of secluded bays or shaded nooks, into which the little row-boat may glide, nor rugged promontories covered with stately trees, beneath the shadow of which one may luxuriate, safe from the noonday heat, and refreshed by the cool breeze that sweeps over the water. Midway between Penn Yan and the head of the lake is Bluff Point, around the base of which the lake sweeps, and which forms a peninsula, separating the east from the west branch of the lake. This point, as it is called, is a hill of some thousand feet in height, rising with a steep acclivity, but cultivated to the water's edge. On the top it is comparatively level, and presenting for some eight or ten miles a beautiful farming country. At the highest elevation stands a pleasant farm house, overlooking the lake and all the country round. Seen from the water, it stands out in bold relief against the sky, like some ancient castle of the barons of old. From Penn Yan to this dwelling, is a pleasant ride of some ten or twelve miles over a plank road most of the way. When there, the traveller will have a view worth a day's ride to look upon. He will be far above the surrounding country. On three sides of him will be the lake with the beautiful scenery that skirts it. To the East he will overlook a country of forest and farms for miles and miles, within which he will see two or three smaller lakes; to the north he will see Penn Yan, and the rich agricultural district that surrounds it, and beyond, the Seneca Lake. Away to the south he will be charmed by the beautiful valley that stretches away from the head of the lake, and is lost among the hills that hem in the valley of the Conhocton; while to the west his eye will wander over a country more wild and rugged, but still rich and beautiful. No traveller should leave Penn Yan without visiting Bluff Point. Nor should he fail to take a passage over the lake in the pleasant little steamer Steuben. In Captain John Greig he will find an intelligent and courteous gentleman—one who loves his boat and the lake he navigates, and the country and the people round it; who loves to point out the beauties of the scenery, and hear the tourist respond to his own enthusiasm. He is, as I said, an intelligent man, not profoundly educated in scholastic lore, but one who has read and thought a vast deal. Talk about the birds, and you will find him an ornothologist. He will show you his collection of birds, prepared in a superior manner by himself. Among these he will point out to you a loon or northern diver, taken on a hook upon a night line in more than a hundred feet of water.

Talk about the fishes, and you will find him deeply conversant with piscatory lore. Talk of the animals that, when the country was wild, frequented the forests in this portion of the country, and you will find him at home on the subject. In whatever relates to nature, and the living things of nature, he is learned as careful reading and study can make a man of his years.

I go up the Lake with him to-morrow, and shall write you again. I go to visit the old scenes of my boyhood. Though everything is changed, though the old land marks that I loved are all gone, yet I love to linger around the spot where my early youth was spent, and call up visions of scenes long, long past. I love to call back the brave old trees, the fields, the fences, the stumps, the gushing spring, and brushing away the houses and the streets, place them as they stood of old. I love to call up the old maples that stood in the meadow between the old log house and the lake, in all their ancient verdure, and talk with the unseen spirits that people their green foliage. I love to tear away the store houses, the docks, and the great high wall that usurp the place of the little bay at the northwest corner of the lake, that shot landward beneath the spreading arms of the ancient elms and oaks, up whose great trunks the wild grape-vine climbed, and creeping out along the branches, covered them with its tendrils like a net work, and spread out its broad green leaves like a thatched roof, shutting out the light of the sun.

And yet it is a sad thing to visit these old places and see the mighty change that has come over them.

I am on the Crooked Lake, a passenger in the pleasant little steamer Steuben, under the command of Captain JOHN GREIG, of whom I have spoken before. All that I said of him then was true, all that I said of the scenery around this lake is true, unless it be that I have failed to do it justice. I said I was reared upon the banks of this lake, and that as I looked upon its pure clear water, and upon the hills, the gentle slopes, the valleys and the streams that come to it wandering away from the country, a crowd of sad, but pleasant memories come clustering around my heart. It is not now as it was then. Everything is changed. The old forests are gone, the tall pines, the majestic oaks, the maples, the sycamores, the gigantic elms, the lofty lindens, the wild cherry and the butternut trees, old primeval things all, are gone. Let me describe it to you as my memory paints it, before civilization had robbed it of its ancient beauty, as it lay here in the midst of the wilderness, sleeping alone. Let us look upon it as it was years and years ago, when I was a boy. We will talk with the old settlers, the pioneers that first made war upon the forests that stood in primitive solitude about it. They were the vanguard of civilization, and changed by their labor that great wilderness into fruitful fields. True, they have all passed away, dropped into honored graves, but we will call their spirits around us, and they will tell us of the times of old, of the scenes of the early settlements, of their struggles and hardships. They can tell us many a story connected with this lake that has lain here so long unappreciated and unhonored. We will not look upon the beautiful farms, the villages that now are found upon its shores. We will people the fields with the old forest trees, and brush away the houses and barns. We will take away the fences, and remove all these evidences of civilization. Where the flocks and herds are feeding in rich pastures, we will replace the deer and bear, and the other wild animals that roamed there before the woodman's axe frightened them away, or the hunter's rifle doomed them to destruction. We will do as I did more than thirty years ago, when there were but few clearings along the shore, go a voyage around the lake in a canoe made from the trunk of a gigantic pine. I earned my first five dollars by that voyage. I was hired by two English gentlemen to row them round the lake. They were kindhearted men, for when they saw, boy that I was, that I was weary, they relieved me in turn from the oars. We were four days in making the circuit of the lake, but the guinea they paid me made me richer than I have ever been since.

At the northwest corner of the lake was a beautiful little bay, stretching landward some five or six rods by two or three in width. Above it the branches of tall oaks and elms were intertwined, and the wild grapes that crept up their great trunks, spread their net-work all over the tops of the trees, and made with their broad leaves an arbor through the arches of which the sun never shone. The water of this little bay was clear as crystal, and the white pebbles on the bottom, some three or four feet down in the water, were as visible as though nothing but air was above them. At the head of the bay, a cold spring that came gushing up at a few rods distant, entered. From this little bay I have caught, first and last, hundreds of speckled trout weighing from half of a pound to three or four times that weight. But it is all filled up now—stores and shops, and a street, and docks, and a great high wall occupy the place of that little bay, and those old elms and oaks, and that spring, have all disappeared. I killed my first deer as he stooped his head to drink of the water of that little bay. I had watched him from my hiding-place for an hour, as he came browsing along the side of the hill. Just as the sun was going down, he stepped from the thick bushes on to the pebbly beach, and after looking all around him, and snuffing the air, he stepped confidently into the water to slake his thirst. My rifle was upon him, the ball that sped from it penetrated his brain, and he fell dead. Further south, stood a tall sycamore, the roots of which were laved by the water; upon the dead branches, near the top of which, was a favorite perch for the fish-hawk, as he watched for his prey. Occasionally a bald eagle would alight there to plume himself, and watch for the wild ducks that frequented the lake. Further south still, were a few acres of low marshy ground, where the main inlet entered, where the musk-rats built their houses, and the mink and the otter stole along the margin in pursuit of prey. The inlet took its rise some seven or eight miles up the valley, in a multitude of large springs, and it was full of the speckled trout. Let us pause here, and call up some of the old settlers, whose farms extended from this "big creek," as it was called, which flowed along through the centre of the valley, back to the hills. Judge BAKER, I believe, was the first white man who stuck his stake in that valley, and commenced the war against the ancient forests, that has been carried on ever since with such relentless vigor. His farm is now in possession of his son, and a most beautiful one it is—rich in all that belongs to agriculture, and cultivated to a charm.

JUDGE BAKER was a most remarkable man, strong in physical strength, one calculated to endure the hardships of a new country, but stronger still in native, vigorous, common sense. I remember him well. In his latter years, when his early industry had relieved him from the necessity to labor, he was a reading man, and was always a thoughtful one. He was the first who explored that region with a view to settling there. He came from Pennsylvania up the valley of the Conhocton, and reaching the place where the village of Bath now stands, struck off through the valley towards the head of this lake. The forest around the lake was exceedingly dense, and before reaching it he climbed into a high tree, to take a look about him. He was not aware of its proximity, and when he had reached the topmost branches of the tree, there it lay within fifty rods of him, its waters calm and still, unruffled by a wave or a ripple. Two Indians were paddling their canoe along the shore, going down the lake, while several deer were feeding among the grass and water lilies that grew about the mouth of the inlet. I have listened often and often to the old man's description of this beautiful sheet of water, as he then saw it for the first time. How he descended from his perch on the tall old elm, and worked his way to the pebbly beach, and how calm and still it was, how the tall forest trees cast their shadows out over the water as the sun was sinking in the west. How solemn and moveless the hills stood around. How the trout leaped in their gleesomeness from the surface, and schools of the yellow perch made the water boil in spots around. How he shot a deer that was feeding along the margin; how gently but gloomily the night shadows gathered around him; how the fireflies flashed their little torches in the darkness; how he slept on his bed of boughs, in a brush shanty built by himself; how gloriously the sun came up in the morning over the eastern hills, casting his brightness on the rippling waters, and making them glisten in the sunlight, like a sheet of fire. I remember, as I heard him describe the scene, how I thought I should like to have been with him on his exploring tour that time, and looked upon the lake as it lay there all alone, surrounded only by those old forests, and navigated only by the wild men of the woods. It would have been a thing to remember always.

My father came there some years later, but while the lake was still surrounded almost entirely by woods. True, there were at long intervals clearings along the shore. But its primitive wildness was gone. Civilization began to develop itself there as long ago as I can remember, and I could only watch its progress as it moved forward.

My father had become security for a friend in the loan of money, and to indemnify himself from loss, had taken a mortgage upon a negro, (slavery existed then in this State.) The debt fell upon my father, and he became the owner of a man. Old Shadrach was a Virginian by nurture, but an African by birth, having been imported in his infancy. He had a mortal fear of snakes and toads, and he could be frightened into anything by the threat of putting a snake or a toad in his bed. I call him old, because he was between forty and fifty at my earliest recollection, and of course became older before he died. Old Shadrach ran away regularly two or three times a year. He would stay away sometimes a fortnight, sometimes a month, and on two or three occasions so long that my father began to congratulate himself upon being rid of him entirely. But some morning old Shadrach would come crawling out from the hay mow, and promise "massa" that he would never run away again as long as he lived. Shadrach, as I said, stood in mortal fear of snakes. He was one day fishing in a canoe on the lake, and drew up what he took to be a rattlesnake. He dropped his pole in horror and leaped overboard, yelling and screaming for help as if a thousand Indians were scalping him. He could swim like a duck, and he struck out, screaming in horror at every pull. Upon reaching the shore he broke like a quarter-horse for the house. My father, who was at a short distance, hurried up, to know the reason of the outcry. "Massa," cried Shadrach in all the earnestness of terror, "de lake is full of rattlesnakes." "Get out, you woolly-pated rhinoceros," replied my father, "who ever heard of rattlesnakes in the water?" My father went out in another canoe to the one in which Shadrach had been fishing, and upon securing the pole, which was floating about, found that Shadrach had hooked a great eel, a fish by no means common in the lake. But Shadrach regarding it as belonging to the family of snakes, never trusted himself alone after that on the water.

Let us pass along down on the eastern shore, close along under the hill. The land is rugged here, the hill rising in steep acclivity several hundred feet. It is early morning. See how the sunlight first rests upon the hills on the western side of the lake. Remember it is all woods there; see the shadow retreating in a long line down the side of the hill; see, it has reached the water. It is ten o'clock, and we are still in the shade. We are five miles from the head of the lake, in a beautiful little bay under the lee of "Welles' Point." The clearing that we see, is that of Dr. Welles, the father of the Hon. Henry Welles, one of the Judges of the Supreme Court. Dr. Welles was one of the pioneers of the region along the lake. He was a man of energy and learning, and of infinite usefulness in the early settlement of the country. This is the only clearing in sight, save that from which we started. (We are speaking of times "long ago.") His log house stands back from the bay in which our canoe is floating. I have, when a child, accompanied my father and mother on a visit to Dr. Welles—not in a carriage, along a pleasant road skirted by green fields, but in a canoe or skiff; my mother seated in the stern with a trolling line in her hand, with the hook a hundred feet or more behind her; myself seated in the bow and my father rowing. I have travelled that way more than once, listening to the songs that my father and mother sang as we sailed along, and have seen her draw in many a trout on the way. Good old times those, when the men in that region "chopped down and chopped up" acres and acres of woods; when they "sheared their own fleece and wore it." Let us rest in this little bay and talk of the times of old, when everything was wild and natural, before steamboats came ploughing their way through these waters, or the scream of the steam-whistle was heard.

Dr. WELLES was the first settler within miles of this locality. He came from Columbia county, in the summer of 17—, cleared a few acres, and put up a log house, and the next summer brought his family to reside here. Boards were scarce in those days. When he built his house he had enough for the roof and the floors, but not for the doors. When his family took possession, they hung blankets at the opening for doors, and the family for several nights slept on beds made up on the floor. The Doctor brought with him a negro slave, who rejoiced in the distinguished cognomen of Scipio Africanus, which by such liberties as white people take with the names of colored persons, was stripped of its euphony, and reduced to simple Sip. Old Sip, with the rest, had his bed in a corner. One morning it was discovered that his face was paler, and his hair straighter than common, his great white eyes had a bolder prominence. His hand trembled like that of a man who had indulged in a debauch over night, and his words were tremulous and incoherent. Something was evidently wrong with Sip. Nobody knew of his having been sick; he had made no complaint, he had uttered no groan, he had lain abed after the others were stirring, with the blanket drawn partly over his head, leaving only his great eyes glistening the more brightly in contrast with the ebony of his skin. The Doctor roused him from his bed, got him up on end, questioned and cross-questioned him, but could get nothing coherent from him, and it was not till a strong application of old Jamaica, that Sip's recollection came back, and enabled him to tell his story. He was laying awake long after the others had gone to sleep, when, as he affirmed, a great black animal pushed aside the blanket that hung in the place of a door, and walked around to the beds that were ranged on the floor, paused a moment at Sip's bed, and then walked leisurely out. There were two things confirmatory of Sip's story. First, he was frightened by something as near out of his wits as it was possible for a human being to be; and secondly, there was found on the boards of the floor several tracks resembling those made by a bear, when his foot is wet with dew, and the bottom of it covered with earth. Whatever the truth of the matter may have been, the Doctor believed the assertion of Sip, and the collateral evidence of the tracks, and always supposed that a bear had invaded the privacy of his dwelling that night. This anecdote I had from Judge WELLES, who is not a man to indulge in fictions.

It was a common thing for the deer to swim the lake in the summer time, and many were taken by the Doctor's family by pursuing them with a canoe in the water. On one occasion, a deer, as was supposed, was seen swimming across the lake, from the west, towards the eastern shore, and a daughter of the Doctor, who subsequently was the wife, and is now the widow of the late General GEO. MCCLURE, together with Sip, put out in a canoe in pursuit. Away off in the forest, among the new settlements, young ladies are more courageous than they are in the cities, and come to understand woodcraft, and love the wild sports of the forest and lake almost as well as their brothers do. I have seen those who could fire a rifle with the precision of a marksman, who could row a skiff or paddle a canoe with the best, who were successful anglers for the speckled trout, and could take the salmon trout with a trolling line on the lake. And yet, they lacked nothing of the natural refinement and innate modesty that belong to the true woman. I said the daughter of Doctor Welles and Sip started in pursuit of the deer that was swimming the lake. He swam but slowly, and they easily overtook him. The young lady was in the stern of the canoe, and Sip was in the bow. As they approached the game, Sip's eyes began to open with astonishment. "Golla, Missus," he cried, "dat deer am black—my! he ain't got no horns, he ain't got no long ears, nudder." As they approached nearer, Sip's paddle was suspended, and his teeth began to chatter—"Dat no deer, dat de debil," he shouted, as he tumbled over in the bottom of the canoe in utter affright. But whatever it was, the canoe was close upon it, and then it turned to give battle. It was a huge bear, and such a set of ivory as it showed was a sight to see. In the astonishment of the moment, the canoe had floated within reach of the now furious animal, and he threw his great paw up on the bow. "Let go dat," cried Sip, as, with a last effort of despair, he struck a furious blow with his paddle. The bear caught the oar with his paw, and hurled it to a distance in the water, but his hold of the canoe was loosed, and by a skilful movement, the young lady sent it beyond his reach. A spare paddle was in the canoe, and the way Sip and she pulled for the shore, was astonishing. They arrived in time for the Doctor to return with his gun and axe, and dispatch the animal before he reached the shore. See those stately old elms on the point, how they tower up towards the sky, stretching abroad their leafy arms in dalliance with the summer winds, and casting their morning shadows away out on the water. They grew there from the seed planted by the hand of nature, and where they stand others as gigantic have grown, till weakened by decay or riven by the lightning, the storm hurled them to the ground, to rot where they fell. In the times of old the deer crouched in the heat of noon in their shade. The elk may have browsed upon the tender plants beneath them, or the bear clambered up their great trunks. But they are gone now, and the willow, and smaller shrubbery planted by the hand of man, occupy their place. Strange that those stately old elms should have been removed to give place to trees of a lower dignity, and a meaner growth. Strange that when civilization sweeps away the old forests, it does not leave more of the ancient monarchs of the woods standing where they grew, as memorials of its triumphs over nature, and as witnesses of the achievements of human strength and labor.

Let us pass on down the lake. I must remind you that we have swept away these fields, and houses, and barns. We have restored the forest in its primitive grandeur. We have banished the horses, and cattle, and sheep, and have called back the wild animals that belonged here in the times of old. Five miles below "Welles' Point" we enter another little bay or cove, formed by a point of land running far out into the lake. I was here more than thirty years ago. It was all wild then, all woods. There was neither farm-house nor clearing in sight. On the voyage round the lake with the two Englishmen, as before mentioned, we rowed silently round this point, and saw a noble deer swimming out from the shore, as if starting across the lake. He had antlers like a stag, and when we came in sight, he wheeled towards the shore with the snort of a war-horse. The Englishmen had a rifle along, and as he was almost at the shore, one of them fired upon and killed him. He was a noble animal. We dined upon venison that day, and a more delicious meal I have never tasted, though it was cooked in a primitive way, by a fire built on the shore of the lake. From this little bay let us cross over to Bluff Point. We are opposite to it now. See how it looms up towards the sky, covered with a dense forest. The top of that hill is the highest land in sight, by hundreds of feet. It is no mountain peak, piercing, in stately barrenness, the heavens, but a rounded promontory, rising on three sides from the water, and seems to us, as we look upon it, like a great island in the midst of the lake. It seems close by us, and yet to reach its base we must row a mile and a half. See how the "West Branch" winds around, and seems to hide away behind and among the hills. Look away off towards Penn Yan. There, too, the lake seems to steal around behind high promontories, to lose itself in the forest of great trees. It was a beautiful view from this point "long ago," and it is beautiful still. Then it was romantic and wild, as nature made it, with all the old things standing round, as she placed them when she threw this earth finished from her hands.

Now it is robbed of its ancient dress, and decorated by the ingenuity, the labor, and the industry of man. Fields are where forests stood, and the things that civilization gathers around it, make up the landscape. Which is the more beautiful, I leave others to determine. For myself, I love nature in her old primitive garments, and I love civilization with her smiling, though painted face. I love the old woods, and I love the fields. I love the wild things, and I love the tame things too. All I bargain for is to leave me the birds, the happy, the free, the sweet-voiced birds. You may sweep away the forests. It is best that they should be removed. It is necessary for the progress, and to meet the necessities of humanity. Launch your steamboats upon lake and river, and send forth your iron horse, thundering along the valleys, spread out your farms, push back the woods with the fields, build your cities and towns, destroy the deer and the wild animals that must perish with the forests, but leave me the birds, the happy singing-birds, and I am content.

We will now row westward, around the base of Bluff Point, six miles to the head of the West Branch. On both sides of the branch the hills rise with greater or less acclivity, but nowhere so steep as to prevent cultivation. At the head of the branch is a beautiful valley stretching away to the northwest, through the centre of which winds a small stream alive with the speckled trout. Pines, and elms, and oaks, with the wild cherry, butternut and maple trees, constitute the principal growth of timber. Remember we are speaking still of "long, long ago." There is a neat village here now surrounded by rich farms. It was all forest when I passed a night on the banks here on my first voyage round the lake. We will pass along south again on our return to the head of the lake. The hill on the west side of the lake and the rising grounds for miles were covered with a forest of pines. High-growing stately trees, like the masts of a tall ship. No axe had as yet marred their beauty, and they stood here clothed in fadeless green, and murmuring softly and solemnly as the breeze stirred in their foliage. This forest of pines has been swept away, and you see fields of grain and pastures, and meadows where they stood.

We pass along to Ingersoll's Point, three miles from the head of the lake. We will land here, and see how this point of land was formed. We go a few rods on the main land, and we enter a ravine or gulf as it is called. The hill-side is steep, but we walk on a level, straight into the hill. A little stream goes laughing along over the smooth stones. It is tranquil and pleasant now, good-humored and gay; but when the snows are melting and the spring freshets come, it is a mad and a mighty torrent, roaring and foaming down the gorge, vast in volume and resistless in power. The rocks begin to rise on either hand higher and higher, and as we advance a perpendicular wall of slate rock rises on either side to the height of a hundred feet. Before us now the little stream trickles with a gentle voice down the shelving rocks, from away up towards the top of the hill, leaping from ledge to ledge. Our progress is stayed here, unless we choose to climb where a false step or a slip on the smooth rock would send us skiving in the gulf below. It is a goodly sight when the "stream is up," to see how it cascades down from the plain above into the gorge below, rushing, and tumbling, and roaring in white foam over the beetling rocks. "Ingersoll's Point," and the acres of flat land stretching out into the lake, were made by the earth excavated from the hillside by the stream when its back was up.

Captain GREIG is in his element to-day. He has a pic-nic party on board from Penn Yan, and they dine here on "Ingersoll's Point." He has a company of a hundred "fair women and brave men," married and single, all cheerful and happy. They have a band on board, and quadrilles, and waltzes, and polkas occupy the young people, while the elders look on, and like myself, think of the times when they were young, when they "went out a gypsey-ing," and were merry in the dance. The dinner was spread on "the point," under the shadows of the brave old elms and on the green grass beneath their spreading branches. Towards evening all were on board again, and the steamer started out on her return voyage. As the sun went down we swept across the head of the lake, in view of the pleasant village of Hammondsport, and then headed away for Penn Yan. The darkness came down calmly and stilly. The winds were hushed, not a ripple was on the water save the long wake in the rear of the boat. It was a pleasant thing to hear the echoes that came back from the hills, returning with a mellow harmony the music of the band; and it was pleasanter still to look upon the happy faces of the young people as they glided about in the mazes of the dance, or chatted in the fulness of their glee. That was an evening to be remembered, the return of that party from their pic-nic on "Ingersoll's Point."

I bid good-bye to the Crooked Lake with regret. I could linger here for months, busy with old memories and scenes of the "long, long ago"—scenes that like our youth belong to the returnless past, to be recalled only in fancy, that can come back to us only in dreams of the night.

I am at Bath, the county seat of Steuben. This is another beautiful village, nestling quietly among the hills of the Southern tier. It was among the early settlements of what was once called the Western Country. It was located by CHARLES WILLIAMSON, the first proprietor of several millions of acres, known as the Pultney estate. A pleasant farm that—one that might afford an industrious man, who exercised a proper degree of economy, a good living, and enable him to portion off with a fair number of acres a reasonably large family of children. It was not so valuable when Sir WILLIAM PULTNEY became the proprietor as it is now, as it passed into his hands, as I have heard, for something like a shilling an acre.

Bath is a pleasant and a thriving village, remarkable for its neatness and healthful location. On the East is a high mountain, rising in steep acclivity some eight or nine hundred feet, whose rugged sides can never be cultivated, and along whose base the Conhocton river flows. In the early times, before the Erie Canal was built, Bath was the outlet to market for the grain of a broad sweep of country. It was regarded as the head of navigation, and was to be the site of a great city. You will not of course suppose that great ships visited its port, or even the periogues, formerly so common on the waters of the great West. There was but one direction to navigation from Bath, and that was down stream. Arks were built of pine planks, which would carry some thousand or fifteen hundred bushels. They were queer-shaped craft, not very well calculated to stand a rough sea, but they were made water-tight, and cost from $75 to $100 each. These were floated to the storehouses that stood down by the river, and when the spring freshets came, the grain was turned into them in bulk, and covered from the rain; with a pilot, and a hand at each long oar that projected away out at bow and stern, started with their freight on a returnless voyage towards the Chesapeake Bay. Their course was down the Conhocton to the Chemung river, down that river to the Susquehanna, and down that noble river to tide water. These frail vessels did not always reach their destination. About one out of ten emptied its contents in the river as it was dashed against some unknown obstruction, or was stranded on the shore through the unskilfulness of its pilot. Thousands upon thousands of bushels of grain found their way to market through this precarious channel, and Bath was looming up, when the canals were built and its glory departed. The ark of the Conhocton passed into history, the rats took possession of the storehouses, board after board fell from their sides, the roofs caved in, the beams rotted away; at length what was left of them tumbled to ruin, and the place where they stood is now a meadow where the mower swings his scythe, unconscious that he treads on historical ground. The course of trade from Bath for more than a quarter of a century, has been to the North, through the Seneca and Crooked Lake, and the Cayuga and Seneca Canals to Montezuma, and then on the Erie Canal to the Hudson, and so to New York. It is now changing again, not to the ancient channel of the river, but to the New York and Erie Railroad, and so to New York by that great thoroughfare.

The mountains about Bath were famous, years ago, for deer, and I have spent many an exciting hour in the chase after them. It was a pleasant thing to start for the hills while the light was just breaking in the East, while a few stars glimmered faintly in the sky, and the grayness of twilight lingered in the valleys. To feel the grass crisp with frost beneath your footfall, and see the mist rising from the river, and creeping up the sides of the hills. It was a pleasant thing to stand on the brow of that high green hill over against the village, just as the sun was coming up from his resting-place, and see how he threw his early light on the tops of the hills on the east and west; to mark how the shadow retreated from their sides down towards the valley, and when he rose above the forest trees, how gloriously he started on his course. It was pleasant to look upon the clustered houses away down below you, and watch how the smoke came up from chimney after chimney, and went wreathing upward towards the sky. It was a pleasant thing to look upon the farms, the fields, and watch the flocks of sheep as they started from the fold, wending, in the early morning, in a long line towards their pasture, and the cows gathering around the place of their milching. It was a pleasant thing to look upon that little lake, sleeping so quietly just east of the village, and afar off to the north the Crooked Lake, stretching away and hiding itself among the highlands that surround it. All this I have looked upon more than once, while a pair of noble stag hounds were crouched at my feet, impatient for the chase. Turning from the pleasant landscape beneath me, I would strike into the woods. The forest extended back unbroken for miles then, and when I had passed a short distance from the brow of the hill, I would lay on the dogs. Glad enough they would be for the freedom to hunt. Far off in the woods, perhaps, the voice of the staunch old hound would be heard, deep and long drawn out. After a moment it would be heard again. The interval between his baying would become shorter and shorter, until the voice of both dogs would break out in a fierce and continuous cry, and then I would know that the game was up and away.

I need not tell you of the music there is in the voice of a pair of stag-hounds in the deep forests of a still morning. How it echoes among the mountains, and swells up from the valleys; how it comes like a bugle from the forest dells, and glancing away upwards, seems to fill the whole air with its joyous notes. Now the sound of the chase grows fainter and fainter, as it recedes, until it is lost in the distance, and the low voice of the morning breeze, whispering among the forest trees, alone is heard. Again faint and far off is heard the music of the chase, swelling up, and then dying away, like the sound of a flute in the distance, when the night air is still—clearer and more distinct it comes as the dogs course over some distant ridge. Now it is loud and joyous, making the woods vocal with the melody of voices. Again the music dies away as the dogs plunge into some hollow way until it seems to come up like the faint voice of an echo from some leafy dell. Again it swells louder and fiercer, as the chase, changing its direction, sweeps up the valley towards you. Louder and louder grows the music. You hear the measured bounds of the deer as he goes crashing on his way to the river, fleeing from the destruction that is howling on his trail. He passes beyond the range of your rifle, in his frightened course, and the dogs rush by you, running breast high on his track, and your Tally Ho! gives fresh impulse to their speed, and a fiercer and more joyous strain to their music. You hear in the distance the sharp crack of a rifle, that comes echoing up from the valley beneath you. In a few minutes the music of the hounds is still, and you know that your friend stationed at the river has secured his game.

The public buildings and the best residences of Bath are fronting its beautiful square of some six or eight acres. In the centre of the square "long ago," stood a tall pine that for years was known as the "liberty tree." It was left when the old forest was swept away, and stood there solitary and alone for nearly a quarter of a century. But it faded in seeming sorrow over the fate of its companions, that had been so ruthlessly destroyed. Its green branches died, one after another, till a bare trunk with leafless arms stretching out, as if in hopeless and barren desolation, was all that was left of that once stately monarch of the woods. It was at last hurled to the earth by the strong winds, and the place of the "liberty tree" was vacant.

I studied law in this pleasant village, under one whom I can never cease to respect. He resides here still, an honored, and justly honored citizen. A sore affliction has recently jarred among his heart-strings. May the wound that was inflicted be healed by the affectionate kindness of those that remain to comfort him, and may he find consolation in the memories that come up from the graves of the good, who pass away in the pride and strength of their early manhood.

There are "solid men" in Bath, too, as well as in Canandaigua. Men who, by their indomitable energy, have risen from comparative poverty to great wealth. Who started in life with only strong hands and stout hearts, but who have mastered fortune. Men who are still in the vigor, the strong time of life, and who can reckon their dollars by hundreds of thousands. The old settlers, the pioneers of Bath, are all gone. Many of them I knew "long ago." The tombstones that stand in the quiet grave-yard, that record their virtues, bear no lying epitaphs, nor lines of bitter irony respecting their worth.

I said I studied law in Bath. Let me relate an anecdote connected with the first suit I ever had the honor of appearing in as counsel. My friend, H. W. ROGERS, now of Buffalo, was my fellow-student then, and he will pardon me for relating the triumphs of the genius of two young men who were seeking distinction under some difficulties. A worthless scamp had been arrested for some misdemeanor—assault and battery, I believe—and being too poor to employ other counsel, applied to my friend ROGERS and myself to defend him, promising to pay us a small fee for assisting him in his trouble.

We readily undertook his defence, promising ourselves no light harvest of reputation from our first effort at forensic eloquence. A jury was summoned, and three magistrates sat in solemn judgment to hear the evidence against our unfortunate client. We had a day to prepare, and the speeches with which we intended to astonish the court, and confound the jury, were profoundly studied and reflected upon. Well, the evidence was closed, and, as was arranged beforehand, I rose to address the jury, and my friend was to follow. I got as far as "Gentlemen of the Jury," and there I stuck, like a pig in the fence. Not another sentence of my great speech could I utter, to save me. At length, in despair, I told the jury, "that as I was to be followed by my elder and abler associate, I would occupy no more of their time," and sat down in perfect confusion and shame. Friend Rogers then rose to deliver his maiden speech. He, too, got as far as "Gentlemen of the Jury," and there *he* stuck, as I had done before him. There was no use in trying to go on. The great speech was gone, not a word of it could he catch, not a sentence could he bring to mind. He was in a hopeless dilemma, but he extricated himself by saying to the jury that "the case had been so ably summed up by the counsel that had preceded him, that he felt it unnecessary to add a word to the argument," and he sat down with the big drops standing on his forehead. We were laughed at *some*, by those who gathered to hear our maiden efforts. The best of the joke was, that friend HARRY was several years in finding out that he had perpetrated a good thing at my expense.

There were formerly many excellent trout streams around Bath. Spalding's run, Neal's creek, the Campbelltown creek, the Michigan creek, the Twelve-mile creek, and Townsend's run, and many other pleasant streams that came down from the hills were famous in their day. That was before sawmills and high dams, and the other utilitarian devices of civilization poisoned the waters, or the multitude of anglers had destroyed their speckled inhabitants. Just below Bath, within a mile of the village, is Lake Salubria, a beautiful little sheet of water of some two or three hundred acres. It has neither inlet nor outlet above ground, but its waters are clear and pure. I was one of three or four that "long ago" put a hundred or more brook trout that we caught in the Townsend run with a net, alive into this lake. I remember the day well. We rigged a half hogshead with water on a lumber wagon and started for the run. We waded around in the water, and punching with long poles under the old logs and caverned banks, and having secured over a hundred, started for home. The heavens gathered blackness, and one of the severest storms I have ever known overtook us. The lightning flashed and the thunders rolled through the heavens, and the rain came rushing from the clouds in a deluge upon us. My Panama hat hung like an elephant's ears about my shoulders, and my very boots were filled with the drenching rain. We persevered, notwithstanding the storm, and got our hundred trout, all alive and active, into Lake Salubria. They did not, however, multiply as we hoped they would. For years one would hear occasionally of a great trout being caught in the lake, till at last they were all gone. They lacked the ripples and the running water. They lived to be old, and then died without progeny, "making no sign."

I am at Hornellsville, where the Buffalo and New York Railroad forms a junction with the

New York and Erie, in the valley of the Canisteo. Steuben is my native county, and I am at home among its high hills and beautiful valleys. Thirty years ago this town was a hamlet. A store, a wood tavern, a dwelling house or two, made up the village, and a solitary stage coach bore the only visitors, and constituted the only means of conveyance to and from its sequestered location. In the winter an army of lumbermen swarmed in the forests around, and the sound of the axe and the crashing of the tall pines as they thundered to the ground, broke the frozen silence of the woods. When the spring freshets came, the raftsmen started on their long journey down towards the Susquehanna, and away to the broad Chesapeake, and when they departed, Hornellsville was alone for the balance of the season. But now it has its brick blocks, its long streets, its tall steeples, its machine shops, its factories, and its mills, and the hum of business and the clank of machinery is everywhere heard. Long trains of cars, drawn by the iron horse, are rushing along almost hourly; the old stage-coach, with its fat driver, is gone, and the sound of his horn will be heard there never again. Broad farms are spread out in the valley, and the fields are creeping up the sides of the hill. Blessings on the valley of the Canisteo; blessings on the streams that come down from the mountains in which I have so often, in days that are past, angled for the speckled trout. Blessings on the pine-clad hills over which I have hunted the wild deer, and whose echoes I have so often wakened by the thrilling music of my hounds. Those brave old hills are here yet, covered with their summer foliage—defying by their steepness the farmer's plough, and laughing at what here I call the desolation of civilization. Fields may be green in the valleys, and flocks and herds may eat lazily of the rich pastures, but the rugged sides of these hills will remain unchanged. The tall pines may fall victims to the lumberman's axe, but the sides of these hills as they rise in steep acclivity towards the sky, will always, when the summer smiles, wear their garments of green in spite of human progress, and the wasting of the beauties of natural scenery that marks its career. Let me tell you a hunting anecdote. I was, many years ago, on a hunting excursion with my old friend Andrew Helmer (as staunch a woodman as ever "sighted a rifle") on the hills that skirt this beautiful valley. We were driving the ridges, as it is termed. From the logway at the brow of the hill, down which the pine logs were rolled, a timber road ran straight back, into what was then a forest of many miles in extent. In this road we stationed ourselves some sixty rods apart, but in plain sight of each other. There were two runways for the deer, one of which was beyond him and which he was to watch, and the other on the opposite side of me, which I was to take care of. Having taken our positions, a boy was sent into the woods to lay on the dogs. In a short time we heard the cry of the hounds—the game took a turn over a distant ridge—the hounds in hot pursuit—and their music was a pleasant thing to hear in that calm autumnal morning. In a short time the deer swept round the base of a hill, and instead of taking to the usual runway, dashed forward between Helmer and myself. The woods were thick, and we could only judge of his whereabouts, by his measured bounds and the crash of the brush, as he sped in his terror from the cry that was close behind him. I knew that he could be seen only as he crossed the timber road, and what was done for his destruction must be done quickly. I stepped into the middle of the narrow road, and raised my rifle to my shoulder. As I did so, there stood Helmer with his rifle poised and pointed straight at me, and it seemed to me that I could look into the barrel, away down to the ball, which, if it should chance to miss the deer, would stand a smart chance of hitting me. I knew Helmer too well to doubt of his taking the chances of firing whether he hit me, or I hit him, or we both hit the deer. A large pine stood invitingly close by the road—I lost no time in getting behind it, but as the deer came crashing up to the road, I leaned out, and as he leaped across, fired and dodged back. Helmer's rifle answered to mine like an echo, and the deer fell in the edge of the brush, dead; but one ball struck him, and that I claimed.

Helmer claimed it as his, and though I never gave up the point, yet truth compels me to admit there were two slight circumstances in his favor. *The ball-hole was on his side of the deer, and we cut a rifle bullet from a tree, slightly out of range of the deer, and the side of that tree where we found the bullet was towards where I stood.*

II.

NIAGARA—PORTAGE—WELLSVILLE—COUDERSPORT.

I AM here in sight of old Niagara, and within the sound of its thundering voice. I have never before seen this exhibition of grandeur spread out here, to humble the pride of man, and show forth the power and majesty of God. I look for the first time upon this stupendous panorama, so full of all that is grand and glorious, all that is beautiful and sublime. Here is the drainage of more than 150,000 square miles of the great lakes, those inland seas that lay out West and North, the hundred rivers and streams that come into them from the hills and broad plains, and the thousand springs that bubble up away down in their silent depths—all these "mighty waters" are concentrated into a narrow gorge of less than half a mile in width, and, impelled by a resistless hand, they go boiling and heaving, roaring and struggling, like some gigantic monster in his wrath and agony, rushing forward in their matchless power, to plunge in wild fury down beetling cliffs into the returnless depths below. The voice of the cataract is never silent. In summer and winter, in the brightness of noonday and the darkness of midnight, its roar is on the air. When the great flood subsided, from the time when the dove brought back the olive branch, and the raven went forth on his solitary and returnless flight—when the Ark rested on Ararat, it was heard, shaking the earth with its roar; and the sound that then startled the wilderness will be heard till the crack of doom—that mighty flood will roll on, over the shelving rocks and down the stupendous precipice, till the time appointed for the earth's destruction shall come. I have stood on the brow of that precipice, and looked upon the rushing waters as they were hurled into the deep abyss; I have stood at its base, and looked upward at the beetling cliffs, and seen that flood as it seemed to me rushing in appalling grandeur from the sky—around me was the mist and the spray, and arching above me was the rainbow, glowing in prismatic brightness, like that which spans the rear of the retiring storm. I have looked upon the cataract in the calmness of a clear night, and seen the stars as they stole out one after another from the deep vault of the sky, as if to watch its eternal flow. The voices that elsewhere break the stillness of nocturnal repose are here forever silent, as if awed by the sublimity of its power. But one sound is heard, deep, solemn, and ceaseless—never changing, never losing its intensity. When the storm rages, it is heard above the storm. When the winds rave and the tornado sweeps by, it is heard above the winds, and the wild fury of the tornado. 'Tis the voice of the Cataract!

But who shall describe Niagara? Let it flow on in its majesty, till man shall conquer its fury, and make it subservient to his will; till he shall "lay his hand upon its mane" and tame it into subjection; till human genius shall chain it to the great water-wheel, and make it a motor to endless machinery—grind corn to satisfy human hunger, and throw the shuttle and spin. Unless some new discovery shall render valueless water-falls as motors, even Niagara will, in the course of human progress, one day be compelled to become utilitarian, and perform an active part in the great drama of life.

There is one thing in regard to Niagara that strikes. It can have no rival. Saratoga may become antiquated—the sea-shore a resort only for invalids. Fashions may change in regard to pleasure resorts. Rival locations may compete by opposing attractions. But Niagara can have no rival. The flood will sweep on over the precipice, the waters will boil and foam, they will struggle and heave down the rapids, rushing on forever, and the roar of the cataract will be there through all time. Its deep, thundering voice of power, will be heard in its solemn intensity; its ceaseless sermon of the majesty, the omnipotence of God, will be preached while the waters flow, and stupendous precipices confine them within the changeless gorge. In all the world there is but one Niagara, and all the world will visit the mighty show. You may build up a city there, you may make long streets, and line them with houses, and crowd them with people; you may rob it of its wild scenery, and strip it of the things that nature spread out all around it, you may construct canals and erect machinery, but still the great cataract will be there, and the world will travel hundreds and thousands of miles to see it. They will go to the brow of the precipice to look down, and to the base of the precipice to look up. They will involve themselves in the mist and the spray for the sake of gazing upon the rainbow that is above them. They will ramble on Goat Island by moonlight listening to the roar of the waters, or enjoy its cool and pleasant shades at noon-day. You may roll your great water-wheels in their ceaseless rounds; you may harness your machinery and set your great hammers in motion; your hundred strong hands may hurl the ponderous sledge against the ringing anvil; you may set your ten thousand puny machinists at pounding the iron and driving the spikes, make all the noise you can, and the roar of the cataract will drown it all.

I am at Portage, and a wild place it is too—Niagara in minature. I am standing on the high bridge. A train of cars has just rushed by me away up in the sky, higher than the top of the tallest forest tree, two hundred and fifty feet above the surface of the water below. Think of a train of cars thundering through the air, higher than the weathercock on the loftiest steeple, hurled forward at a speed of forty miles to the hour. It passes within six feet of me, there is a blast of wind, a rushing, roaring sound, and the train is gone—it vanishes around a point of the forest, and while I stand in mute astonishment, the snort of the iron horse is heard miles away. But the bridge remains firm; there is no swaying or yielding; a slight tremor, and the deep rumble, is all that tells you you are not on the solid ground. The genius of man has conquered the "great gulf" that intervened between the perpendicular precipices, and you pass in security over the mighty chasm, as on a level plain. Just below the bridge, the river leaps down a precipice of sixty feet. Further down, but in sight, it leaps down again some eighty feet; and lower still, it plunges again down a precipice of the same depth. You will remember that the surface above these falls is level. You look down from the bridge, and your companion in the gorge below looks like a boy, and you wonder why the lady that is on his arm is not in pantaletts and kilts; that a child so small should dress like a woman, and carry a parasol, surprises you. Pass down to the lower falls, take your stand by a dwarfed cedar that grows out from the rocks and shoots upward, and look over the cliff into the fearful depths below. You are nearly five hundred feet above the level of the water, and there is nothing but air between you and the boiling stream. You can plunge down from that dizzy height, if you will, and rest in quiet beneath the wave. There will a voice whisper in your ear to take the fearful leap. Beware of the tempter and stand back, for there's a fascination in the whirling waters, and your brain may yield to its power.

> "Come on, sir, here's the place. Stand still—
> How fearful and dizzy 'tis to cast one's eyes so low
> The crows and choughs that wing the midway air
> Show scarce so gross as beetles: half way down
> Hangs one that gathers samphire; dreadful trade.
> Methinks he seems no bigger than his head.
> The fishermen that walk upon the beach
> Appear like mice. The murmuring surge,
> That on the unnumbered idle pebbles chafes,
> Cannot be heard so high. I'll look no more,
> Lest my brain turn, and the deficient sight
> Topple down headlong."

I am at Wellsville, a village in Allegany county, on the Erie Railroad, and on the borders of the State of New York. It is situated on the Genesee river, which here is a comparatively small stream. It is the lumber depôt for a broad sweep of country. Boards and plank are piled up here in vast quantities, waiting transportation to the east, and long lines of teams are drawing more from the country beyond. I counted twelve loaded wagons pass the door of the public house where I am stopping, within half an hour. I have been here, too, years since, when there was not an acre cleared for miles below this, towards the north; when it was all wilderness from a few miles south of Angelica, away to the southern and eastern slope of this portion of the Allegany mountains. I once came with a party of fishermen, among whom was SAMME FITZHUGH, Esq., of Livingston county, a man known for many years through all the Genesee country, for his social qualities, and his skill and science as a sportsman. He has gone to his rest now. We left Angelica on the occasion spoken of, and went up the Genesee to where Philipsburgh now stands. There was a dam there which had been constructed years before, in connection with which a mill and fulling mill had been built; but the mill had been burned down, and the place deserted. There was no one living within several miles of it. We followed the river for some three or four miles above where Wellsville now stands, and then camped down for the night. In the morning we started down the stream again; our object was in part to examine the timber land, which one of our party had bought, or was about buying, and in part to have a good time with the trout in the river. It was no trick, then, to take trout in the Genesee river weighing from a quarter of a pound to a pound and a half, beautiful yellow-finned fellows. The country was wild enough then; I have never seen it since until now, and can hardly believe, as I look upon it, that it is the same locality that I saw then, covered with gigantic pine trees, and away beyond civilization. I have been wondering, as I heard the cars passing, what we would have thought, as we lay in our blankets, sleeping on boughs that night that we "camped out," away off here in the woods "long ago," had we heard the scream of the steam-whistle, and the roar of a train of cars coming thundering along the gorges of the mountains, as they now do, startling the sleeping echoes, and chasing slumber from our eyes. I've a notion we should have stared *some.*

I am at Coudersport, the county seat of Potter county, in the State of Pennsylvania. I have crossed the high ridge that separates the waters of the Genesee from those of the Allegany. This is a sequestered little place, nestling among the hills, on one of the remote branches of the Allegany. The people here have a semi-weekly mail, and some of them take a weekly paper, but not many. They are engaged in building a very large court-house for so small a place, and upon inquiry I find it is built mainly by taxes levied upon the immense tracts of non-resident lands of the county. I say mainly by such taxes, because, although the tax purports to be general and equal upon all lands according to their value, yet a shrewd assessor, who knows the resident from the non-resident owners, can so discriminate as to lay the burden upon the shoulders of those who own immense tracts and live at a distance. This, it strikes me, is no bad way of providing means to erect good public buildings, without burdening, to a very serious extent, those who are encountering the difficulties incident to the settlement of a new country.

We leave Coudersport *en route* for the Sinnemahoning, a river that has its source in the same range of highlands with the Genesee and the Allegany. This ought, "upon principle," to be the highest land east of the Mississippi. It can be proved to be so by a very simple, and apparently conclusive course of argument. The Genesee river rises here, and flows off north to Lake Ontario, and so through the noble St. Lawrence to the ocean. The Allegany flows west and south, and is the remotest eastern and northern branch of the Ohio, that finds its way to the ocean by the Gulf of Mexico, while the Sinnemahoning reaches "the great deep" through the Chesapeake Bay. But high as this region is—and it is high enough and cold enough for all practical purposes—it is by no means the highest region of the Alleganies.

III.

LAKE CHAMPLAIN.

BURLINGTON — KEESEVILLE — AU SABLE FORKS—FRANKLIN FALLS—SARANAC LAKE—ROUND LAKE—TUPPER LAKE—BOG RIVER—ON THE BANKS—THE BLACK FLY.

I AM on the Champlain, in the steamer *America*. She is a staunch and beautiful boat, under the command of Captains Flagg and Mayo, two as intelligent and gentlemanly commanders as can be found on the American waters—men who understand their business thoroughly, and whose attention and politeness to their passengers are worthy of all imitation. This steamer is a most staunch one, furnished with great elegance and care, and she goes ploughing on her way with a steadiness and speed rarely equalled. I write this in a stateroom, while the boat is in motion, and you may judge of the quiet way in which we move along.

I have been for hours on the deck of the boat, watching by the moonlight the changing scenery along the shore. On the one hand are the mountains of Essex looming up dark and shadowy, their bare heads glistening in the moonlight, and the forests along their base and up their rugged sides resting in sombre blackness like a shroud, save where here and there some bluff and bare rock shines out midway up the mountain. Away off on the right are the Green Mountains, standing out in bold relief against the sky, upon which the starry covering appears to rest, or behind which it seems to hide itself. Away off in front of the vessel are islands, seeming with their green trees like gigantic war vessels floating darkly on the Lake. While behind is a long stream of light, where the moonbeams are thrown back by the agitation of the waters. By the way, why is it that nobody praises Champlain? Why have tourists neglected to chronicle the charming scenery around it? To my notion, it is one of the most beautiful sheets of water in the world.

There are a thousand romantic bays, that steal landward around jutting promontories, lying in the deep shadow-like entrances to immense caverns; a hundred beautiful islands; green fields stretching away to the base of the hills, tall precipices rising in ragged and beetling cliffs right up from the deep waters, upon the tops of which stand old primeval trees, like sentinels upon the battlements of some ancient castle. As we ploughed along in view of Ticonderoga and Crown Point, the chimneys of the ruined fortifications stood up in solemn stillness, while Mount Defiance, on the top of which Burgoyne planted his cannon, looked grimly down upon the desolation and decay beneath it. Did you ever try to call up the ghosts of the dead men whose names history has linked to the ruins upon which you may be looking, and locating them in imagination, as history locates them—make them do again the deeds that gave them immortality? While I sat on the deck of the steamer as we passed the ruins on these points, I saw in imagination the little army of Ethan Allen, emerging from the forest on the Vermont side of the Lake; I saw them crossing the narrow channel from point to point; not a word was spoken, not an oar splashed in the water, not a sound disturbed the stillness. I saw their muskets lowered, lest the sheen of the moonlight from their bright barrels or from their bayonets, might attract the notice of their enemies. I saw them as they landed noiselessly upon the beach and formed into columns for attack. I looked away to the fort. The ruins were gone. The fortification stood there in its strength. I saw the cannon as they were ranged along the top of the walls looking threateningly over the waters. I saw the sentinels as they marched back and forth, unsuspicious of danger. I read their thoughts as they tramped their lonely rounds. Their hearts were away across the ocean to their homes in their native land. Parents, brothers, sisters, perchance their little children were about them, and I could see the tears gather in their eyes while memory was bringing loved faces around them.

Suddenly a tumult, a wild cry of alarm, a shout of triumph broke the stillness of the night, as Allen and his sturdy followers came plunging over the walls into the very heart of the fort. Resistance was in vain. The surprise was complete, and with the firing of but four or five guns and the death of two soldiers the stronghold of the English was lost and won. I saw the astonished Briton when the surrender of his post was demanded in the name of the "Great Jehovah and the Continental Congress." I saw him as he stood in his *deshabille* surrendering his sword to the conquerors, and the stars and stripes as they were run up to float in the night winds, and while the shout and hurrah of victory echoed among the mountains and went floating over the Lake, the vision melted away. The dead men went back to their graves, the ruins as they have stood for fifty years, battling with time, resumed their solemn shape, and desolation and decay again came over the place where brave men fought and bled and died.

I am at Burlington, the largest and most flourishing town in Vermont. It is not a city. Vermont *has* but one city, and that of the smallest. This is her only port. She lays away from the Ocean, inland, and the Champlain, until recently, was her only outlet to the markets of the great cities. This is a most beautiful town, situated on an elevated plain, overlooking the lake. From the College green you look away over the water, on the one hand, and beautiful rural scenery on the other. There are many pleasant situations, fine gardens, and splendid residences in Burlington; and there are many "solid men" here, too; solid in wealth, in business capacity, and in the hospitalities that adorn life. Looking out on the lake, you see many beautiful Islands, conspicuous among which is one on which stands the light-house, some three miles from the main shore. On the left of this, and mid-way between it and another beautiful Island, a solitary rock lifts its sharp head, some twenty-five feet from the surface, remaining there always, treeless and shrubless, all alone, throwing back the waves when the winds sweep over the waters, and moveless and solemn when the moon looks down on the still surface of the lake. Further off, still, are two small Islands, covered with tall trees, that seem to rise right up from the water. No brush, no water-grass, no sandy shore surround them; but they appear to go straight up from the deep water, and in the distance, with a haze in the atmosphere, look like great war-vessels with a press of black canvass spread from invisible masts. Burlington is a busy place. I see far out on the lake two steamers, coming in opposite directions towards the docks, and I hear the roar of a steam-whistle off to the South, as a train of cars comes thundering in from

Boston, while another iron horse is rushing with a ponderous train from Rouse's Point. Here and there, all over the lake, as far as the eye can reach, are seen the white sails of smaller craft, moving in every direction; some up the lake, some down, and some beating across, all seeming bent on progress towards or from a market.

Burlington must be a most delightful summer residence. The air is so pure, so bracing, the drives so pleasant in every direction; the scenery around so enchanting, that I wonder it is not preferred by everybody to the crowded and cramped-up places of fashionable resort.

There is good lake fishing at Burlington. In the early morning before the sun had come up over the eastern hills, I went out with a boatman on the water; I saw the first rays of the morning as they lighted on the peaks of Essex. I saw them chase the shadow down the sides of the mountains, and I saw them when they first glanced across the surface of the lake, making it shine like molten silver as the fresh morning breeze swept over it. I hauled in some three or four noble fish on my way to the light-house Island, and as many more on my return, on a trolling line of three hundred feet in length. It was a glorious morning; the breeze was so fresh and the air so bracing, that I was tempted to shout and hurrah with gladness, as I floated over the water. It made me young again. The spirit of boyhood came over me, and I felt as of old, before gray hairs had gathered upon my head, or stiffness had seized upon my joints. A beautiful and a pleasant town is Burlington. The lake that lays spread out before it is beautiful. Its mornings are glorious, its summer breezes bracing, exhilarating, healthful; everything around it is beautiful, heavenly in the summer time, and between you and I when I become rich, I shall have a country seat somewhere in the neighborhood of the College parks, with my fine horses and carriage, my boats on the lake, my rowers dressed after the latest sailor fashion, strong-armed, and skilful in the use of the oar. I shall have my trolling lines, and all the apparatus for fishing in perfection, and every morning while the last stars are shining dimly in the sky, struggling with the morning beams, while the grayness of twilight lingers in the valleys, I'll be out on the water, to welcome the rising day, and haul in the bass, the pike, and the pickerel. Towards evening, I'll ride round the country, and at night gather my friends around me and be jolly, (not with wine or strong drink. I have parted company with them.) Won't we, my friend, have a good time when I get rich?

I am at Keeseville, a pleasant and thriving village, five miles from the Lake, on the Au Sable River. Immense quantities of nails and bar-iron are made on this stream, at, and within a few miles of Keeseville. There is a capital water-power here, which is fully occupied. The water-wheel travels its ceaseless rounds. The bellows are puffing, the fires are blazing, and the gigantic rollers are in motion. The nail-making machines are constantly at work, day and night—the clank of machinery is mingling with the roar of the waters. It is a hot day, and great drops of sweat are chasing each other down the cheeks of the stalwart operatives, as they handle the blazing iron, drawing it at a white heat, sparkling and throwing off scintillations from the furnaces, and passing it through the great rollers, or lifting the melted ore from its bed of fire, and placing it beneath the gigantic pressing machine which converts it into blooms. This operation requires strength of muscle, as well as of constitution, and powers of endurance. It requires some skill, too, and a raw hand would make small progress, till experience has taught him wisdom.

It is a pleasant thing to see one of these great workshops in the night time. The glare of the forges, the intense light of the chunks of iron as they came at a white heat from the blazing furnace, to see them pass through the immense rollers as they are formed into fitness for nail-making, coming out from the pressing machine longer and longer, increasing in length, stretching out and running along the floor like fiery serpents, while the stalwart operatives handle them with iron tongs, as if they were harmless things.

The Gorge is some two miles below Keeseville —one of the greatest curiosities of this country. The river goes roaring, and plunging, and cascading, more than a mile, through a chasm some thirty feet wide, on either side of which the rocks rise in perpendicular precipices from one to two hundred feet in height. On the top of these ledges you may stand, on the very verge of these great high walls, and look away down upon the boiling waters as they go surging and roaring on their way. This chasm does not seem to have been worn out by the river in its everlasting flow, but to have been made by the parting of the hills. The rocks on one side are counterparts of the rocks on the other, as if pulled apart. Rock matches rock, and shape is fitted to shape. An indentation on the one side, is matched by a prominence on the other, and you can see plainly that if the river could be withdrawn, and the chasm pressed together, the two sides would fit like the halves of an apple that had been cleft by the blade of a knife. Above Keeseville are evidences that a lake once covered what is now a beautiful valley, stretching away for miles to the southwest, and through which the Au Sable now flows. Where now are rich farms, was once the bottom of this lake, and fishes sported above the fields that are now rich meadows, or covered with grain. Some mighty power, centuries upon centuries ago, struggling in the remote depths of the earth, upheaved these hills, till the surface parted, leaving this Gorge, through which the pent-up waters rushed, emptying the lake of its contents, and giving its foundations to the world as a place for man to beautify, over which the ploughshare should pass, and his flocks and herds feed.

Some three miles west of Keeseville is Halleck's Hill, standing on which, and looking to the north, you see, not a rugged mountain scenery, where giant ranges stretch away, and tall peaks lift their bald heads to the clouds. There is no desolation, no wild and rocky sterility, but a beautiful, level plain, a valley reaching away for miles, rich in agricultural products, and teeming with the evidences of wealth and civilization. Away off to the right is the Champlain. The spires of Plattsburgh may be seen in the distance, seeming to rise like white pillars from the depths of a belt of forest, while in front of them can be viewed the spot where was fought the naval battle of Lake Champlain, in the last war. The beautiful landscape before me is the valley of the little Au Sable. It was settled by Quakers, men of peace, who till the ground in quiet, and never go up to the wars with weapons of destruction in their hands. The spot where these peaceful people, startled by the booming cannon, went up and stood to view the conflict on the Lake, when McDonough and Downie fought against each other, is near me. These men of peace were patriots. They loved their country, and while from principle they refrained from the shedding of human blood, yet their hearts and their prayers were with their countrymen, against their country's foes. When the smoke of the battle floated away, and the triumph of American arms was manifest, there went up a shout of gladness, a loud hurrah from these honest Quakers, which showed that the "old man" was strong within them.

In plain view from where I stand is the little Island on which the killed in that memorable battle were buried. There, in the midst of the lake, side by side in amity, rest the bones of those who struggled against each other on that day of mortal strife. Death is a queller of animosities, and the hands that struck at each other in life are quiet enough in the grave. Brave men are sleeping on that little island. It should be regarded as consecrated ground, and a tall monument should be erected to their memory. It should be made to speak of the noble daring of the men who perilled and lost their lives for their country. There are no rich men buried there. No titled men. They were the sailors, men who stood by the great guns, and whose breasts were bared to the foe. They were what the world calls common men, and who, had they survived the battle, would have lived and died without fame; but they are just the men who win victories, and bring fame to commodores and generals, and upon whose bravery hangs the result of battles. Over these bones of these brave men buried here, these poor men, these sailors, these "common men," should be erected what will save them from desecration, and tell to the far-off generations how stoutly they fought, and how bravely they fell in the cause of their country.

I am at the AU SABLE FORKS, a small town in extent but great in respect to the business done in the way of manufacturing iron. The ROGERS' have their principal forges and nail factories here. Almost every man is an operative, or connected with the business of iron-making in some way. You meet the coal man with his face blackened by coal dust, and you meet the bloomer, (not those of the short gowns and pantaletts), but those who handle the blazing iron, covered with the dust and rust of the forge. You meet the teamster with his short pipe and California hat, and you admire his independence as he sits upon his load of nails or blooms, or bars of iron, sending the smoke from his tobacco-pipe wreathing gracefully upward, and his voice has a cheerful ring as he cries "gee whoa" to his sober team. You meet the lumberman, with his bushy beard and long whiskers, with his axe on his shoulder, and his great boots on the outside of his pantaloons. He is just from the woods in the far interior, where he has been making war upon the pine forest trees, hurling them to the earth, shaping them into logs, and transporting them in rafts down the rivers and over the rapids and falls, to the mills. His labors are over until the fall snows come again. He will work in the harvest fields, or fish or hunt till then, when he will dive again into the forest, to winter in his cold shantee, and make war on the old pine trees. Of these lumbermen's shantees I shall tell you more hereafter. They are a great feature in the Chateaugay, the Saranac, and the Raquette woods. You meet the miner, covered with the debris of the ore, among which he delves away down in the bowels of the earth; a man who spends twenty out of the twenty-four hours in darkness, either that of the night or that of the mines into which the daylight never looks. Everybody in this little town is busy.

I am on the elevated plain between the Au Sable and the Saranac rivers. A broad sweep of country, bare of timber, yet without fields or houses. Here is a tract of thousands of acres, that of old was covered with great pine trees and other timber of a large growth. First the lumberman attacked and swept away the pines—then the charcoal men swept away the other large trees, and last of all the fire went rushing and roaring over this plain completing the desolation, leaving blackness and utter lifelessness behind it. No living thing, whether animal or vegetable, remained on its tract. The fire had extinguished or driven them all away. An old resident told me of the "great burning," as he termed it, of this plain. "It was," said he, "of a hot September morning, the wind blew fresh and strong from the west. Somehow the fire got out from the coal pits, on the western border of the plain, among the dry tree-tops and dead limbs, and brush, and spread out sideways, and every way for miles. By-and-bye as the wind rose to a gale, it started on its career across the plain. It was a glorious as well as a fearful sight, to see it leaping forward and upward, swirling and flashing onward, crackling and roaring like thunder, and sending the smoke in dark and dense columns, curling, and wreathing, and rolling towards the sky. The deer and other wild beasts fled wildly and madly before it, towards the mountains, or across the cleared fields of the valley. Fortunately there were no people inhabiting this plain, and the few that chanced to be along the road, fled to the settlement below. It was a grand sight that burning, a thing that is to be seen but once in a man's lifetime."

The view from this plain is a magnificent one, if we regard as such only wild and desolate grandeur, where no sign of civilization crosses the vision. On the south and east, lofty peaks loom up towards the sky. The highest and boldest of them all, is the baldfaced mountain, the head of which stands glistening in the sunlight, like the white locks of some ancient giant. Away off beyond this, dim and hazy against the sky, are the peaks of the Adirondacks, Mount Marcy, and Mount Seward, the loftiest of these, while on every side, peaks of a lower stature, mountains of less notable height, bound the vision. It is a goodly thing to pause here of a clear morning, and look upon the things around you, standing as they do in everlasting silence just where God placed them, and no land mark of civilization, no cottage or field, to tell of the destruction to natural things, which marks human progress. I love these old mountain ranges, and the Lakes that lay sleeping under their shadows, and the streams that wind around their base.

I am at Franklin Falls, a little village some eighteen miles from the AU SABLE Forks. It is situated on the Saranac River. There is a fall in this stream here, of some thirty feet, across which a dam has been thrown, and the water has been made to operate one of the largest and finest saw-mills in the State, a mill capable of turning out some forty thousand feet of lumber per day. There is here a large tavern house for so small a place, which is well kept, a larger store, and a score or more small but neat cottages clustered around them. Two years ago the present summer, this little town, with the mill and everything in the shape of a building, every out-house, shed, and fence, was clean wiped out. A "fire in the woods" came sweeping down from the southwest, driven forward by the gale, hurled onward by the strong winds in resistless fury. In an hour it had passed on, leaving in its track only smouldering ruins and the blackness of desolation. Every vestige of houses, mills, great lumber piles, stables, barns, everything that would burn had been given to destruction, and the villagers were grouped about congratulating each other on their own fortunate escape from a terrible fate. But enterprise has conquered the desolation, and a better mill, a better store, better hotel and better houses, now stand where those that were swept away by the fire stood. These fires in the woods are fearful things in this section of the State. You will remember that this was, of old, a lumber region, or rather there were thousands and hundreds of thousands of pine trees scattered all over the woods. These have been mostly chopped away, and their dead branches, dried tops and foliage, as they lay where they fell, make rich food for the flames. The foliage of the spruce and hemlock, green though it be, is combustible, and when a fire chances to get loose, and the winds are on the wing, the flames move forward with a speed and power which nothing can resist. I witnessed one of these fires in the woods years ago. It was in the night-time, and I was floating on the waters of Tupper's Lake. It came rushing and roaring around the base of a mountain, flashing and leaping upward and sideways, and every way, as the wind impelled it onward, or in gustful eddies laterally among the combustible materials in its reach. For a few minutes it would dash forward before the wind, and then seem to pause as if for breath, the flames going straight up among the foliage of the fir-trees, like gigantic torches. Again it would leap forward as the wind returned, pushing the flames in long streams onward among the branches, like the fiery tongues of great serpents. The surface of the lake was lighted up like the day, and its waters was the barrier at last, against the progress of the fire. When it reached the lake, it died gradually away, and when I awoke in the morning, a track of blackness a quarter of a mile in width, trees standing up in charred and leafless desolation, and here and there smoking logs and chunks among which the burning lingered, marked the track of this "fire in the woods."

I am at the Saranac Lake, at the "Saranac House," kept for the accommodation of sportsmen in the summer, and lumbermen in the winter. This is a decent, respectable country tavern, standing literally at the end of the road, and kept by pleasant and obliging people. It is on a beautiful little bay, of some hundred acres, at the north end of the lake. All around are the old woods, the ancient forest standing as it grew, and as it has stood for thousands of years.

The shores of this bay are bold and rocky, save a few acres at the head of it, where the inlet enters. Here the pond lilies spread their great round leaves over the surface, and the brilliant yellow and white blossoms shine out like stars of silver or gold, on the water. We arrived here a little after sundown, while the glad songs of the day were being hushed, and the night voices were coming abroad on the air. High above all was the music of the frogs, that was kept up all the long night, making the woods and lakes vocal with their deep sepulchral notes. By the way, I have seen frogs in my day, that might claim to be sizeable animals, but I have seen nowhere else this kind of amphibia at all comparable in dimensions to those of the Lower Saranac. Great plump green fellows, that would weigh a pound or two, and thousands of them, having voices deeper and louder than that of the bassoon or the brazen serpent; and when they strike up together, the whole air is full of sound. The leaves of the pond lilies are the largest I have ever seen, some of them being full a foot in diameter. On one of these great leaves, some patriarch frog will seat himself towards night, with his great round leaden eyes protruding from his head, his long limbs gathered under him, his wide mouth stretched in a changeless grimace, and as the twilight gathers, he will inflate his ponderous and pouched jaws like a bellows, and send forth sounds that would astonish the puny froglings of the marshes of the Hudson. There is a peculiarity about the melody of the frogs here, that I never noticed before. For a little while all will be still, save the shrill note of the little peeper close along the shore. Then from his leaf, away out on the lake, some deep-mouthed croaker will bellow out, while from every direction, voice after voice will fall in, until as it were a solid roar fills the air. Gradually this will die away and for a minute or two all will be still, and this succession of sound and silence goes on until the sun lights up the day again.

Directly opposite the Saranac House, and across a low ridge, through the forest a half mile or more, is a little lake say of two thousand acres, which is a perfect gem. Its waters are clear and cold, the banks, save a little patch at the south, bold and bluff, the hills rising gradually from the water's-edge, little bays stealing around and hiding behind rocky points, laying there in eternal shadow; as a whole it is one of those beautiful little sheets of water, which is the more charming because the eye can take in at once all its delightful scenery. As we rowed around it, we saw on a natural meadow of some three or four acres, two noble deer feeding. We paddled silently to within eight or ten rods of them, when they seemed to scent us. They raised their heads and looked all around, but as we were perfectly moveless at the time, they did not seem to notice us; still, they were alarmed and uneasy, evidently satisfied that there was danger some-

13*

where. At length we rose up in the boat, and shouted, and it would have done you good to see how they hoisted their white flags, and with what prodigious bounds they went snorting and scampering away.

I am at Round Lake, ten miles from the Saranac House, on my way to the Raquette River, Tupper's Lake, and the wild regions that lay around the sources of Bog River. We left Martin's this morning, in a little water-craft, made of thin cedar boards, and which weighs perhaps a hundred and twenty pounds. This little boat, light as it seems, and tottlish and unsteady as it may be when unloaded, will carry four persons, and a reasonable amount of baggage, with perfect safety, over these beautiful waters. These rivers and lakes are the highways, the turnpikes, the railroads of these high and wild regions, and these little boats are the carriages, the stage coaches, and the cars, in which everybody must travel. You start from the head of the Lower Saranac, and with a few carrying places, over which the sturdy boatman trudges with his boat on his back, you go a circle of a hundred miles in diameter; you traverse the Lower Saranac, Round Lake and the Upper Saranac; you cross the "Indian carrying place" of a mile, along a pleasant and beaten path through the woods. Then you launch again, on a series of ponds and down Stony Brook, to the Raquette River, and then up or down that beautiful water-course, as your fancy dictates, to the lakes beyond; you meet every little while a boatman, returning from a journey to the woods, alone or with passengers who have been on a sporting trip among the lakes and forest streams. The rowers rest a moment on their oars, kindly greetings are passed, news of the sports and from the outside world are exchanged, and each passes on his way. A turn in the river, or an island in the lake, hides him from your view, and you are alone again.

While we were packing our traps in our boat at Martin's in the morning, an incident occurred which occasioned some amusement, at whose expense I will not now say. The shore where the boat was landed was bold, going down steep into the water. The bow of the little craft lay upon the bank, and the stern on the water some four feet in depth. The party were all in the house save one who stepped into the boat for the purpose of placing a small pail of butter under the stern seat. His weight tipped the bow clear of the land, and the boat started out on the water. Turning to see what the difficulty was, and forgetting for a moment the care necessary to steady the craft beneath him, he lost his balance, the boat glided out from under him, and he went down like a great frog, head foremost into the water, and came up in five feet depth, wet as a drowned rat. Fortunately the water was not cold, and what was better, nobody happened to see him as he crawled out upon the shore, every hair of his head and every thread of his garments dripping like an eave-trough. It was a goodly sight to see him there, shaking himself like a Newfoundland water-dog, or standing up straight and stiff, to let the water run off from his saturated garments. When the discovery of the facts was made, a hearty laugh was indulged in at his expense, and countless were the jokes to which he was subjected. Do you ask who it was that took this involuntary plunge into the Saranac? Sir, there are questions which people, though they possess all the knowledge necessary to the solution of them, do not like to answer, and this is one of them. All I choose to say is, he was a man of about five feet nine in height, somewhat rotund in shape, of fourteen stone and a little over in weight, and somewhat given to grayness about the head. Perhaps you may know him. If you do, you will confer a special favor on me by saying nothing about the matter.

I am at Tupper's Lake, a sheet of water which I assert has no peer in beauty in this country. It is some ten miles in length, and varying from one to three miles in width. Its waters are pure and cold, though less transparent than some of the lakes in this region. This is owing, probably, to the iron ore, which doubtless underlays and which we know abounds around it. At the foot of the lake, a few rods from the bank, the ore crops out on the surface, and you can easily trace it from an eighth to a quarter of a mile. The ore appears to be very rich, and from the indications on the surface, extensive. I have no doubt that long years hence, maybe centuries, this and other rich mines of iron, known to exist in this now wild locality, will give employment to thousands of men, and send out their portion of metal to meet the immense and always growing demand for iron, required by the operations of civilization. The great features of Tupper's Lake, those which give it its principal charm, are its islands and bays. These are the most charming imaginable, always remembering that we leave out of view civilization, regarding only wildness, solitude, and primitive grandeur. These bays stealing around behind jutting and craggy promontories, winding away in the deep shadow of forest and mountain, they lay there unrippled almost by a breeze, always. Floating into one of these, you are hid from a view of the lake; above you is only the sky, while the tall trees, and hills that surround them, limit the vision, as though you were in the bottom of a great bowl, and could look only upward. The islands are of various size and appearance. Here a bare rock, an immense boulder, lifts its brown and moss-covered head, right up from the deep water, standing all solitary and alone, with no tree, shrub, grass or vegetable thing growing upon it. There one, maybe, of a few rods only in circumference, covered with fir trees and pines, standing clothed in everlasting green, with no rocks visible to the eye. Then again, there are others containing maybe hundreds of acres, covered with timber, among which great boulders, larger than haystacks, stand, with here and there precipices rising straight up, fifty or sixty feet, gray and gloomy, while occasionally a bare rocky peak rises above even the tree-tops. As you float by one of these islands, and see the great boulders, the walls, and rocky peaks, struggling as it were for mastery with the forest growth above and around them, you can hardly divest yourself of the idea that you are looking upon some gigantic ruins of the olden times. The crumbling walls, the decaying and deserted battlements of ancient castles, and strongholds built by people of a rude and vanished age, when physical force, and strong arms, conquest and plunder, were the great landmarks of the times. You can almost mark the spot where the lofty towers stood, where the ponderous gates swung upon massive hinges; where were draw-bridge and moat, and you think how impregnable the sturdy old Baronet was in his stronghold against everything but Time. And then you think how that same Time demolishes the strongest and proudest works of man, how it topples down castle and hold, how it sweeps away at last, by its strong, slow, but sure process, the most massive works of human energy.

There are two settlers on the shores of this lake; the one at the outlet, and the other near the head of the lake. The first, a fisherman and hunter, who has some two or three acres cleared, raising simply vegetables for his family, taking the world easy, as most frontier men do, seldom sweating from hard labor, or tired by real work. The other is a lumberman, energetic and industrious, has small taste for hunting or fishing, or any of the wild sports of the forest or lake. He has some forty acres cleared, a good log-house for his family, and another of larger dimensions, fitted up with tiers of berths all around, like the cabins of the large steamboats, but not by any means with the same degree of elegance. Here, during the Winter months, and until late in the Spring, an army of lumbermen congregate, occupying this as their sleeping apartment, and boarding with the hardy settler in this wilderness. This family is eight miles from a neighbor, some fifty miles from a doctor, the same distance from a church or school-house, and you will readily see that whatever pleasure there may be in isolation, they enjoy it to the full. Speaking of school-houses reminds me of a matter that I omitted to mention in a former letter, a thing that I "booked for discussion" on my way, but forgot to mention it in its proper place.

Between the AU SABLE FORKS and FRANKLIN

FALLS, as I said to you, is a high region of country, cold and uninviting for agricultural purposes, desolate by nature as a place of residence, but covered with a large growth of timber. This timber is a mine of wealth to the manufacturers of iron, furnishing them with charcoal for their furnaces and forges. Occasionally you come to a city, almost, of coal-pits. Hundreds upon hundreds of them clustered around. Some smoking in the slow progress of combustion, some just covered, and some just being piled ready for covering, and some already burned, from which sooty, and *charred* men, I had almost said, are raking away the coals, and loading them for the forges. As a matter of fact, it requires people, to chop the wood, build and burn the pits, and carry away the coals; and they are to be found in plenty, in log-houses along the road. As a corollary from these facts, it follows that children will be born to them. And you will see the sturdy, knotty, and hardy-looking little wilderness-born chaps, swarming in what you and I might consider inverse ratio, so far as numbers are concerned, to any apparent necessity for their presence, or provision for their support. Now, in this country, as a general thing, wherever you find a dozen children, you will find a school-mistress and a school-house. These three institutions seem to be inseparable, growing along up together, and it is a glorious thing that it should be so. It develops the native energy of the American character, and brings forth its inward might. Well, some three or four miles south of FRANKLIN FALLS, in the "coal formation," as geologists would say, stood a log-house. There were some fifteen or twenty barefooted, healthy-looking boys and girls, playing and scampering, and shouting around the door, and I wondered at the evidences of a prolific reproductiveness, which seemed to characterize whoever inhabited it. While we were some distance from it, however, I heard a loud rapping on the window-sash, and the little ones disappeared with a rush into the house. That sound was too full of old memories, recollections of long ago, not to explain the problem that had puzzled me. That log-house standing there all alone in that little clearing, was a school-house, a "seminary of learning," a small branch of a great system, that has thrown and is throwing this country forward, with a rush of progress such as finds no parallel in the world's history. As we passed it, the door stood open, and I took an observation of the inmates. There was the plain but neatly dressed mistress, with her clean calico dress and black apron, her white neckerchief over her shoulders, and crossed gracefully over her bosom; her hair combed modestly and smoothly from her forehead, and fastened in a knot on the back of her head, standing with book in hand, and a class of little girls before her, about hearing them read. One chubby little fellow, of say eight or nine years of age, was standing by himself in the middle of the floor, with a paper cap on his head, his pantaloons rolled half-way to his knees, his legs and feet bare, and the fore finger of his right hand in his mouth, and his face down in a ludicrous-sheepish, and shame-faced fashion. There was no mistaking *his* position. He was undergoing punishment for some sin against the laws of the school, demonstrating the great truth that reaches all the way from the cradle to the grave, that the way of the transgressor is hard. There was something so old-fashioned, so familiar to me in all this, that I was tempted to laugh and cry at the same time, as the present and past stood out so palpably before me.

Do not think me capable of ridiculing these primitive people, or primitive schools. They are too important, too essential to the prosperity and progress of this country, in my estimation, for that. I remember with feelings of profound veneration the log school-house of my own boyhood days. It was the foundation of the small progress I have made in life. The teachings begun in these log school-houses have given direction to, and roused the latent energies of many a great and good man of our country, whose names have passed into the history of these States, who will live in the world's memory when thousands of graduates of the Colleges and Universities will have perished. Blessings on that log school-house in the Saranac Woods, on its schoolmistress, and the little children, whose "young ideas" she was teaching "how to shoot."

We leave Tupper's Lake by a direct road to go up the Bog River, to the ponds and lakes towards its source. There are beautiful trout in this lake, and abundance of them. We did not care to take them, for we could not get them out to the settlements, and we had more of the brook and river trout than we knew what to do with. We saw some taken by the settler at the lower end of the lake, weighing from eight to twelve pounds. These he salts for winter use, though he can take them at all times. The trolling season is nearly over, and but few can now be taken in that way. They are caught now by what is called deep fishing. Buoys are made in water from fifty to one hundred feet in depth, where the fish are baited. Long strips of bark are peeled and tied together, to make a sort of cable, to one end of which a stone is fastened as an anchor, and at the other a piece of light wood is made fast, and left to float on the water. About this, chub, shiners, and suckers, cut into small pieces, are thrown for a day or two, and then the fisherman goes out in his boat, fastens to his buoy, drops his long line and great hook, baited with a minnow, and naturally draws in the six, eight, and ten pounders, that have been fattening on the fish he has been furnishing them.

I am at the upper falls of Bog River. This large stream, but small river, forms the inlet to Tupper's

Lake, and comes down from a plateau some sixty feet above it, in three cascades over shelving rocks, of about twenty feet each, and shoots off in a powerful current far out into the lake. Across this current, where it enters the lake, and in the eddies formed by it, are great places to throw for the river trout. They may be caught in great quantities and of a large size, and their play is beautiful. They are, however, at this time, caught both larger, and if possible faster, by trolling, with a minnow for bait, back and forth, a few rods from the shore, across the current. Beautiful yellow or orange-bellied fellows, of from one to three pounds in weight, and their activity and strength is exceedingly exciting to those who have a taste for that method of taking them. For myself, I love the fly or grasshopper, or even the vulgar angle-worm, best; and when I can use them, neither deep fishing for ten-pounders, nor trolling, will tempt me to forsake them.

Our boatmen carried our boat and what a Hoosier would call our plunder, from the lake, a few rods up a steep ascent, and launched it on the river, above the falls. For some three or four miles above, the river flows in a deep and tortuous channel, with but a light current. We then entered a region of boulders, lying in mid-channel, around which the currents wound, and went twisting and eddying away. Here I threw my fly, by way of experiment, and found the trout abundant. Some half a mile further on, we came to a rapid, half a mile in extent, around which the boat had to be carried. And I may say here, that during the day we encountered nine rapids, of greater or less extent, around which our little vessel had to be transported. These carrying places where, however, short, and as we had two boatmen, occasioned but little trouble or delay, and afforded rather a relief from the fixed posture which we had to assume in the boat. There has been a vast amount of lumbering done on and in the neighborhood of this stream the last winter. Twenty thousand logs have floated down it, to the lake below, during the Spring freshets, and there are a vast many lying scattered along the banks, which must await the Spring freshets of next year. On each of the falls (and there are seven of them) dams have been built, to hold back the water, until all is ready, when the flood-gates are opened, and the mighty rush of waters carries everything before it. We could see the mark of the flood, six or eight feet above the present level, on the trees along the bank, and the water is yet greatly above low-water mark. I can imagine with what tremendous force the river goes thundering through the narrow gorges, and down the rocks among the great boulders fixed as mountains in the channel; and the wonder is, how even the great logs can withstand its mighty power, and not be splintered into shreds, among the gigantic obstructions against which they are hurled. The shanties of the lumbermen are seen every few miles along the banks, and they constitute a great feature of this region. They are built of long logs, covered with shingles split from the pines and spruce. Tiers of berths are built one above another, on each side, and across the ends, save where you enter the door. In the centre is a rude fire-place of stone, but without a chimney, while a hole in the roof is left for the escape of the smoke. In some of them are immense cooking stoves, instead of fireplaces.

The bed of the hardy lumbermen was of hemlock, or spruce boughs, or of hay or straw, and here they managed to live comfortably, according to their notions, through the cold winters, though the chill winds whistled through a hundred openings, and the snow drifted in through the crevices. These shanties are deserted now, and they stand there tenantless, with most of the tools remaining which were used by the lumbermen during the winter. These tools are entirely safe from plunderers, for there is a sort of faith among woodmen, that is a surer protection than bolts and bars. We entered one of these shantees, the door of which was on the latch. There, in the centre, stood a great stove, with the utensils for cooking upon and around it. In one corner was piled up axes, crowbars, log chains, iron dogs. On a shelf was a cask of vinegar, and another that smelled mightily like whiskey, a great pile of codfish, and bread hard and dry enough to answer for cannon balls, pewter dishes, knives and forks, selected for strength rather than elegance, and on a little shelf in the corner, a pack of cards, so soiled and greasy, that one could safely bet they had been through ten thousand games of "Old Sledge." The whiskey and the cards brought out a strong characteristic of the lumbermen of these woods in bold relief, while the hundred black stubs of pipes, and the codfish, added a sort of commentary to the card and whiskey text. And yet, probably there was neither a confirmed drunkard nor a gambler among them all. They drank whiskey upon principle, and played cards, and smoked, and eat codfish by way of giving relish to the "rye." I remember an eccentric old gentleman, who was a member of the Legislature for two or three sessions some years ago, from one of the down-river counties. He was a jolly, pleasant, companionable, and withal, an intelligent man—but he had three weaknesses in rather a remarkable degree. These weaknesses were a game of whist, a gin sling, and a cigar. He could indulge in his favorite game from eve till dawn, provided the gin was good, and the cigars all right. He would play, and drink, and smoke with a zest that defied weariness or desire for sleep, and yet he was never intoxicated, and never staked a cent on the cards. He claimed to be a temperate man, and was principled against drunkenness and gambling. He would, however, stow away more gin, and smoke more cigars of a night, and go to bed soberer, than any two men I ever happened to know. He used to say he loved to drink because it made him relish a cigar so, and he loved to smoke because it made him so dry. It is, doubtless, so with the lumbermen of this region. They like to drink, because it makes them relish their pipes, and they like to smoke, because it makes them so dry.

We have mastered all the rapids and falls, and are now in smooth water, and shall be until we reach a series of nameless ponds, lying between us and Mud Lake. We have seen several deer on the route thus far, since we left Tupper's Lake, but there are no grasses or food for them along the river, and our meeting with them has been entirely accidental. It is said we are now entering upon a portion of the river that affords abundance of pasture for them, and that we shall have a sight at a great many on our passage up.

I am on the banks of one of the small lakes, the outlet of which goes to help to make up Bog River. These ponds or little lakes are without names, so far as I can learn. They have some, but not all of the beauties of the waters further north. They are in part bordered by marshes, and they lack the bold and striking outline of rocky bluff and hillside, nor have they the charming bays that steal around, as it were, from the broad lake, to sleep in the shadow of the forest trees. We are very near the "top of the house" here, and though we can see in the distance mountain peaks going up towards the sky, yet there are no ranges, no highlands, as distinguished from these peaks in sight. We must now be some four or five hundred feet above Tupper's Lake, and a single rise of some fifty feet in all, around roaring rapids, will bring us to the upper level, beyond which there is in this direction no higher plain, no more elevated river or lake.

After leaving the upper falls, the river flowed with a sluggish current through broad marshes, where the wild grasses skirted the shore, and the broad leaves of the pond lilies covered the water. We saw abundance of deer feeding upon these aquatic pastures. I was exceedingly amused by one of these animals, a noble buck. In many places the channel is narrow, and exceedingly crooked, turning suddenly around wooded points. Soon after leaving the upper falls, the oars were unshipped, and the paddles only used, that when we came upon these deer pastures, we might not frighten the animals by the noise of rowing. As we rounded noiselessly one of these short elbows, we came suddenly upon a large deer, that was feeding only some four or five rods from us. He was standing with his nose and a part of his head, including his eyes, for the moment under water, apparently trying to loosen the stem of a pond lily from the bottom, the water being a foot or more in depth. These stems are of the same pithy and fibrous character as a cabbage stalk, rough and knotty like it, and when loosened at the roots, will float on the water. The deer are fond of these lily stalks, and you will see fragments of half-eaten stems floating in the ponds and eddies where they grow. We were perfectly silent and motionless, as we saw him feeding so near us; not a hand was moved. He raised his head carelessly from the water, and as his eye fell upon us, he straightened himself up, then throwing forward his ears, looked in utter astonishment upon us, as if saying to himself, "What, in the name of all that is wonderful, is that?" Presently he hoisted his tail, snorted in amazement, and trotted a few rods towards the shore, looking with arched neck at us over his shoulder. Still, as we did not move, his curiosity seemed to overcome his terror, and he stopped, and turning towards us, stood gazing with a peculiar intensity of look at us. He would stamp with his foot, and whistle, as if to arouse us from our fixed and motionless attitude, if we were living things. Presently we swung our hats and shouted, and he was off like the wind. The discharge of my rifle, and the whistling of the ball near him, added vigor to his terror, and new wings to his flight, and he plunged madly into the thick brush along the margin of the river, and went crashing and snorting up the mountain.

I am now on the banks of a small lake, the principal source of the west branch of Bog River. We are shanteeing here in the old woods, in a house made of bark peeled from the trees around us, composed of a single room, with the whole gable end for a door, and just large enough to accommodate two men if disposed of horizontally, and laid along lengthwise on a bed of boughs rolled up like sacks of potatoes in their blankets. Before it are blazing logs, for the nights are cool, and were it not so, the smoke and the flame are needed to keep off the mosquitoes, that in these woods and around these lakes have each a proboscis that an elephant might envy, and they have a mighty insinuating way with them too. Our boatmen lay wrapped in their blankets in the open air, with their feet to fire and their heads resting on blocks of wood for a pillow, and it would do you good to see how soundly they sleep and to hear them snore. From out in the forest comes the solemn hooting of the owl, and the wild voice of some solitary night bird floats upon the ear, while at long intervals the clarion voice of the loon comes clear and musical from the lake. The hoarse and guttural bass of the frogs comes roaring deep, sonorous and solemn, from among the pond lilies that grow along the shore, and yet with all these noises sounding on the ear, you feel an impression of silence, and you are soothed into a desire for repose. With the air full of noises, you sink away into slumber, and in the morning awake fully refreshed, the weariness of the previous day all gone, and you feel a degree of buoyancy of spirit and limb, which no night's rest in the city can give you.

The pure bracing air of this high region has an effect upon the system which it is impossible to describe. Such at least is its effect upon me. You feel as you inhale it in the morning, an exhilaration, a hilarity that tempts you to shout aloud, hurrah, sing, and be jolly as everything around you seems to be. I have seen people while under the influence of Champagne, cut strange capers, and perform most ridiculous antics, and the mountain air of these wild regions so pure, so bracing, so full of freshness, so deliciously sweet, that though rigid in your observance of the temperance creed, you become almost drunken with excitement, as if you had been worshipping at the shrine of Bacchus.

We saw a great many deer yesterday, caught all the trout we wanted, and we can see the deer this morning feeding on the shore over and across the lake. We intended to stay a week in this region, laying around in a loose promiscuous way, fishing as we needed the trout, and knocking over a deer when we needed venison, telling stories, and hearing them told, of life in the woods, indulging in fact or fiction, in fact, being jolly in a natural way outside of civilization, away from books and newspapers, away from highways and the thoroughfares of life, away from the thunders of railroads and the roar of the steam whistle, outside of paved streets, outside of green fields, and outside of the fences, untrammeled by the conventional proprieties of life, to be wild men in fact away off in the old woods, renouncing for a time the guardianship of the laws, the companionship of the world, alone with nature and the wild things with which God has peopled the forests, the lakes and streams. I have thus far written only in the singular number, and have in this, as it strikes me now for the first time, done wrong. There is with me an intelligent gentleman, who is a keen sportsman, one who relishes a tramp in the woods, who loves to throw the fly, and be among the deer, to hear the forest sounds, and look upon the wild scenery of nature, as much as I do myself; and I have been indebted to him, all the way, for pleasant conversation and "interesting debate" on many subjects besides woodcraft. His skill in all that pertains to the sports of the wilderness, is quite equal to my own. I may as well say here, that I do not excel in any branch of woodcraft. I can throw the fly with only a medium skill, and am not remarkably successful with a baited hook. I am no great shot with the rifle. What I love most is to float along the romantic shores of these secluded lakes, to glide into their shadowy bays, be rowed down or up the secluded little rivers that have flowed here in everlasting solitude through the old forests, and around the base of these mountains. I love to commune with the primeval things all around me, to go back in imagination, to the time when this vast Continent was one great wilderness, hid away here across oceans by the Creator, given to the possession of wild men and wild things, till in his own good time he should open it up to the knowledge of the world, making it the field of a regenerated and renewed civilization; where the great principles of human freedom could be planted in a virgin soil, and man's capability for progress be fully developed. This must have been a glorious hunting ground for the Indian, and admirable residences, too, for his brother the beaver. There was no need of these latter building dams to accommodate themselves with still water. The lakes and ponds spread all over the country, were prepared for them; and when they and the wild men of the woods lived in amity, before the greed of the white man had set a value upon their fur, and tempted the cupidity of the Indian to contrive their slaughter, the beaver must have had a good time of it here among these waters. And yet these industrious and provident animals were not entirely satisfied with the natural ponds and lakes alone. There are occasional localities pointed out along the streams where there are unmistakable evidences still existing that they had in the olden times their dams. There are, too, water-ways, narrow channels across low marshy grounds, from one pond to another, that are called by the woodmen "Beaver Canals," which, it is said, are the works of the beaver. These "Canals" are some three or four feet wide, the water with scarcely a perceptible current, and in some none at all; winding across the marshes, skirted by tall grass or flags, and you feel almost certain that they are not natural water-courses. You can easily persuade yourself that they are the work of art, have been excavated for the purpose of opening a convenient passage way, and the many muskrats that are seen constantly swimming to and fro in them prove that they are still regarded as highways of travel. There is one across a neck of land on the Racquette River, just above a noted locality known as the "driftwood." This "Canal" is some quarter of a mile in length, leading from the river to a body of water containing probably three thousand acres, known as Isham's Pond. This pond connects with, and is on the same level with the river, and the "Canal" across the Isthmus saves a journey of some four or five miles round. It is from four to six or eight feet in width, through a dense forest of lowland timber. The water is about two feet in depth, though the excavation, if excavation it be, is from four to six feet in depth. We passed through this canal with our boat. There was scarcely a perceptible current. Whether it is the work of the beaver, hundreds of years ago, or a natural canal, I do not undertake to say, but to me it appeared like an artificial channel, made for convenience of communication between the river and pond, and our boatmen seemed to have no doubt on the subject.

I have thus far given you the romance of a journey into these woods, the sports that abound here, the abundance of trout and deer, the beauty of the lakes and rivers, the romantic and wild scenery which you will find spread out all around you. It is, in sober truth, a charming region to visit, for the purpose of whiling away a fortnight or a month. But—and what a pity it is that this disjunctive should always steal in, standing forever in the way of fulness of enjoyment, obstructing our pleasures, and casting a shadow on what should be all brightness, all sunlight, all glory. Yet so it is, there is a BUT in this case, and at this season of the year, during the month of June, the freshest, greenest, brightest, loveliest, most glorious of all the months, when the birds are merriest, the forest foliage most beautiful, the air balmiest, and all nature is clothed in its gayest garments, decked with its sweetest smiles, *the black fly* greedy for blood, hungry, relentless in cruelty, swarm in millions around you, and spite of your most active exertions, your most ingenious devices subject you, especially if your skin is thinner than that of the rhinoceros, to a protracted torment, to which crucifixion would almost seem a positive pleasure. I am a reasonably courageous and persevering man in pursuit of pleasure in the woods. I can bear a great deal of positive hardship, labor, for which, were it encountered for hire, a very large "pile" would have to be paid. I have before now been hungry and cold, I have fought the musquito and the midget, been out in the rain and the chill winds, in pursuit of game. I have tramped in hot days long miles over mountains, stumbling over boulders and among tangle-brush, weary and dripping with perspiration. I have encountered the black fly before in these same woods and in the same beautiful month of June without a thought of surrendering, but I never, and the oldest hunter of these woods never encountered them in such myriads, absolute swarms, as they have appeared the present season. I have been compelled to surrender, acknowledge myself vanquished. I said we intended to stay here a week. We came here last evening and we start for home this morning, absolutely driven from the woods by the BLACK FLY, a little insect not larger than the head of a pin, but with teeth like a tiger's. If I live to get out to the settlements, a problem the solution of which the next two days will solve, if there is enough of me left to make it an object worth preserving, I'll tell you in my next all about it. If I should be clean eaten up, a catastrophe by no means improbable, do not charge it to the panthers or the wolves, lay no blame upon the bears or any of the beasts of prey, but to the BLACK FLY. In that unhappy event, my last injunction is: KEEP OUT OF THE SARANAC WOODS IN THE MONTH OF JUNE.

APPENDIX.

A.

—

SUNRISE IN THE COUNTRY.

"I've seen the sun rise. I saw his vanguard of light that preceded his ascent from the other side of the world. I saw him when he leaped into his chariot and started westward across the sky."—*Letter from a Correspondent.*

WE have witnessed the same phenomenon three times during the present month. Once we were on the St. Lawrence, along the island that lays opposite Cape Vincent. Once we were on Lake Champlain, opposite Burlington; and once sitting on a venerable, moss-covered boulder overlooking a beautiful meadow just by the village of Lenox, in the State of Massachusetts. It is a glorious thing, the rising of the sun of a calm, clear summer morning. At Cape Vincent we rose while the larger stars were yet shining faintly in the firmament, and the moon was still visible in the sky. The morning was warm and still, the river unruffled, and we started with an early waterman in a rowboat from the dock, to troll for the pickerel, bass or muscalange, if they choose to make the acquaintance of our baited hook. We heard the first morning song of the wild bird, and saw the last star vanish in depths of the sky. We saw the light grow brighter and brighter in the east, as the twilight faded into day. We had just hooked a famous pickerel, and were drawing him in on a line 250 feet in length, as the sun came up over the eastern hill in all the brightness of his glory. It was a splendid thing to look upon, and so was the pickerel that had our hook in his jaw. The sun blazed along the surface of the water, dazzling the eye by his sheen, and the pickerel floundered in his astonishment, while we looked first upon the one and then upon the other, rejoicing in the double favor that was granted us, and thinking

> " How happy could we be with either,
> Were the other dear charmer away."

We admired the sunrise, and hauled in on the pickerel. We made prey of the fish, and let the sun go on in his course.

At Burlington, we were out on the lake alone in a skiff by the time the first rays of the sun illumined the Eastern horizon. It was a calm, beautiful morning, the air was balmy and full of invigorating freshness. A light breeze rippled the surface of the water, as we rowed out from the shore to watch the departure of the darkness, and see the lighting up of the world by the sun, as he came up from his resting place. We saw how he first gave his rays to glow on the tops of the mountains away off in

Essex, while in the valleys at their base the grayness of twilight still lingered. We saw the sunlight chasing the shadows down the sides of the mountains, and we looked upon the sun as he seemed to hang for a moment, like a great torch among the trees that stood out on the eastern summits against the sky, and then how he rose above them to go forth on his course, like a charioteer of old, with his steeds of fire. He seemed to rejoice in the greatness of his strength as he leaped clear of the hills and mounted aloft in the sky. The darkness vanished from before him, and the moon and stars hid themselves from the glory of his presence. We breakfasted on a yellow bass that morning, which was but one of a half-dozen we caught before the sun was clear of the tree-tops.

At Lenox, among the mountains of the Old Bay State, we saw the sun rise again. Lenox is a sweet spot, surrounded by an amphitheatre of hills. Beautiful farms are spread out all around the town. Beautiful roads, lined on either side by the sugar maple; beautiful streams and beautiful lakes are within range of a morning walk, or an evening drive. It has pleasant fields and shady groves in sight, and deep ravines where the grass grows to the edge of the soft-toned brooklet, as it sings faintly over the smooth pebbles, and the deep shadows of the arching trees cool the heat of noon. We rose, as at Cape Vincent and Burlington, while the twilight yet hovered over the fields and town. We saw the thin mist rising from the meadows, and creeping up the sides of the hills, hiding their shadowy verdure, and making them look like the fair face of a maiden shining dimly in its beauty through a veil of gauze. We heard the wild matin songs as they broke in their gladness from the stillness of night, and watched the swallows as they started from the barns and chimneys on their arrowy flight. We heard the first note of the meadow-lark, as he flew from his night perch, and the last song of the whip-poor-will, as he folded his wings to rest for the day. We sat for half an hour on a venerable boulder that overlooked a meadow. On our right, at a few rods distance, was a half-grown elm, on the topmost branch of which sat a brown thrush, singing his morning song, and swaying gracefully in the breeze while he sang. On our left was a thorn bush, among the thick branches of which the catbird mocked the brown thrush, while over against us, perched upon a fence stake, was a quail, whistling in his clear and silvery notes to his mate, as she brooded in her fondness over her treasured nest.

'Twas a pleasant thing to watch the departure of the night shadows, to hear the voices of the morning breaking into harmony, and look upon the sun as he came up from behind the eastern hills. It seemed to us that the gladness grew in intensity, and that a new song burst forth as he came into view. The brown thrush sang with a clearer voice, and the catbird in his thorn bush mocked with fresh vigor, while the bob-o-link darted up from the meadow-grass with a freer bound, and while he shook the dew-drops from his wing, and balanced himself gracefully in the air, sang with a prolonged lay, and a gladder energy.

Sunrise in the country is a glorious sight, a vision infinitely more pleasant than those which visit the pillow of the sluggard while indulging in his morning sleep. Go out into the country among the mountains, or among the fields, where everything is fresh, where the dew-drops glisten on the grass, or sparkle on the forest leaves—where the morning breeze comes to you fragrant from the meadows or the foliage of the old woods. Look upon the stars as they depart from the sky, and upon the sun as he comes up from his bed of darkness. It is a glorious exhibition, and open for all. It can be seen without money, and enjoyed without price. Go into the country and see the sun rise.

B.

—

THE "SAINTS' REST."

You need not take down your map and look for the location of "The Saints' Rest." It is not laid down on the map. You need not look into your gazetteer. It is not in the gazetteer. You need not inquire of the oldest inhabitant about its locality, for he has never heard of it. It is not the place that good people have been looking for, for ages, the place where Christian people hope to repose when earth, with its cares and sorrows, shall have passed away. And yet "The Saints' Rest" is a veritable locality. It occupies a place in the world, and is not inaptly named. First let me tell you how we got here, and who I mean by *we*, for I am not alone.

At Coudersport we took a lumber wagon, and packing our movables, consisting of provisions, fishing tackle, and a rifle, took to the woods, over a road such as *you* have probably never travelled. Great bags stuffed with hay, as compactly as they could be, and laid in the bottom of the box, constituted our seats. I said we took to the woods and we went up and up for hours, towards the top of a range of hills that seemed to have no summit, over a road that was good, at least for dyspeptics, if jolting over roots and topling down into deep holes is beneficial. Once in two or three miles we would come to a clearing of a few acres, with a log-house, or maybe two or three near each other, composing a little settlement surrounded by a dense and sombre forest of great hemlocks, from the limbs of which the lichens hung, and above which mountain peaks went looming up towards the sky.

Towards four o'clock we came in sight of a little settlement of three or four families, the entire of whose clearings may have amounted to a hundred and fifty acres. A log house for each family, and two or three barns, constituted all the buildings in sight. The day had been excessively warm and sultry. The tree frogs were piping all along the road; the leaves on the trees as they stirred in the sluggish breeze, lifted their leaves fan-like to the sun, making the tree-top shine all over like silver. As the day advanced, clouds came flying over in solemn procession from the southwest, indicating that a storm was on the march. As we entered this little clearing dark and heavy clouds came heaving solemnly up over the western hills, the low growl of the thunder was heard in the distance, faint flashes of lightning glanced across the sky, while around us was the gloomy stillness that precedes a summer storm. We were some dozen miles from the "The Saints'

Rest," seven or eight of which lay through woods without a house. We applied at one of the houses in sight, and were accommodated for the night. We had got ourselves and our team comfortably housed, and the storm came on. It was a goodly sight to see the rain come down as it did then, as if the clouds had been torn asunder to empty their contents at once in a rushing flood upon the earth. It was a goodly sight to see the lightning, flashing and streaking, in a ragged, zigzag from the clouds down to the forest-covered hills, and it was a goodly sound to hear the sudden boom of the thunder as it burst like artillery upon the ear, and went rolling and dying away among the mountains. In an hour the rain was over, and the bow of promise hung arching upon the rear of the storm. In the morning we breakfasted with our entertainer, compensated him for his trouble as far as money could do, and grateful for his kindness, took up our journey again for the "Saints' Rest." You may judge of the quality of the road when I tell you we were some seven hours in going less than a dozen miles. We passed over a high range, and went singing and jolting, whistling and laughing down towards the Sinnemahoning, in the pleasant valley of which is the "Saints' Rest." Our last mile or two lay along a stream that came down from the hills, beautifully clear and cold, and I left my companions with the promise to procure a mess of fish for our dinners. I redeemed that pledge, for within two hours of their arrival at the "Saints' Rest," I was there with a basket literally full, of as beautiful speckled trout as an epicure would wish to see.

And now you ask who compose the *we*, of which I have been speaking, for you are aware that in these letters I indulge in no editorial plurals. Well, first and foremost, there is the Dominie, a pleasant and a Christian man, one who, while he never forgets the dignity of his high calling, is neither a zealot nor a bigot. He is a man of varied reading and ripe scholarship, full of pleasant anecdote, and of a cheerful wit. He is no ascetic, moving along through the world with a brow of solemn severity, who "will not smile though Nestor swears the joke is laughable." Then there is the dominie's wife, a cheerful-hearted, pleasant and accomplished lady. Then there is my friend the lawyer, a man whose weakness is a pleasant trout stream, a rod and fly—one who takes to the water like a duck, as if he were amphibious, who, with rod in hand, will stalk boldly into the stream, and throw the fly with the water rippling around his knee-pans, defying all the spirits of neuralgia, rheumatism and lumbago; a man, too, of giant sympathies, and a big heart. And then, there is his wife, who sings like a bird, and loves nature with the strong affection of a devotee —a most sensible and excellent woman, younger than the dominie's wife, and less serious, perhaps, as if fitting for a lawyer's lady. Then there is my own wife, of whom it does not become me to speak, save that we started in life together before either had numbered twenty years, and have walked quietly and peacefully through many dark days and sore trials, to the present time, and no repining or unkind word has she spoken, to me at least. Here, then, we are, six of us, at the "Saints' Rest," in the sequestered valley of the Sinnemahoning, and here we propose to stay for a week. By the way, shortly after I left the wagon, and while the ladies were talking about the wild animals that belong in these old forests, a fine deer stepped from the covert of the woods, on the other side of the river, into an open space on the bank, and having gazed for a moment upon them, hoisted his white flag and bounded away. It was a pleasant and a new sight to them. They described, with enthusiasm, his symmetry of form, and his graceful movements, as he bounded into the forest.

To you, who profess only a love for brick houses and paved thoroughfares, who prefer the long vista of a street, with the rumbling of carriages and a moving panorama of sidewalks covered with people, to tall mountains and old forests, and streams and fields, there would be nothing inviting here. Every locality has its legends and every place its history, and why should not this quiet spot have its history and its legends, too? The "Saints' Rest" has its history as well as the largest city. It is only a clearing of some five-and-twenty acres, having a house of the composite order of architecture, being a log house and a frame one conjoined. My friend, the lawyer who is with me, a year or two since furnished its owner with the means of building an addition to his log-house, to accommodate him and his friends on their fishing excursions to the valley of the Sinnemahoning. While he and his male companions came, without their wives, it was called the "Sinners' Home." Last season they brought their wives, and so glowing were their descriptions of its charms, that the old name was expunged, and it was christened the "Saints' Rest'."

We are here, six of us, as I told you in my last, in one of the most primitive and secluded spots in the world. In front of the door runs the Sinnemahoning, a most pleasant little river, on its way to the noble Susquehanna. In the still night, and in the early morning, you hear its gentle song as it flows along in ripples over the smooth stones. To the right, a mountain peak runs upward towards the sky to the height of some fifteen hundred or two thousand feet, covered with gigantic hemlocks to the summit. In front is a mountain range, regular in form, extending north and south, which forms the eastern barrier to the narrow valley of the Sinnemahoning, rising to the height of fifteen hundred feet, with a steep acclivity, covered with dark evergreens, the mountain birch, and gnarled maples to the top. To the left, the valley stretching away to the north, and from among the arching trees, that reach their long arms out over the water, and the dense willows that grow thick and luxuriant along the shore, the river comes quietly out as from a cavern, and is lost to the view in its solemn shades. In the rear of the house is another mountain, lifting its sombre head to the clouds, to the left of which a little stream comes down through a mountain gorge, while on the right is a pleasant valley reaching away up between the hills, where the old forest stands in all its primeval grandeur, and through the centre of which a cold stream carries its tribute to the river, in sight of the "Saints' Rest." Here, then, in this bowl, this valley, surrounded by high mountains, is the "Saints' Rest." Pleasant fields are around the house. A foot-bridge consisting of the long trunk of a great pine, hewn on one side, spans the river, beneath which the water spreads out still, placid and lake-like. Just below, there is a ripple where the river goes singing along over the smooth stones, swirling away under caverned banks, and then hiding itself in deep eddies among the piled-up drift wood that bridges it when the water is low. The owner of this spot has been here some nineteen years, and is one of nature's nobility, an honest and a Christian man. He is the owner of a hundred and fifty acres of land, and was the first man that ventured into this wild region as a settler. He is an Irishman. He came from Philadelphia at that early day as an agent for a large land owner. He erected for his principal a dam across the river, and a log-mill. The dam is standing where it was built, and the log-mill is there but it has gone to ruin—the rafters decayed, and the roof fallen in—the water-way has become filled up, and willows and alders grow around the doors, and reach their arms in at the windows, and hang them over the logs that formed the outer walls of the mill, hiding what remains of the structure from view, as if to conceal the decay and desolation that has settled down upon it.

I have been exceedingly interested in hearing his excellent and simple-minded wife recount the scenes through which she passed in the first years of her residence here. On one occasion she took her infant in her arms and went out to where her husband was engaged in chopping down the trees. Let me tell you her story as she told it to me, in her own simple language. "I was lonesome," she said, "in the house, and I took Lizzie" (her daughter, now a wife and mother) "in my arms, and went out to where my husband was at work. She was a little baby then, but a few weeks old, and I wrapped her in a shawl to keep the wind from blowing upon her. When I came out to where my husband was, I told him I'd help pick up the brush, and he told me to lay Lizzie down by the side of a stump. She was asleep, and I wrapped her up carefully and laid her down among the bushes, and went to gathering up the brush and piling them in heaps. My husband was cutting down a large tree at a little distance, and I went up to where he was. I asked him which way the tree would fall, and he pointed in a direction different from where my baby lay. I stood by him, seeing the chips fly as he swung his axe, and watched the tree as it began to reel to its fall like a drunken man. It began to shake at the top as if in great trouble, swayed for a moment this way and that, and then started, slowly at first, right towards where my baby lay. You can't tell what my feelings were. My heart swelled with horror almost to bursting as the tree went reeling to its fall. I screamed in agony as it went sweeping along through the air, and, wild with terror, thrust my fingers into my ears to shut out the death-scream of my child, and ran like a crazy woman into the woods. My husband ran to where my baby lay, and was there almost as soon as the tree touched the ground. There by the side of the stump, with the broken and crushed limbs all around it, lay my baby unharmed. He turned and ran after me into the woods, hallooing to me to stop and come back, and that LIZZIE wasn't hurt. That was a glad voice to me, and the words went to my heart at first like a dream. I stopped for a moment to listen again. 'LIZZIE is safe,' cried my husband, 'come back.' I couldn't yet fully understand the meaning of what he said. 'LIZZIE is safe' seemed to be sounding all around me. It came down like a voice from the sky, and upward like a voice from the earth. The great trees all around me all seemed to have voices of gladness, and all seemed to say 'LIZZIE is safe.' 'Come back,' I heard my husband say again, 'LIZZIE aint hurt;' and everything around me seemed full of happy laughter and great joy. I stopped and listened in bewilderment, and as I did so, 'LIZZIE is safe' was anywhere, above, below and around me, everything cried 'LIZZIE is safe.' My husband came up to me and took me by the hand, and said kindly, 'Don't be frightened, LIZZIE isn't hurt;' and then a trembling came over me, and my strength seemed to be all gone. In a moment I was better, and when my mind took in the sense of my husband's words, I thanked God with a full heart that he had turned a great sorrow from me. I went with my husband to where I left my baby, and there lay the little thing, hid away among the broken limbs of the great hemlock, and the bent and tangled bushes, like MOSES among the rushes, fast asleep. The great hemlock had, in its fall, struck the stump by the side of which LIZZIE lay, and glanced off on the other side; but its limbs, broken and ragged, had been forced into the ground all around her, and it was a wonder and a great mercy that she was not crushed.

"I took her up and went home and laid her in her cradle, and then knelt down and thanked the great and good God, that takes care of his creatures, even in the deep forests, and the lone woods. I've passed through many sorrows, and I never wept as long at once as I did then, but it wasn't with grief. I was very happy. My heart was very light, but I couldn't laugh. It seemed as though joy like mine could only speak in a low hushed voice, and be seen only in tears. Lizzie has been a kind, good girl, all her life, and I often tell her how lonely and sorrowful my life would have been, had she been crushed to death by that great tree felled by her father's hands."

We arrived here of a Saturday afternoon, and it being ascertained that one of our number was a clergyman, the good lady of the house urged him to preach to the settlers on the coming Sabbath. To this he cheerfully consented, and word was sent to all the families on the Sinnemahoning, some six or seven in all. On the morrow they came in, husbands, wives, and little children, to hear what was not often permitted them in their wilderness home —the preaching of the gospel, and to mingle in the public worship of God on the day of his appointment. The number was small, but I have never seen a more attentive and seemingly devout audience. When the service was over, they gathered around the excellent dominie, shook him cordially and gratefully by the hand, and then departed quietly and cheerfully to their homes. Blessings on these good people that have made their homes away out here in these narrow and secluded valleys, beneath the shadow of these tall mountains, and amid the gloom and seclusion of these ancient forests.

I have been here a week, and have as yet seen no man or woman, save those who came with me, who belongs outside of this sequestered valley. I have seen no team passing along the road, no traveller winding his way to some remoter spot, or to some settlement further in the wilderness. I have, however, seen the mail boy that comes to this neighborhood once a week on horseback. The post-office is about a mile from us, and is "the last of the series." The post-boy delivers his collapsed mail bags to the post-master, feeds his weary nag, and then turns back towards home. There is no post-office beyond this, on this side of the mountains. There are fifteen voters in the town, and the quarterly receipts at the post-office, I understand, average about seventy-five cents per quarter.

I love this lonely region—I could dally here for weeks among the hills, and forests, and streams. I hear the old sounds that were familiar to me in my boyhood, and see the things that I have not seen since my early youth. In the evening, so delightfully cool, we sit on the foot-bridge, and listen to the old owls away up on the sides of the mountain, talking to each other among the old hemlock trees. "Hoo! hoo! hooho!" says one on the right. "Hoo! hoo! hooho!" says another on the left, and "Hoo! hoo! hooho!" says a third among the branches of a great tree near us, and their solemn voices come out on the night air, like those of the wood demons, as if inquiring who it is that invade their territory and profane their ancient sanctuaries by human footsteps, and the voice of civilization. Along the stream the frogs croak, and the peepers send their shrill voices from among the grass in the damp and marshy places. The raccoon calls from the margin of the woods along the clearing, and is answered from away off in the forest. The fire-flies flash their tiny torches along the meadow, and over the still waters. The voice of the river is heard away below us, as it flows over the riffles, singing as it dances over the smooth stones, in a ceaseless chaunt, and the wind murmurs softly among the thick foliage of the trees. Then, when we have listened to all these forest sounds, so ancient and so primitive, we lift up our own voices in song. I said in a former letter, that we had with us a lady (the lawyer's wife) who could "sing like a bird," and it was a pleasant thing to hear her sweet clear voice swell out on the night air, full and melodious, and to note how the other sounds ceased, as echo prolonged the strains, as if enraptured by the new and pleasant music.

We have many romantic spots to resort to in the heat of noon, where we talk over the things of the outside world in a quiet way, as we sit around on the green knolls or the trunks of the fallen trees. There is a little island near the foot-bridge, covered with great trees, from which the underbrush has been cleared away, so that the ground is covered with a delightful grassy verdure. Above, the arms of the trees are lovingly intertwined, their thick foliage shutting out the sunshine, and making a shade beneath, delightfully cool and sweet, while the rippling waters are murmuring all around. This is one of our favorite resorts when the sun is high; and were all those that we love—our children, and our heart companions—around us, it would be hard to part from the charming spot. As we were sitting on the foot-bridge I spoke of, on the Sunday evening after our arrival here, the inquiry arose as to how many trout would be required for a breakfast for all. We settled upon thirty, as the number that could be safely regarded as a full supply—being five to each person—and I promised to procure them in time. I can never sleep late in the morning outside of a city or large town. I know not why it is, but in the country I am always awake by the earliest dawn. It was so here—I was wide awake before the day-break, and as I lay listening to the ceaseless sound of the river, I heard the first song of the first bird of the morning. I rose and dressed myself, and long before the sun had thrown a ray upon the mountain, I was ready with my rod and basket, to redeem my promise of the night before. I could have caught the requisite supply of trout within sight of the house, but I chose to have a ramble, as well as a pleasant time with the fish before breakfast, and I started off up the stream that came down through the valley I spoke of in a former letter. A pathway led up the valley, which I followed for a mile. I have written so much about the music of the woods, that it may well have become tiresome, but I venture to still say that it seemed to me I never heard the songs and sounds so full, so varied, so gleeful and so happy, as they appeared to me then. On every side, and from everywhere came the voices of wild things, some loud and boisterous, some solemn and deep, some hoarse and guttural, and others clear and shrill, but all blending in nature's harmony, and all full of gladness and joy. There is no sorrowful sound among the voices that one hears in the woods—sounds of terror there may be; the thunders roll through the sky, or burst in startling peals, the tornado sweeps by in its wrath and majesty, the tempest roars in its power—all these speak of the mighty strength and power of God, but there is in the whole range of natural voices that one hears in the wilderness, no accent of sorrow, no note of grief.

A mile up this valley I came to a clearing of some half dozen acres, which, however, was without a possessor. The fences were all gone, the roof of the log-house had fallen in, the chimney had fallen down, and blackberry bushes clogged up the door, while the rank weeds grew where once was the floor. The settler that made this clearing, had abandoned it long ago. The wilderness was too lonesome for him. His wife pined for her kindred, and after two or three years of solitude and trial, he departed leaving this cleared spot in the forest as the only memorial of his former presence. As he left it so it remains, excepting such decay and desolation as comes with time, and, as is sure to be written, upon what is abandoned by the care of man. I sat down by what was once the door-yard of this primitive dwelling—a spring of pure cold water came bubbling up at my feet, and ran away in a little brooklet, to the large stream that I heard in the distance. The sun was just beginning to illumine with his first rays the peaks around. The thin mist was stealing slowly up the sides of the mountains, while around me still lingered deep shadow, and the grayness of the morning twilight. I sat here for half an hour watching the sunlight chasing the shadow in a long line down the mountain sides, and listening to the sounds that were coming from the woods around. From within the old walls of the old log-house, among the rank weeds and broken timbers, a porcupine came stealing out, and unconscious of my presence wandered all around me, seemingly looking for grass-hoppers, and insects or worms that were chilled by the night-damps. He came to the little brook, within a rod of me, and drank; I remained perfectly still, and he wandered carelessly away into the woods, never discovering that the thing he took for a stump by the spring, was a man.

I rigged my fishing apparatus and struck through the woods to the stream that I heard, and which flows towards and empties into the Sinnemahoning, within a few rods of the "Saints' Rest." My hook had scarcely touched the water when it was seized by a trout. I found no difficulty in supplying the promised number. I had caught thirty in fishing less than that number of rods, and that after rejecting all the small ones. I added eight to the number, and then returned by the path along the valley, and by which I had entered the forest. I was back while all my companions were yet sleeping soundly in their beds. I said I hear again old sounds that were familiar to me in my boyhood. They are the cow-bells in the woods, and the sheep-bells along the fences; the woodman's axe, as he battles with the forest, and the crash of the trees as they come thundering to the ground; the cackling of fowls in the barn-yards, and the loud baying of the house dog, as some new sound stirs in the forest—all these are like household words to me, but they belong to the "long, long ago."

It is a curious thing to watch the growth of a region that is young and wild—to see it change from a wilderness into a fruitful and populous country—to look upon the march of civilization, as it moves along with a slow and toilsome progress, sweeping away the old things of Nature, and spreading out all around the things that pertain to its dominion. Some bold-hearted adventurer marches into the woods, with his axe on one shoulder and his rifle on the other, and falls to chopping down the great trees. Presently there is a spot in the forest, on which the sun shines down bright and clear. The logs and brush are burned up, and a field of grain waves in the summer winds. After a little will be seen a log-house, and a woman sitting on the door-sill with a brood of tough, hardy little ones, tumbling and frolicking about her. You will hear the blows of an axe, as the settler battles with the tall forest trees, and you will hear them through the day crashing and thundering to the ground. You will hear the barking of a house-dog, the cackling of fowls, and the quacking of the ducks and geese. You will hear the loud ding-dong of the cow-bell in the woods, and the tinkling of the sheep-bells along the fences. These are new sounds in the forest, and the old woods may know by them that their time is come. Away off, perhaps miles away, another hardy settler puts up his cabin, and makes war on the ancient forest trees. Year after year the woods are pushed back by the fences. Fields spread out wider and wider, until settlement meets settlement, and the old primeval things have vanished away. Painted houses have succeeded the log-cabins. Flocks and herds, feeding in rich pastures, are everywhere seen. The sound of the woodman's axe, and the crash of the falling timber, is still. The burning fallows, sending their dense columns of smoke, wreathing and curling towards the sky, are things that have ceased to be, for the old woods have been swept away. The ding-dong of the cow-bells and the tinkling of the sheep-bells are no longer heard. Stage-coaches are rolling along the highways, or an engine dragging with lightning speed a train of cars, loaded with human freight, goes thundering along the valleys. Villages and great farms, and school-houses, and church-spires, are everywhere seen, filling up the view that once swept over a boundless forest. Civilization has settled down with its train of concomitants, and the things of old have vanished from its presence.

As it has been elsewhere, so will it one day be here. Farms will be spread out in these valleys, fields will creep up the sides of the hills. These streams that have rolled, during the long forever of the past, in untrammelled freedom, roaring and surging in the spring and autumn freshets, and flowing pleasantly and quietly in the summer months, will be harnessed into the service of man—be chained to the revolving wheel, and made to grind corn, or throw the shuttle and spin. True, these tall mountains will stand here in all their solemn grandeur as they now do, but these broad forests that they now overlook will be gone. The great trees that give a sombre beauty to their steep acclivities or crown their lofty summits, will pass into the structure of human dwellings, or edifices erected by human labor.

www.ingramcontent.com/pod-product-compliance
Lightning Source LLC
LaVergne TN
LVHW010146110826
845151LV00002B/435

9781425537111